IMAGES
of America

LEXINGTON

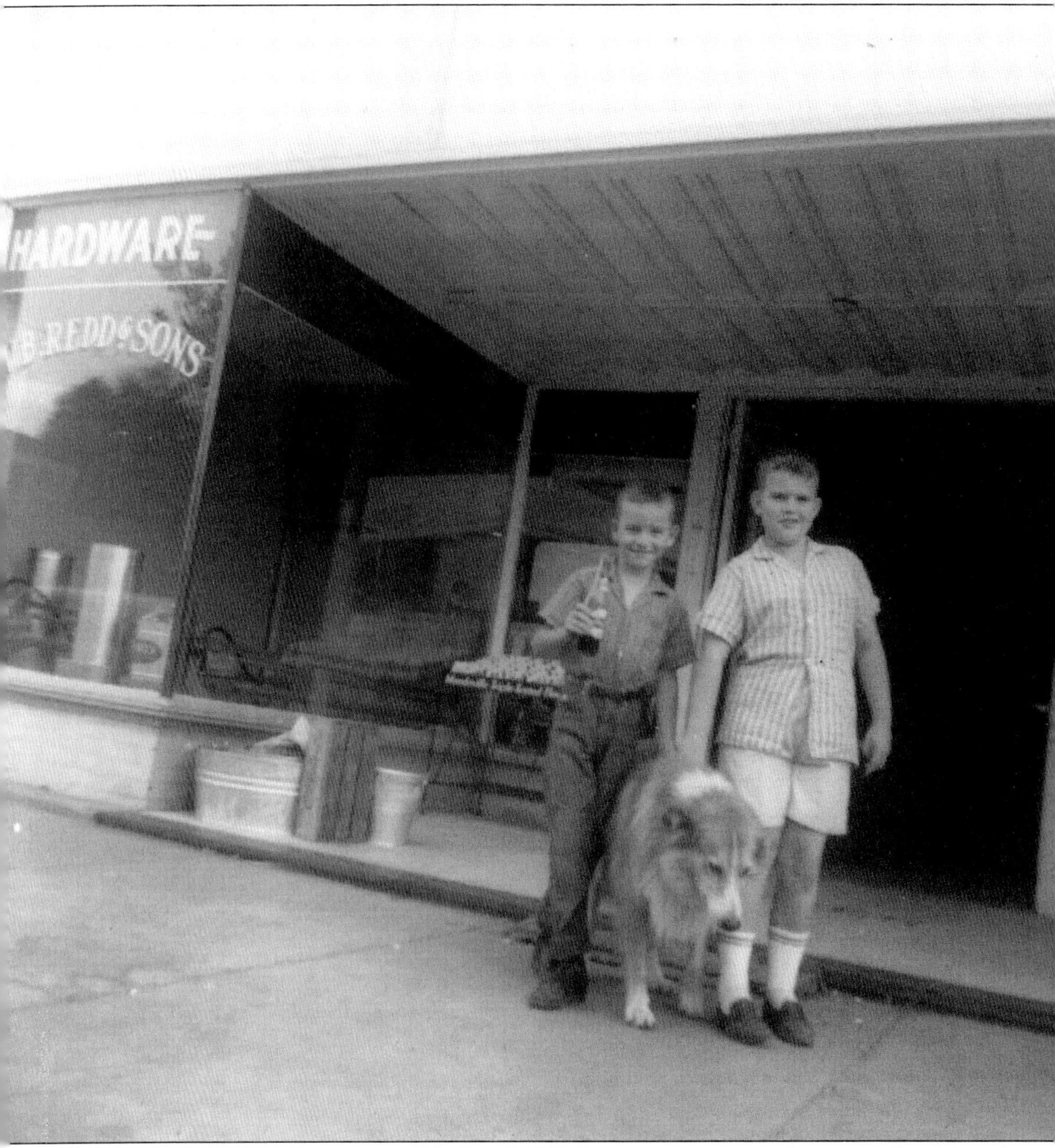

In downtown Lexington in the 1930s, Ron Redd's dog is sitting pretty with some boyhood friends while one enjoys a soda from Ron's father's feed and seed shop on Main Street. (Ron Redd.)

On the Cover: Marching down Main Street, Lexington, SC, are men and women returning from World War II. People lined the streets to honor those who sacrificed in so many ways. A rich military tradition continues today as a deep vein in the central core of duty to one's country in the citizens of Lexington County. (Ron Redd.)

IMAGES
of America

LEXINGTON

Sharon R. Paeth

ARCADIA
PUBLISHING

ISBN 978-0-7385-8597-0

Published by Arcadia Publishing
Charleston, South Carolina

Printed in the United States of America

Library of Congress Control Number: 2010921602

For all general information contact Arcadia Publishing at:
Telephone 843-853-2070
Fax 843-853-0044
E-mail sales@arcadiapublishing.com
For customer service and orders:
Toll-Free 1-888-313-2665

Visit us on the Internet at www.arcadiapublishing.com

I dedicate this book to the people of Lexington County.
The support and unity they demonstrate is the most
inspiring quality a group of people can share.

Contents

Foreword		6
Acknowledgments		7
Introduction		8
1.	The Beginning	9
2.	Key Families Influence Growth	23
3.	Lake Murray	51
4.	Outlying Areas	57
5.	Churches and Traditions	89
6.	Military Involvement	103
7.	Historic Sites and Parks and Recreation	121

FOREWORD

The Images of America series by Arcadia Publishing is a unique way to preserve the heritage of areas throughout the United States. These lovely coffee table books provide rich insight into the lives of everyday people and communities.

Born and raised in the town of Lexington, I was delivered into this world by the late Dr. James S. Liverman at his tiny clinic on Church Street. He also delivered most of the 11 children of my parents, Alice and Michael Aun, along with hundreds of others in the county.

My maternal grandfather, Elias S. Mack Sr., was a Lebanese immigrant who came south seeking a better life and literally ran out of money in nearby Columbia. While peddling his dry goods and in fact trading them for fruit and vegetables with people throughout Lexington County, he fell in love with the area and moved his struggling family here, where he opened several businesses over the years. My grandfather was affectionately called "Jew Mack" because everyone thought he was Jewish, though he was in fact of Arabic bloodlines and Lutheran by faith. He was elected mayor of Lexington but served only briefly after it was learned that he was not an American citizen. Somehow his Ellis Island papers were not in order, but his old friend then-governor Strom Thurmond stepped in to help him out. Almost 40 years to the day later, his son, Elias S. Mack Jr., was elected mayor of Lexington. This passing of the baton so typical of small-town America is what is celebrated so uniquely in this book.

Although there are several other books about Lexington County that provide comprehensive historical information, this one highlights both the immigrants and their descendants who were and are stakeholders in this strong community. Often the shared photographs reflect three or four generations of a variety of families. The diversity of this county speaks volumes for the ways that people lived peacefully together. Over the years, these Lexington residents have kept the end in mind, which by all accounts was to provide a place for their children's children to thrive and succeed.

German immigrants, who came from serfdom, firmly believed that all men were created equal. To this day, their descendants have held true to the thought that each person is entitled to his own decisions, that the law of the land should limit the people as little as possible, and that people should rise to the expectation to act in a faithful and trustworthy manner that would bring pride to their families.

The book also recognizes representatives of several segments of the population who served in the military. This small cross-section reveals the deep loyalty and devotion to country demonstrated by the sons and daughters of Lexington County.

For many, this book is a walk down memory lane. For others, it is a window into a small-town community that has grown into a thriving suburban town determined to follow carefully planned decisions for a successful future.

—Michael Aun

ACKNOWLEDGMENTS

I wish to thank my husband, Brian, for his willingness to support me in every way needed to achieve this lifetime goal. I am grateful for my daughters, Heather and Megan, who share my enthusiasm for finding out about the history of where we live. I want to thank all of the contributors who were willing to share their family stories and photographs with me and the world. Together we created a unique memory of Lexington County. Lexington County librarian Mark Mancuso was very generous and helpful during this project. The museums in Lexington County are each a tremendous resource. I want to thank Leo Redmond and the Cayce Historical Museum, Buddy Sturgis and the South Carolina History Museum, Fritz Hammer and the South Carolina State Museum, and most of all, J. R. Fennell and the Lexington County Museum for sharing photographs, facts, and their suggestions for improvement. I also send my heartfelt thanks to my editor, Lindsay Harris, who has been a joy to work with. Thank you to my friends and family who encouraged me to try and helped me to succeed by believing in me.

Introduction

I wave my hand hello to the car going down the road as I drive by. It is unimportant that I do not know that person. My daughter says, "Mommy, who was that person in the car?" I say, "That is one of our neighbors, baby." Frequently, although not as often as 15 years ago, when I first moved into this neighborhood, people raise a hand in greeting, even if they do not know you. That small gesture speaks volumes for the types of people you will meet in Lexington County, South Carolina. Standing in a line for the ladies' room is never a dull moment. People around you begin talking as they search for common ground. The usual conversation starts with information about where you live then moves into whom you both may know. Most Southerners just fall into this routine as a way of life—yet another telltale sign that they truly care for one another. Instead of just passing along the busy lane of life, they take time to reach out to each other. This simple country style reverberates throughout the entire county. As you read through this pictorial history of this special place, I encourage you to see the many signs of this simple generosity and fellowship that is reinforced daily by many.

The roads in Lexington are quite complex. Once when I was travelling home on a summer afternoon shortly after moving in, I became hopelessly lost. I took a left-hand turn that seemed to run parallel to my normal route. After 40 minutes of country driving and no gas station in sight, I was sure that I would really become lost in the backwoods areas. Thankfully, another 10 minutes brought me to the only gas station for miles. The people all turned to look at me as I stepped into the store to pay and ask for directions homeward. They were very patient with me and repeated their directions three times to be certain I would make it back home. They surely wondered if I made it home or not that day! After 15 years and the amazing technology of my GPS, which I nicknamed "Gypsy," I can finally find my way around. I know where Cooper's Corners used to be and where the corner with the old barn that is ready to fall down is, halfway to the next small town.

While you enjoy this pictorial history of Lexington County, I hope that you too will see the patterns of humility, faith, humanity, and simple kindness I have been honored to enjoy as a citizen of this county. While traveling with me on my adventure, you will visit local businesses, churches, traditions, and meet many families and individuals who have made a contribution to this lovely community. You will also hear about the people of the lake and many of the towns surrounding Lexington, which have unique origins of their own. Finally, we will discuss the current places and activities that Lexington County offers to anyone who decides to visit or perhaps to settle in and become part of this growing family of faith and community in a small-town atmosphere.

One

The Beginning

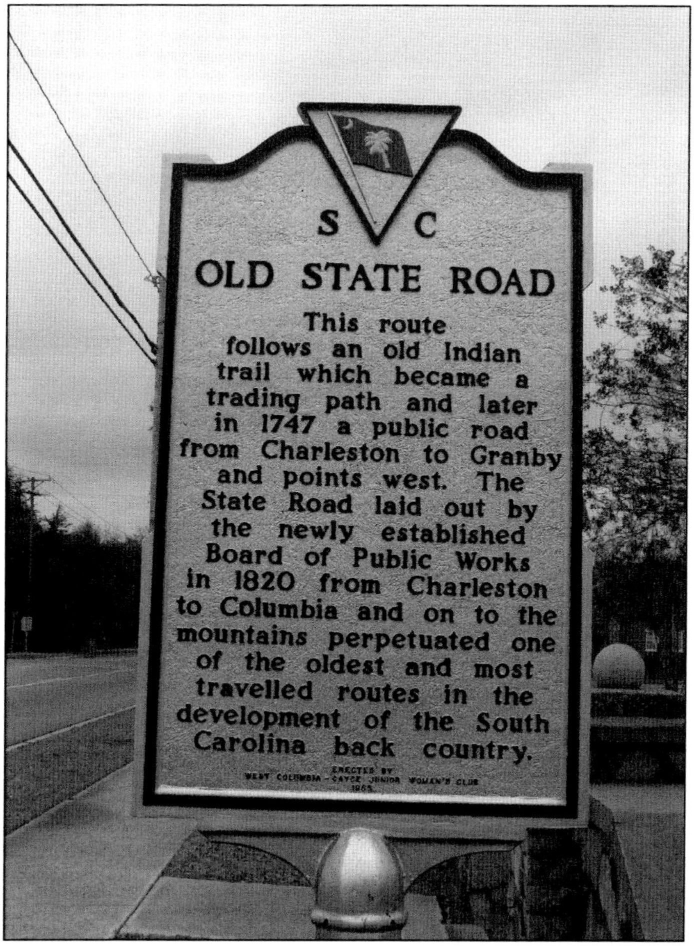

Lexington County began as backcountry, where Congaree Indians were among the established native cultures being disturbed by the growing English colonial presence on the coast. As time passed, citizens of the Lowcountry were anxious to expand their holdings. In 1718, Capt. Charles Russell built a wooden palisade fort called Congaree Fort near the Cherokee and Occaneechi Paths. This haven provided a trading post for the area soon after it was established. This historical marker is located in Cayce, SC, on State Street in front of Brookland Cayce High School. (Paeth family.)

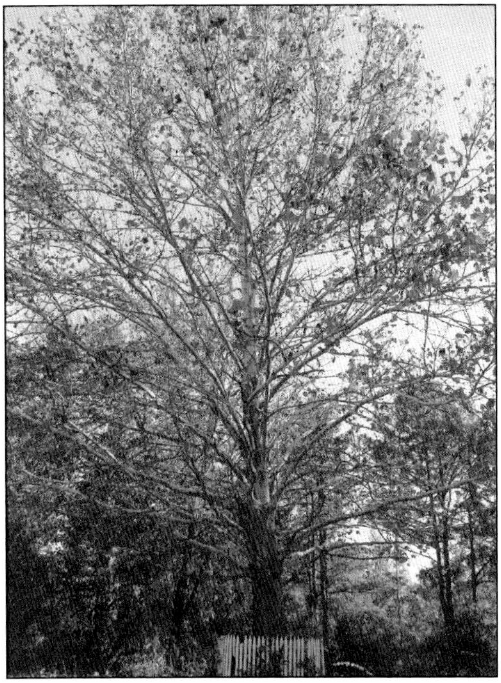

The Cherokee Path was instrumental to the early settlers of Lexington County. This well-known trail provided a route to ferries and other conveniences for travelers, such as the Sycamore Tree, where even today a sycamore tree is still standing. Further along the path's route, one of the first trading posts run by Herman Geiger still stands. Please reference chapter seven for details on these and more historic sites. (Paeth family.)

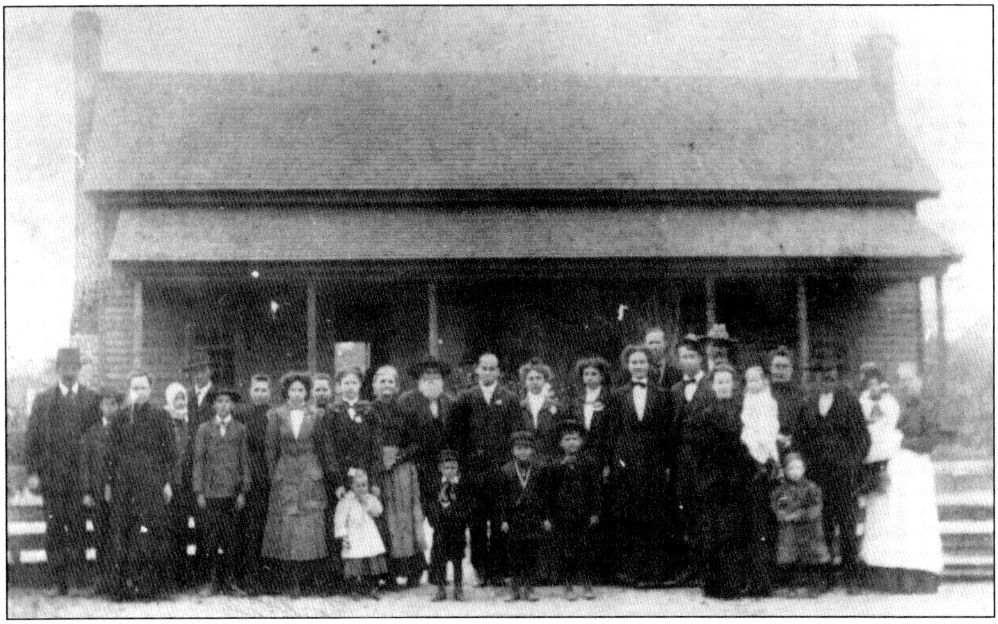

Colonial English traders realized the potential of becoming wealthy if they could trade with the Native Americans for local resources such as deerskins, tar, pitch, and timber used for masts for sailing ships. Cypress was used for barrelheads and clapboards. Goods were traded between the English and American Indian communities at several trading posts located in Lexington County. The Township Act of 1733 encouraged additional settlement by emigrants from Germany and Switzerland to help deter Native American raids. The Roof family (above) were prominent members of the town of Lexington. They are descended from one of the early German homesteaders of this area. (Roof family.)

Over the next 100 years, the residents of this area would face trials unheard of today. The pioneers who settled the backcountry fought the Revolutionary War, with Tories fighting Patriots. At the same time, they had to beware of Native Americans, disease, and starvation. The dedication to build a good home for their families was the quest of these hardworking individuals. (Paeth family.)

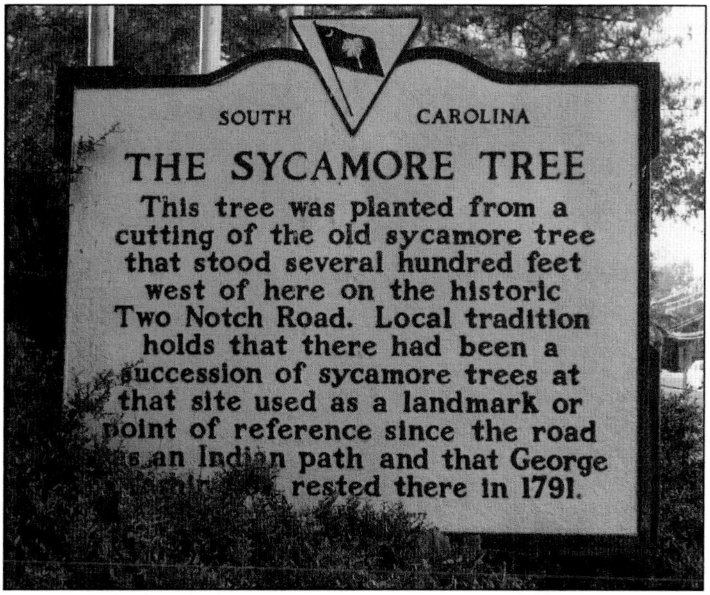

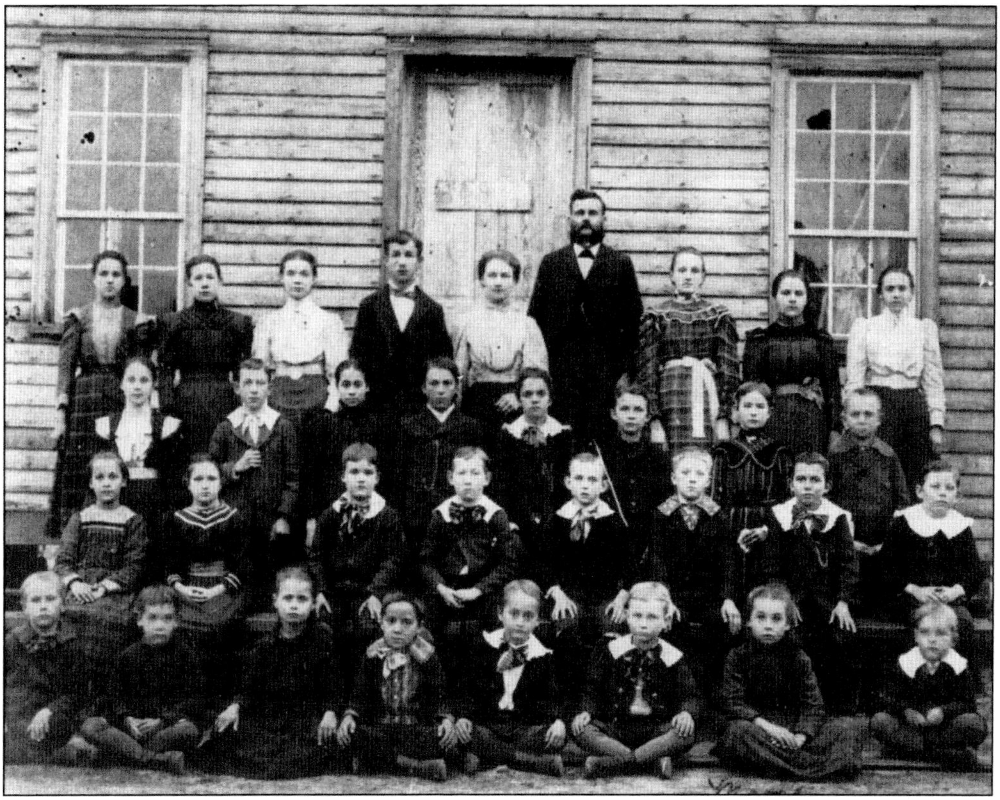

By 1811, Lexington County was a growing community. Small one-room schoolhouses were built to meet the needs of this community. In 1861, there were 20,000 children going to school. During the Civil War, the school system was left by the wayside. Many families focused on both trying to survive after Sherman's ruthless burnings and working through the new laws of Reconstruction. (Bennett Roof.)

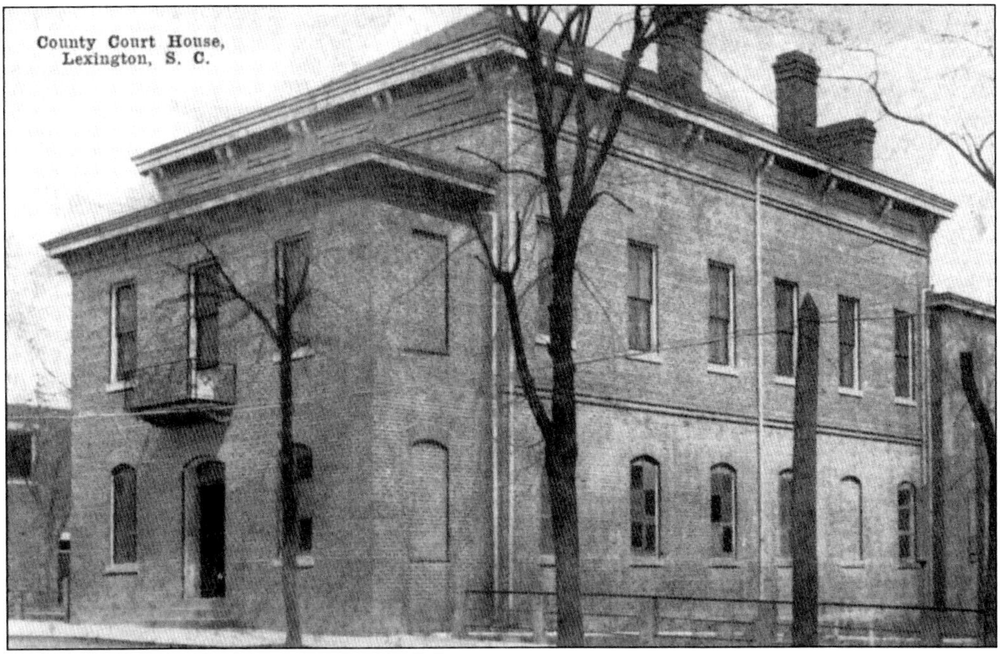

After the Civil War, industries slowly began to thrive again. In the 1890s, the area began to grow and build. Anna Drafts Corley, fondly known as Granny Corley, is remembered as a very generous lady who sold the land in 1819 for the Lexington County Courthouse pictured here. Many local brick structures were built with Guinyard bricks. These buildings were able to remain standing even through the "Great Fire" in 1916, which burned most of the buildings on Main Street. (Lexington County Museum.)

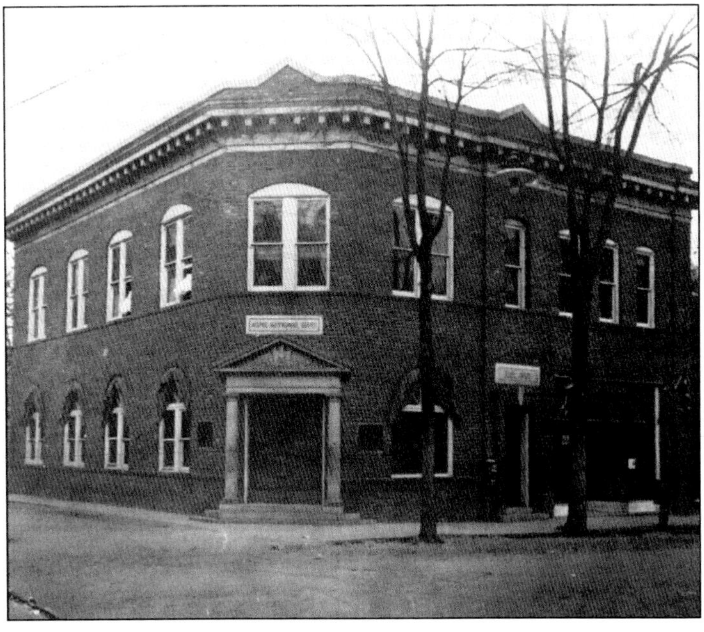

The Home National Bank was started by several of the early entrepreneurs in Lexington County. This bank was built on the corner of Main Street and South Lake Drive in 1913. Notice the structure is built of bricks to prevent burning in a fire. During the fire of 1916, part of the bank burned down. The owners conducted business out of a shoebox until the repairs could be made. The building is still in use today as a law office. (Lexington County Museum.)

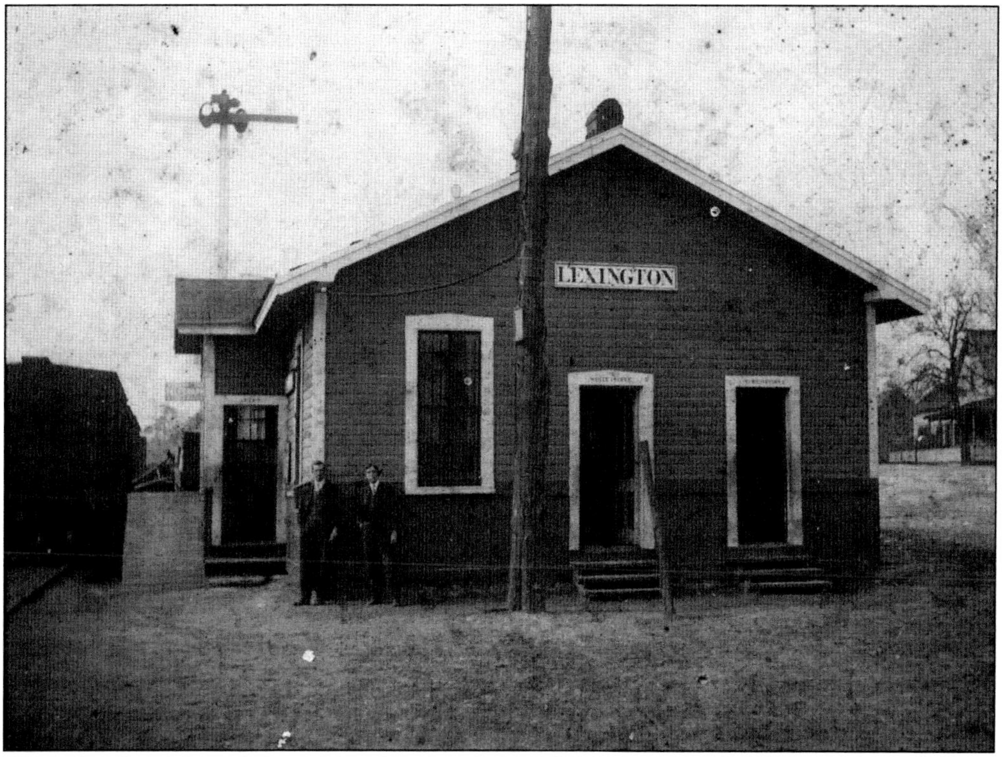

The railroad also came to Lexington County in 1868. The Lexington train depot is pictured above. Along the railroad route is where the outlying areas of Lexington began to grow and flourish. Some towns came alive with industries that thrived on exporting goods to other areas. It is interesting to note that the railroad in Lexington was at the outskirts of the town, not at the center. The businesses in Lexington were standalone enterprises that stood the tests of time and technological advancements. Some of those same businesses are still serving the many generations of Lexington County townspeople. (Above, Lexington County Museum; below, artist Blue Sky.)

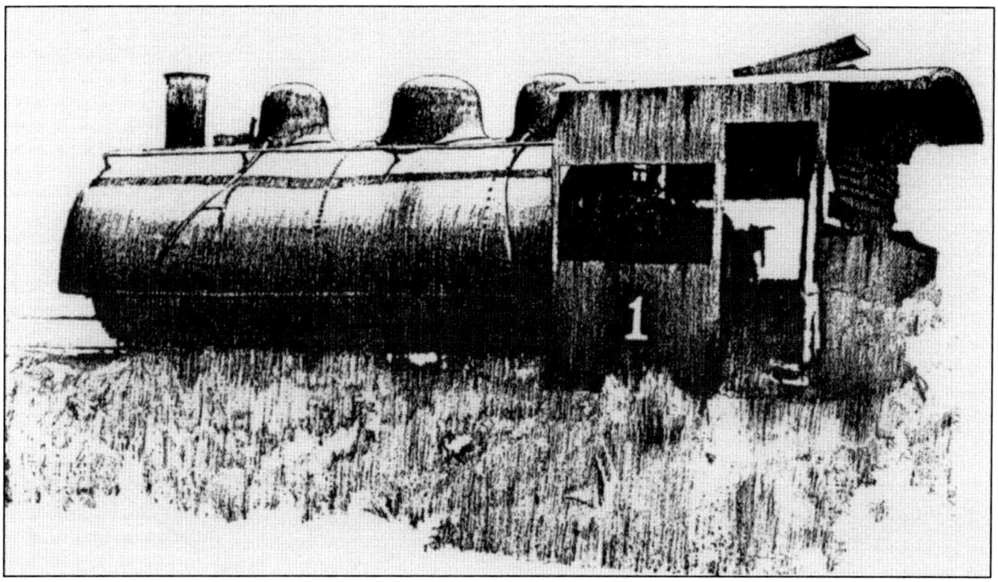

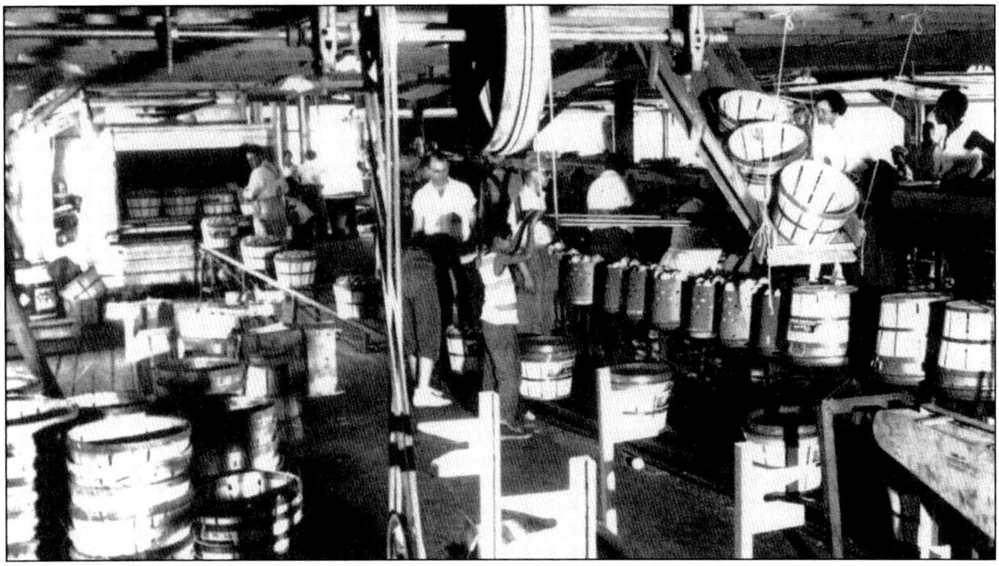

The Walter P. Rawl Farm was begun in the mid-1920s by Walter and Ernestine Rawl. The company remains a traditional family farm, with nine family members in the organization. These family members together represent over 300 years of experience. What began primarily as a peach operation and cannery is now a full-service fresh vegetable operation. Most of these vegetables are available loose and pre-packed. Irrigation has greatly helped farming organizations in the sand hills of Pelion to utilize the many acres of open field left from lumber mills in the early 1900s. (Lexington Main Library.)

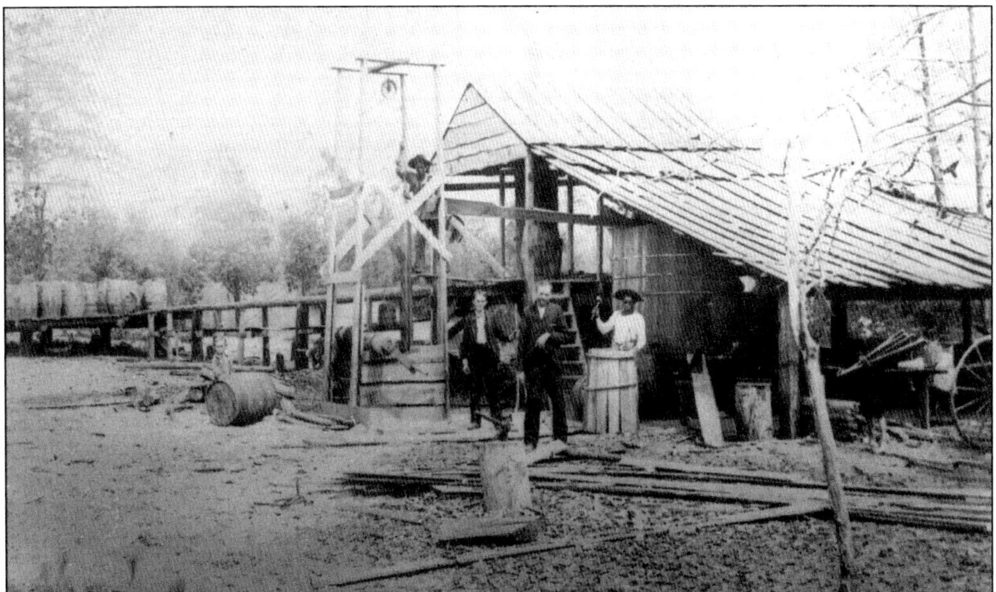

Henry Steele's turpentine still, pictured in 1898, is an example of the early industries in Lexington County. The combined lock system at Granby made transport even easier for products to be purchased and shipped as far as Charleston. Over time the demand for turpentine decreased, and landowners had to seek other ways to utilize their resources. The mill industry was the next industry to grow. (Lexington County Museum.)

Lexington Manufacturing Company was located near downtown. Many people from the surrounding farm areas would move into town, where they would work in the textile factory and live in the small houses there. They found they could rent out their farmland and make more working at the mill. Many people enjoyed the socialization of the mill town area, which was complete with a store, barbershop, and entertainment. The success of Main Street's downtown businesses was founded on this thriving community. (Lexington County Museum.)

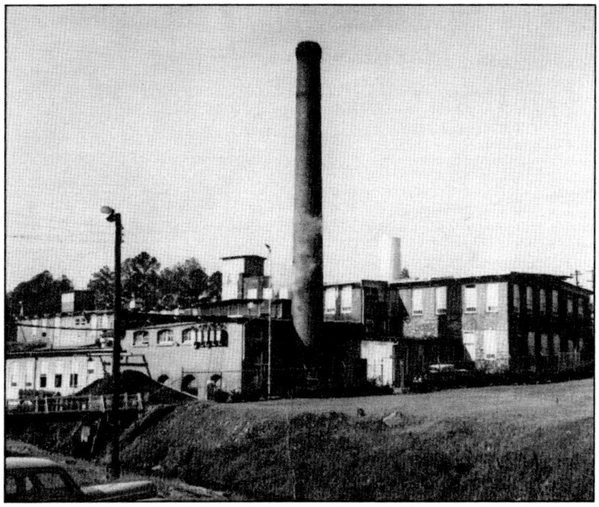

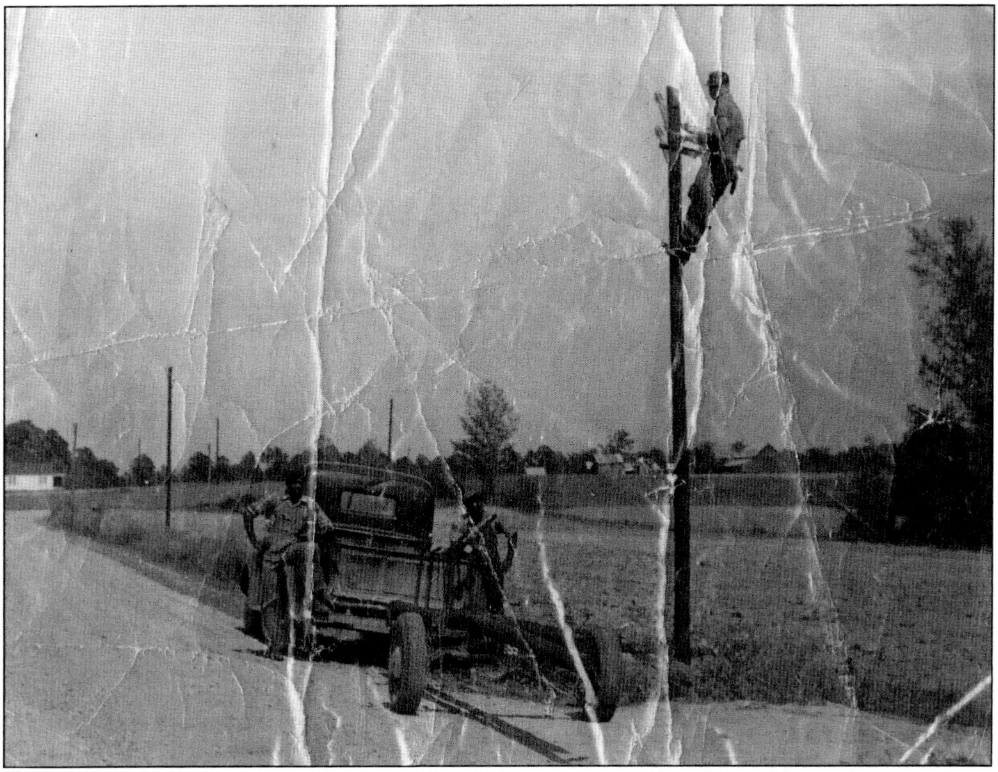

Lexington County had one of the earliest telephone companies in the area, called Citizens Telephone Company, which began in 1903. People in the area applied to have a telephone installed. The company agreed to furnish the telephone lines and telephone as long as the individual agreed to pay for service. The switchboard system, with only 23 telephones connected, was set up by Sam B. George. Within one year, the business grew so fast that new equipment had to be installed to keep up with the growth. During the fire of 1916, the telephone company lost all of its equipment and had to start over. From 1921 to 1948, the number of customers grew from 23 to 707. In 1950, Sam A. George applied for and received two Rural Electrification Authority grants. This allowed over 1,000 people to have telephone service at a reasonable cost. (Annie Laurie George.)

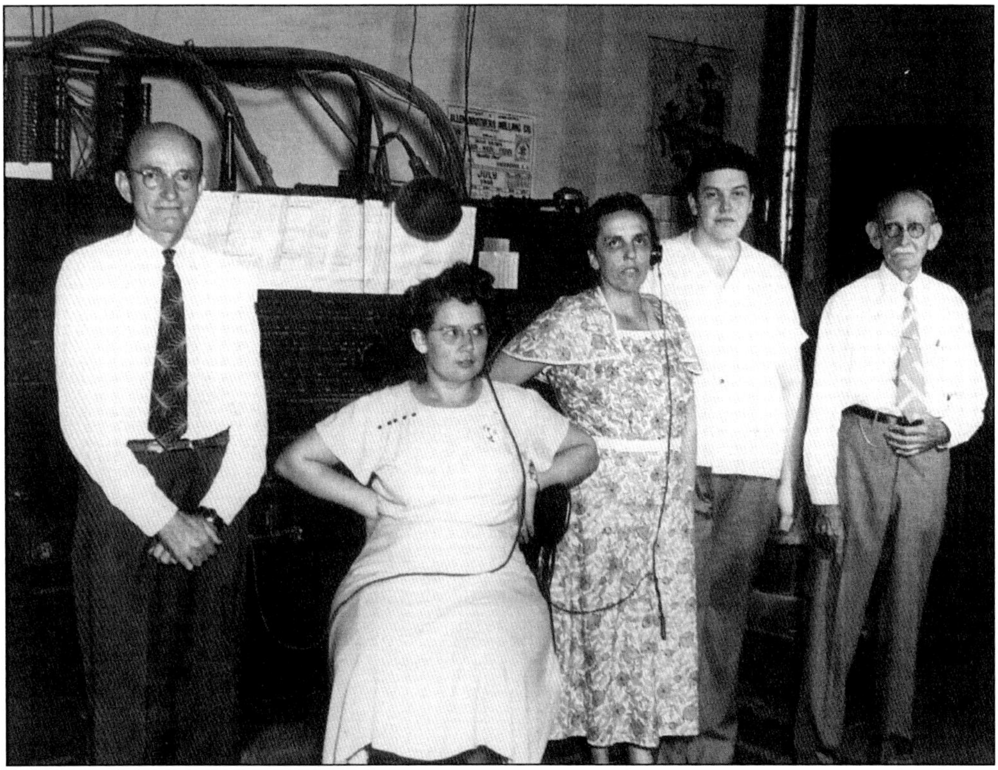

Pictured here are, from left to right, Sam A. George, Mary Lewie, Elese Fields, and Sam B. George. The ladies were the first ones to run the telephone system's switchboard. They knew where everyone was in town. Bill Mathias, son of Dr. Homer Mathias, remembers that the switchboard operators always knew where to find his dad whenever anyone had an emergency. (Annie Laurie George.)

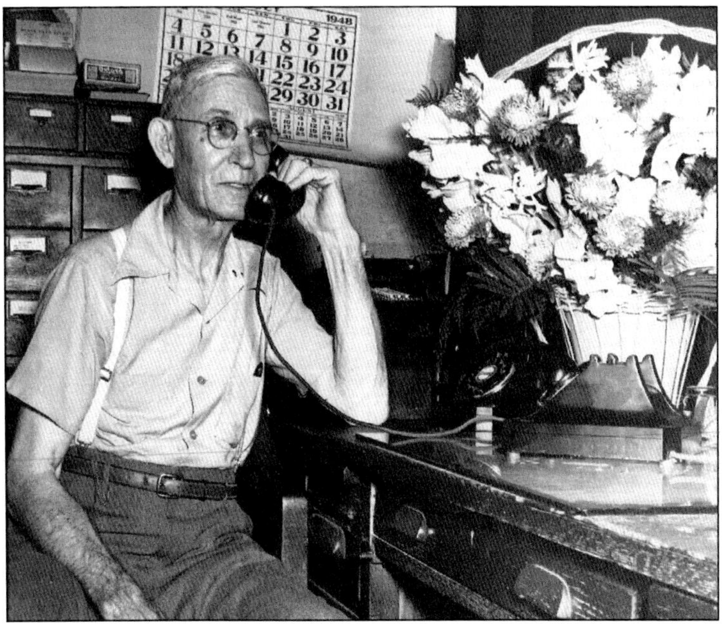

Heber Barr was the first person to make a call using the telephone system. This limited system allowed people within a specific calling area to reach each other through a third party who connected the two parties at a switchboard. Long distance was available but cost more for each call. Barr was also one of the individuals responsible for electricity in Lexington County. (Annie Laurie George.)

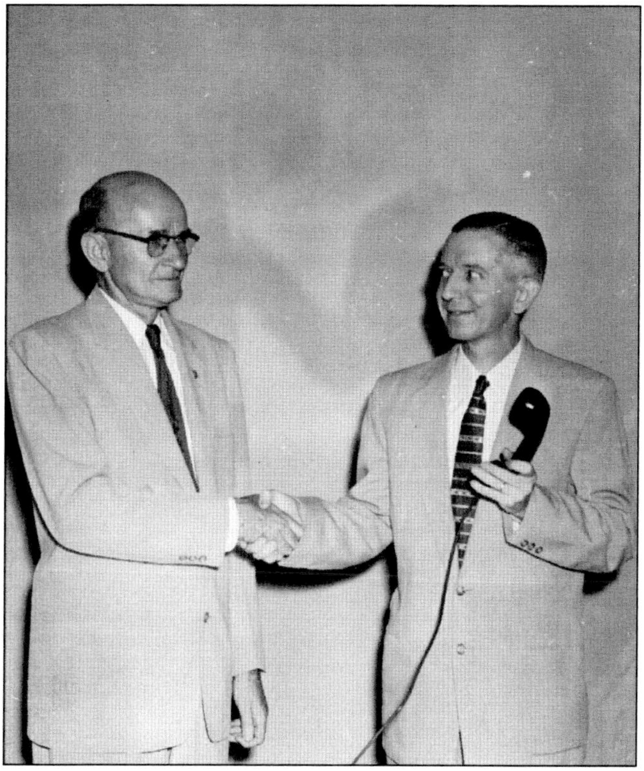

J. C. Shepard, mayor of Lexington, makes the first phone call using the new dial system in 1956. Some people might remember the party line service. People shared lines to receive lower rates and free long distance so they could reach out to more people. Multi-party service of 6–10 telephones was $3.90 per month per customer. One-party service was at the higher rate of $5.95 per month. By June 1960, Citizens Telephone had installed its 1,800th telephone. Some nearby cities did not have this type of efficient and effective service. (Both, Annie Laurie George.)

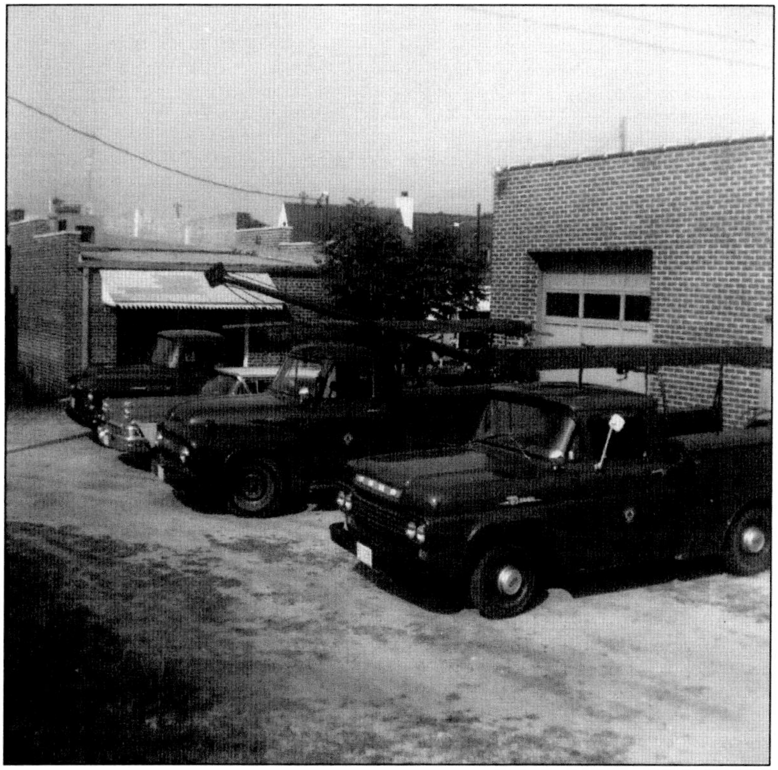

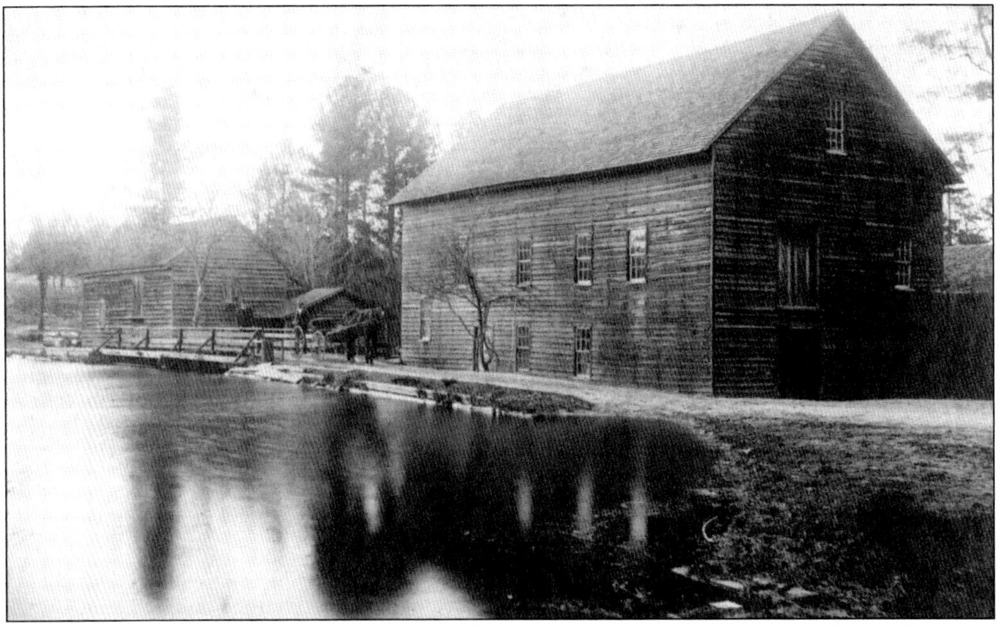

Several mills were the mainstay of the people in Lexington County. People who could not or did not want to farm could come to live in the city and work in the industries here. There were several to choose from. George's Mill (pictured above), Laurel Falls Mill, Lexington Manufacturing Company, and Red Bank Mill were the main factories. Workers like the ones from Red Bank Mill pictured below had to be careful of fires. Most mills had serious fires, which destroyed the buildings. (Above, Annie Laurie George; below, Laura Shumpert McMahan.)

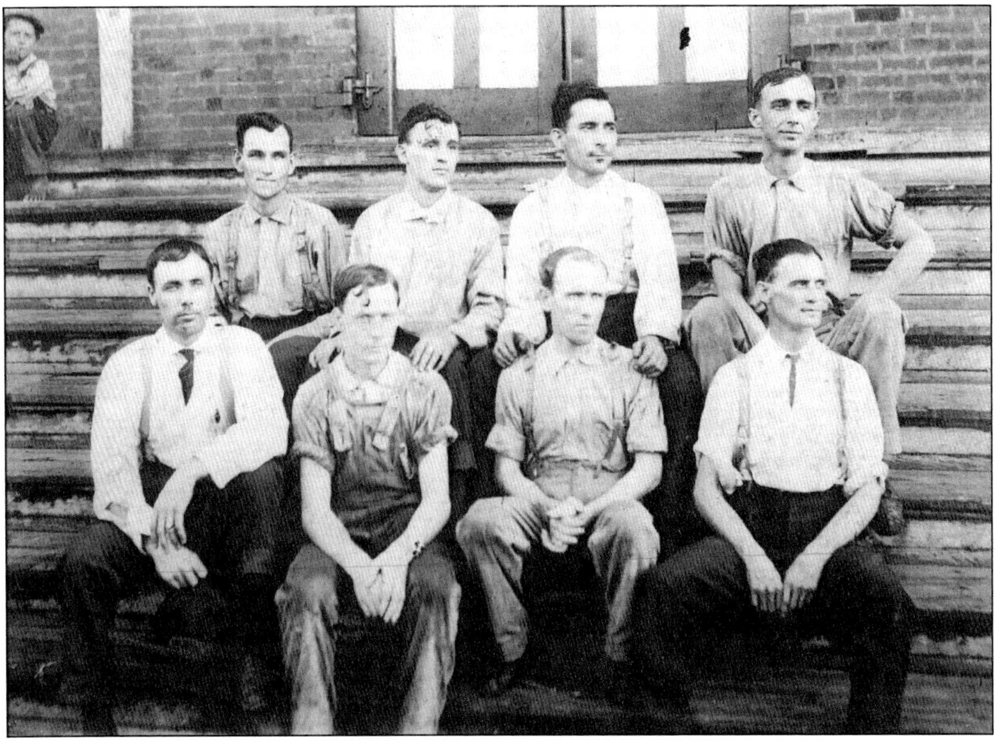

Sam B. George started the Lexington Oil Company. The business was a good investment and helped bring electricity and heat to many customers. Before the Lake Murray dam project, folks had oil burners in their homes. There are still some houses today that rely on oil for heat and electricity. (Annie Laurie George.)

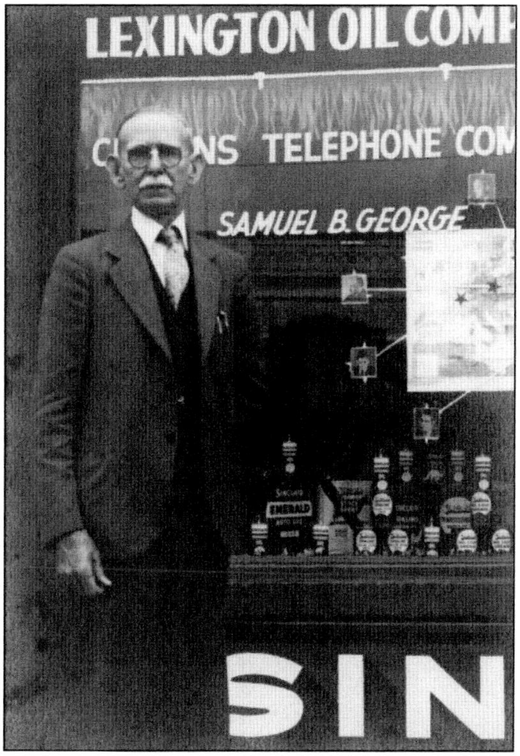

Sarah Taylor Sessions is seated in the second row, far right, with her daughter Ann on her lap. She married Thomas Rountree Sessions from Georgia; they both taught school in Dalton. The couple was married July 21, 1940. Sarah and Tree then moved to Lexington and, in 1949, started Sessions Department Store, which stayed open for 50 years. (Ann Sessions.)

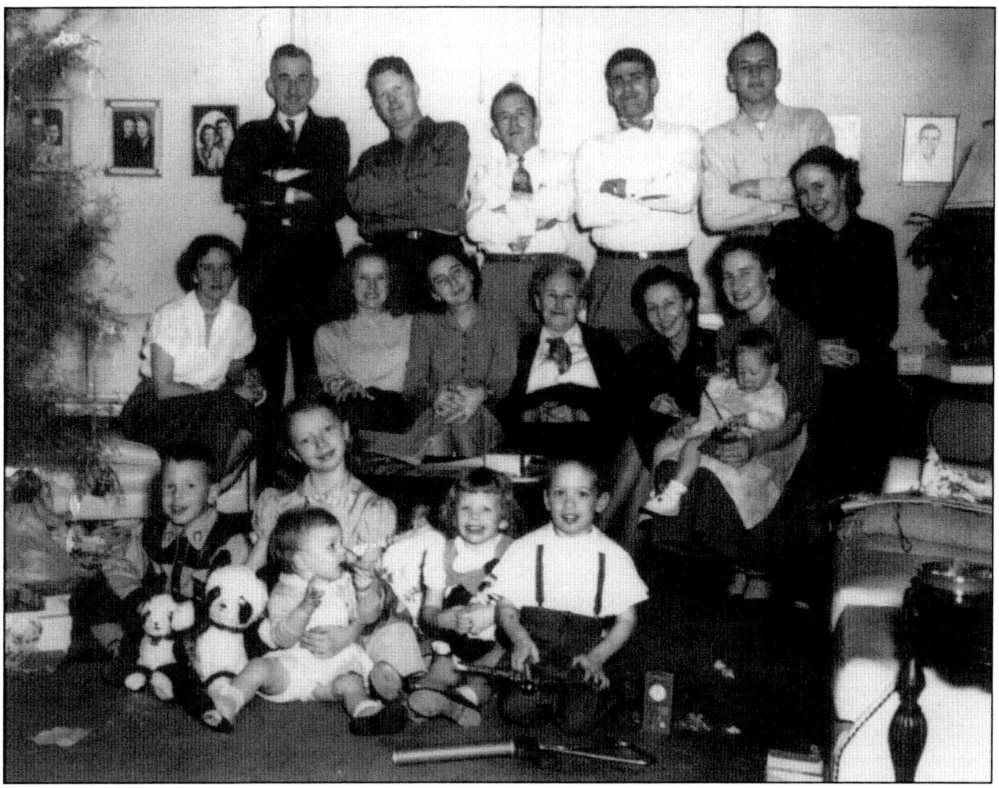

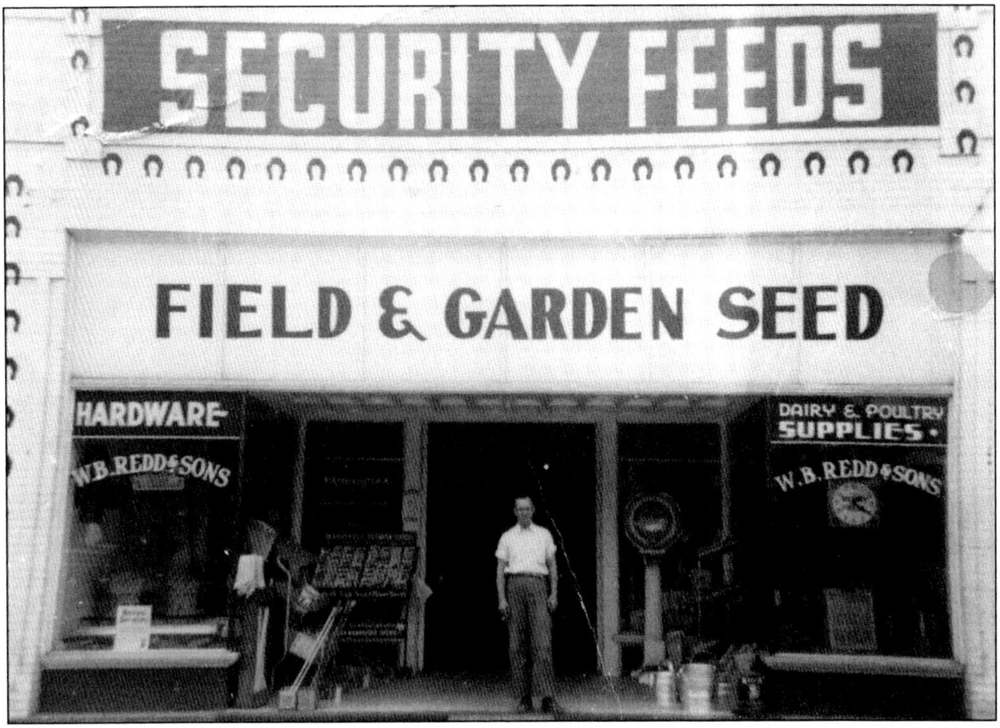

In 1938, Wilbur Redd and Andrew Mathias opened their own feed and seed store at 123 East Main Street in Lexington. Security feed was the primary brand of feed sold in the store. In the 1940s, Wallace Redd joined his father in the enterprise, which changed names to W. B. Redd and Son and stayed in business until 1965. The store had grown into a large phone-order company. Feed was shipped by train from Knoxville to the Lexington depot. Wallace's son, Ron, remembers unloading full cars of feed in the summer heat. They made deliveries with a 5-ton truck and a 2.5-ton pickup to Irmo, Fairview, Pelion, Edmund, South Congaree, and up to Saluda County. Pictured above is Wallace Red. Below, Wallace helps a customer with an order. (Both, Ron Redd.)

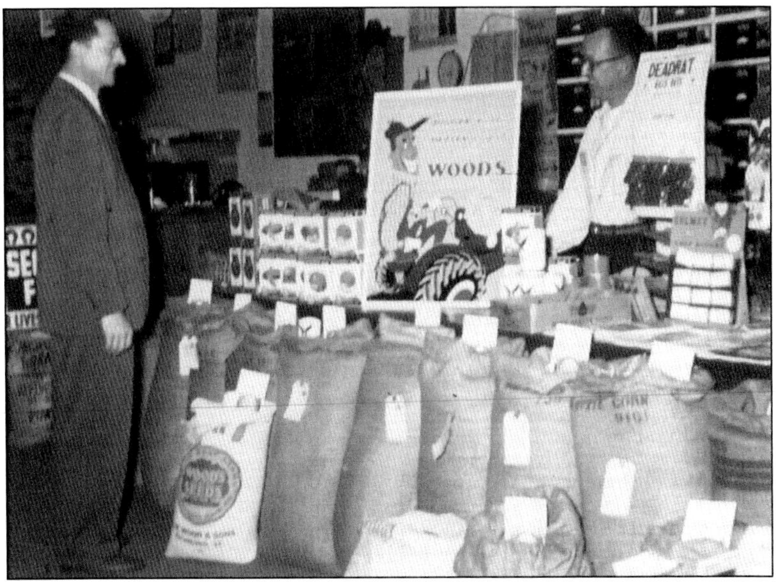

In the winter, at the back of the store was a pot-bellied coal stove. Ron remembers roasting peanuts on top, and visitors would sit back there enjoying peanuts and visiting when they passed through. This casual conversation shared news and ideas for ways to improve the town. One of the interesting parts of business for Wallace became the chicken industry. He taught himself to identify problems with chickens to help his customers. Eventually he had made so many contacts that he was able to pair up customers who raised biddies with other customers who wanted the fryers or layers. If an egg had a slight crack, it would be sold to folks at a reduced cost instead of being wasted. Pictured on the right is a 1930s bill of sale for supplies and feed for a local farm. Below is the Redd and Son store in the late 1950s. (Both, Ron Redd.)

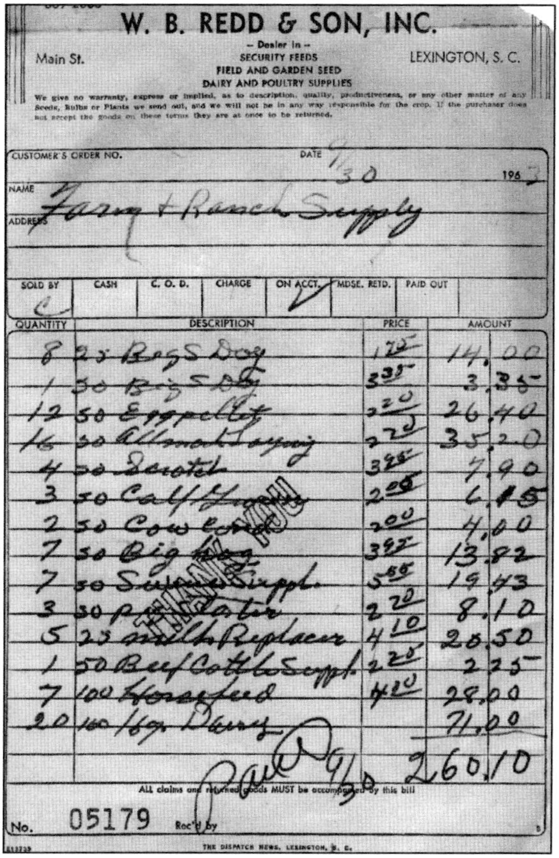

W. B. REDD & SON, INC.

– Dealer in –
SECURITY FEEDS
FIELD AND GARDEN SEED
DAIRY AND POULTRY SUPPLIES

Main St. LEXINGTON, S. C.

We give no warranty, express or implied, as to description, quality, productiveness, or any other matter of any Seeds, Bulbs or Plants we send out, and we will not be in any way responsible for the crop. If the purchaser does not accept the goods on these terms they are at once to be returned.

CUSTOMER'S ORDER NO. DATE 9/30 1963

NAME Farm + Ranch Supply

ADDRESS

SOLD BY	CASH	C. O. D.	CHARGE	ON ACCT.	MDSE. RETD.	PAID OUT
C				✓		

QUANTITY	DESCRIPTION	PRICE	AMOUNT
8	25 Bags Dog	1.75	14.00
1	50 Big S Dog	3.35	3.35
12	50 Egg pellets	2.20	26.40
16	50 [illegible]	2.20	35.20
4	50 Scratch	3.95	7.90
3	50 Calf [illegible]	2.05	6.15
2	50 Cow [illegible]	2.00	4.00
7	50 Big [illegible]	3.95	13.82
7	50 [illegible] Suppl.	5.55	19.43
3	50 [illegible]	2.70	8.10
5	25 Milk Replacer	4.10	20.50
1	50 Beef Cattle Suppl.	2.25	2.25
7	100 Horse feed	4.00	28.00
20	100 [illegible] Dairy		71.00
			260.10

THANK YOU

Paid 9/30

ALL claims and returned goods MUST be accompanied by this bill

No. 05179 Rec'd by

THE DISPATCH NEWS, LEXINGTON, S. C.

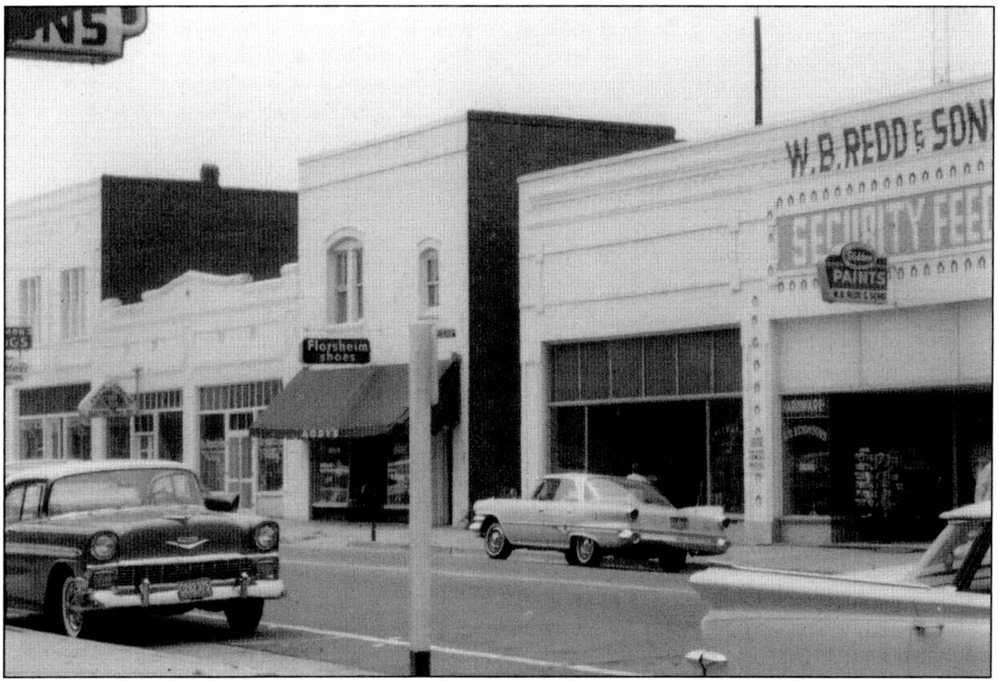

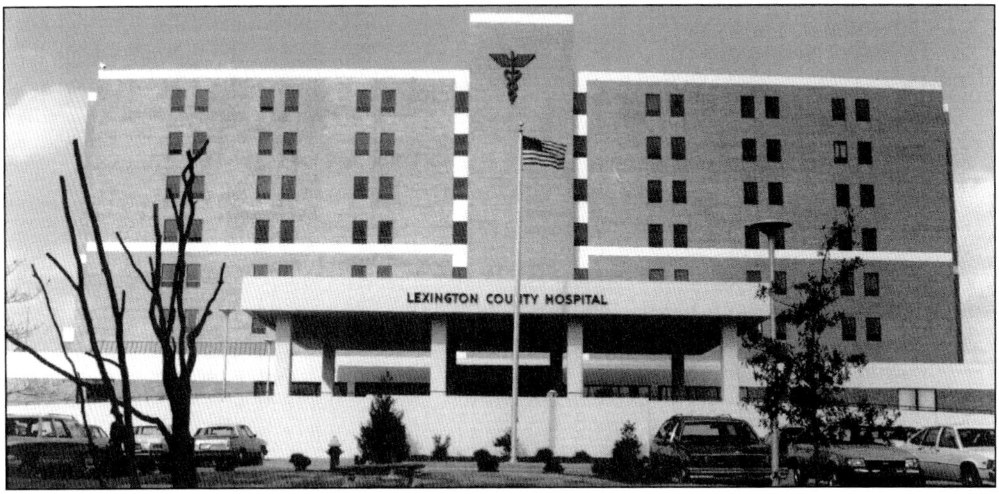

The Lexington Medical Center was a natural result of the area's growth. People had been traveling over an hour to arrive at the hospital in Columbia. A group of concerned citizens formed to begin plans for Lexington County Hospital. The project was financially challenging until Mrs. Harvey Hulon came forward and donated the property to the county. This generous contribution allowed the county to address the additional costs through grants and bonds totaling $3.9 million in 1968. The idea blossomed into a reality in 1971. The hospital board had representation from every major area in Lexington County. Wyman Trotti, from West Columbia; L. Clyde Rauch, from Lexington; Raymond L. Boozer, from Gilbert; David C. Bryan Jr., from Cayce; John W. Parrish, from West Columbia; Frontis O. Smith, from Gilbert; Furman R. Younginer, from Irmo; Curtis M. Shealy, from Chapin; and John Kermit Addy, from Lexington, were the first board members. On Sunday, January 3, 1971, a dedication and portrait unveiling was done by Charlotte and Sally Harman, granddaughters of Dr. Harry Odelle Harman. (Both, Harman family.)

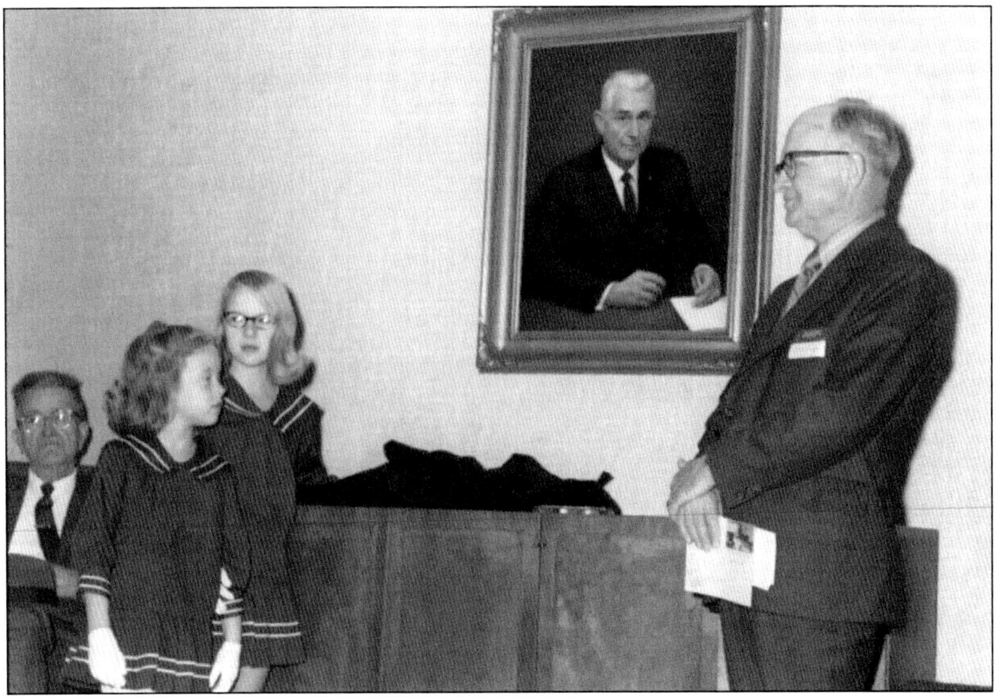

Two

KEY FAMILIES INFLUENCE GROWTH

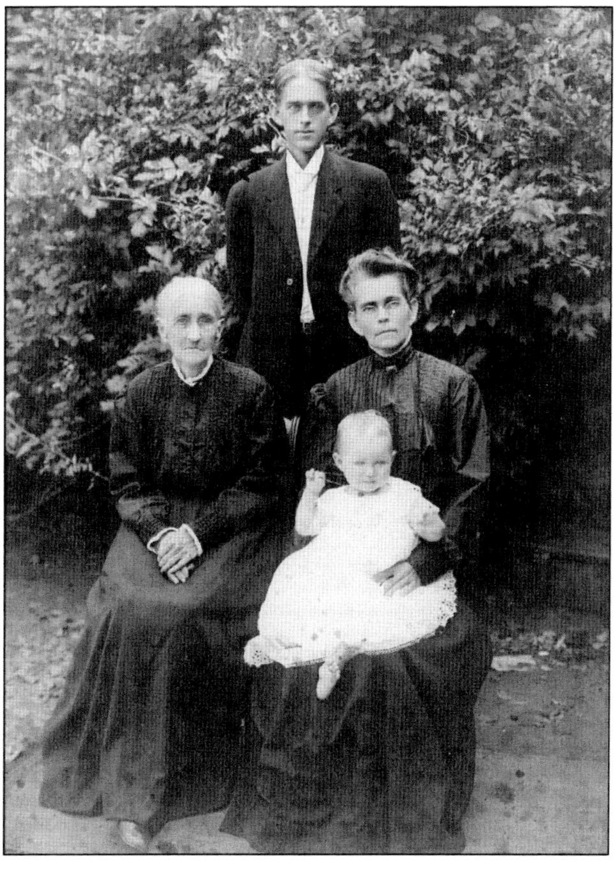

Pictured here are four generations of the Wingard family. Standing in back is Charles Alford Wingard (1887–1959). At right is Charles's mother, Martha Nunamaker Wingard (1861–1937); to the left is his grandmother, Maria (pronounced "Mariah") Schuler Nunamaker. The little girl is the daughter of Charles Wingard, Helen Custis Wingard (1910–1980). Charles was a farmer in the area and served on the county board of voter registration for many years. (Katheryn Liverman.)

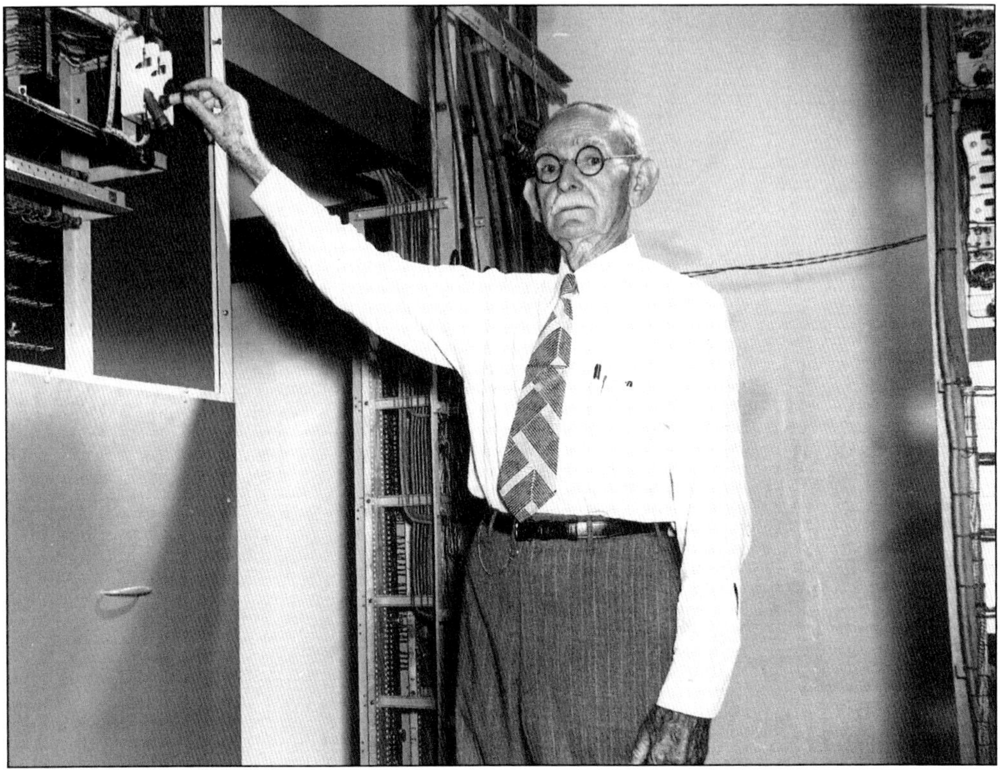

Samuel B. George was a third-generation descendant of Swiss immigrants. Born in Lexington, he worked for Laurel Falls Cotton Mills. Henry Meetze was president and John Caldwell was the chief financier at Laurel Falls Cotton Mills until it was destroyed by fire in 1862. George attended Palmetto Collegiate Institute. At age 14, he learned to manage the roller flour mill, corn mill, and the cotton gin. (Annie Laurie George.)

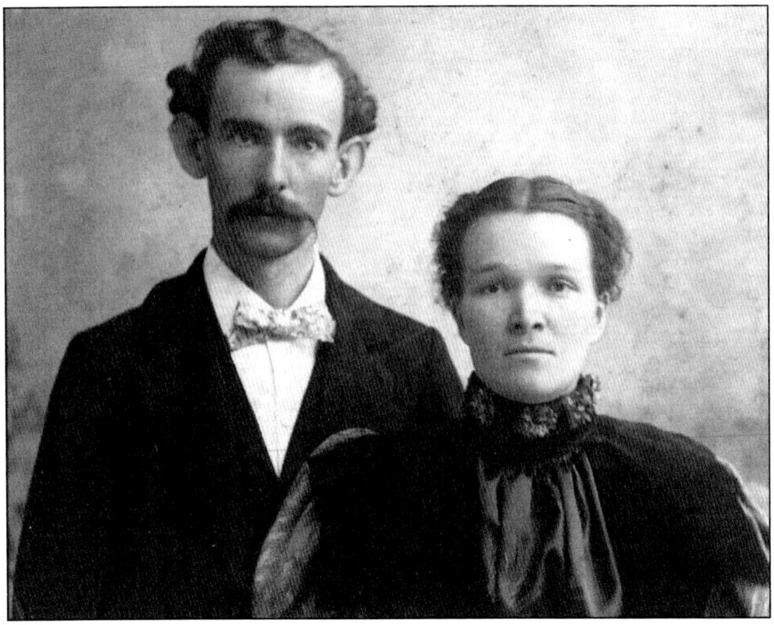

Sam B. George married Olga Hendrix of Lexington Township when he was 25. He was the deputy clerk of court at the time. Olga was a graduate of Winthrop College and a teacher in Lexington School. Both were active members of Lexington Methodist Church. They had five children. (Annie Laurie George.)

Sam George stands here with his smallest grandchild, Lynn, on her tricycle. George was the kind of person who would take time from his busy schedule to tell wonderful stories to his grandchildren. He saw the best in everyone and was very popular because people enjoyed his stories. He was a gentle disciplinarian who thought his grandchildren were perfect in every way. Annie Laurie remembers many afternoons when her daughter Lynn was just a little girl of two; they would hear the beep of the car horn, and Lynn would toddle out to be scooped up in her grandfather's arms for a short trip down the road to Eddy's store. Lynn remembers getting a Coke and some crackers as a treat and riding with her grandfather to the store. Annie Laurie feels certain that her little Lynn was born late in life as a special gift from the Lord to her father-in-law to comfort him after his wife passed away. (Annie Laurie George.)

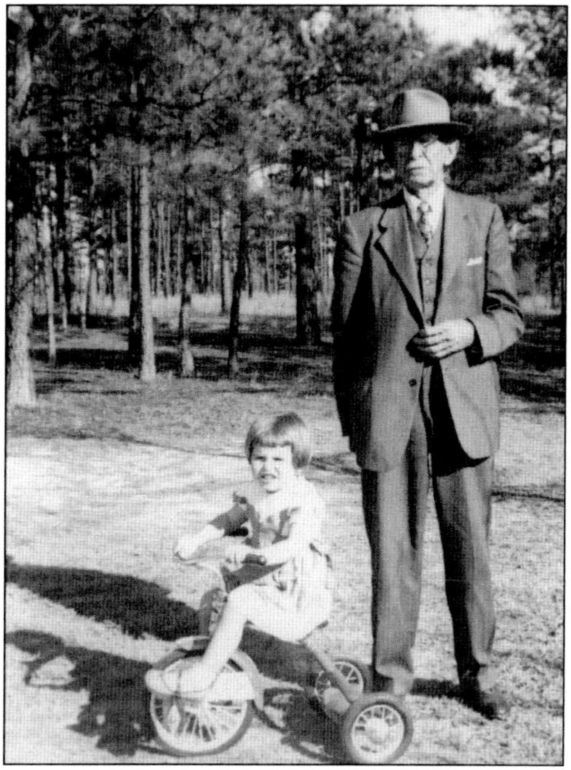

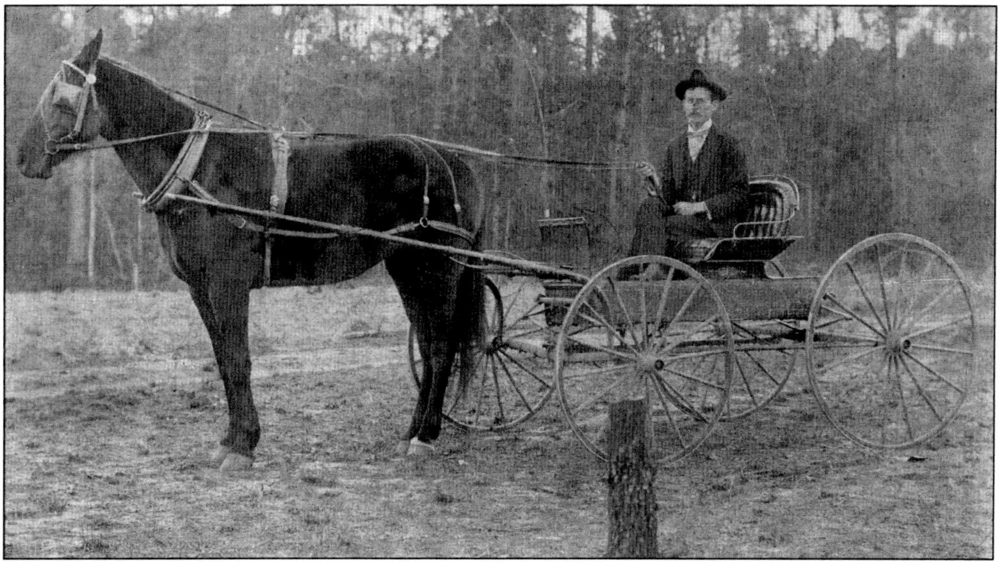

Daniel Drafts came from Germany. His son, Daniel "Darby" Drafts, is pictured here with his mule, Maude. Darby Drafts, a teacher at Leesville School and a farmer, married Mary Emma Wingard on October 18, 1900, and they had four children. He and Mary Emma were very active members at Pilgrim Lutheran Church, where he was treasurer from 1929 to 1943. Their eldest son, Ed, owned and operated the liquor store on Main Street in Lexington for a long time; and their youngest son, Clyde, worked as a conductor on the Southern Railroad until retirement and was also a farmer. (Dorothy Tunstall.)

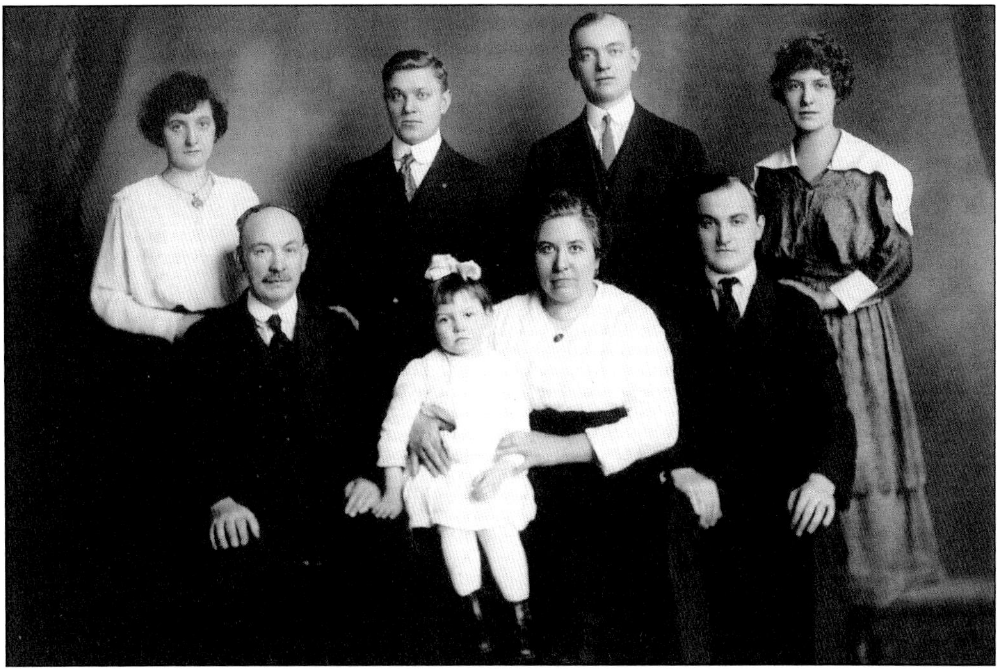

One of Draft's daughters, Julia, married Louie Fiebrich (second row, third from the left), an Austrian immigrant who had settled in Chicago. He is pictured above with his parents, Jacob and Marie, and other family members. Louie and Julia met through mutual friends at Langley Field in Virginia, where he was serving in the Army Air Corps and she was working as a hospital dietician. Julia was a forerunner of the modern-day career woman. Rather than marrying right away and having children, Julia received her degree from Winthrop College. She met Louie Fiebrich later and had two children, Dorothy (Dot) and Louie Jr. The family traveled with Louie while he was stationed at various posts in the States and Puerto Rico. Dot Fiebrich Tunstall remembers moving back to Lexington permanently after her father's death in 1945. In the photograph below, cousins LaRay Drafts (left), Louie Fiebrich Jr. (center), and Donald Drafts are pictured with Julia Fiebrich. (Both, Dorothy Tunstall.)

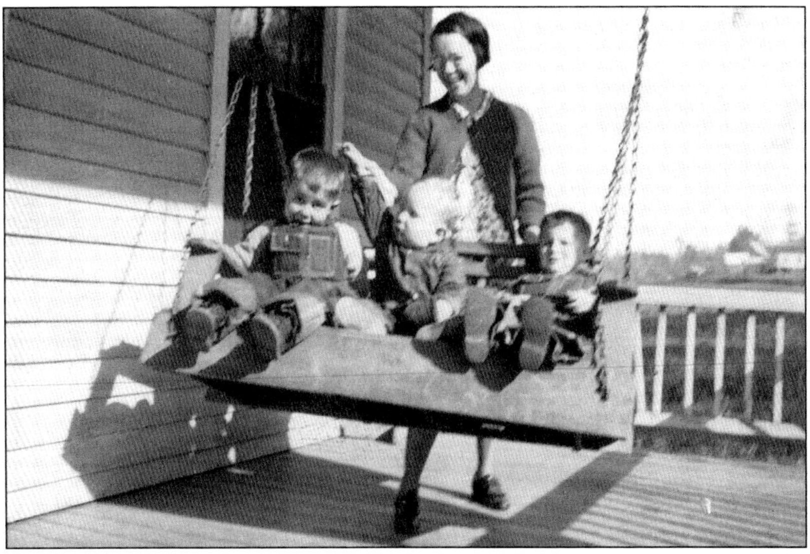

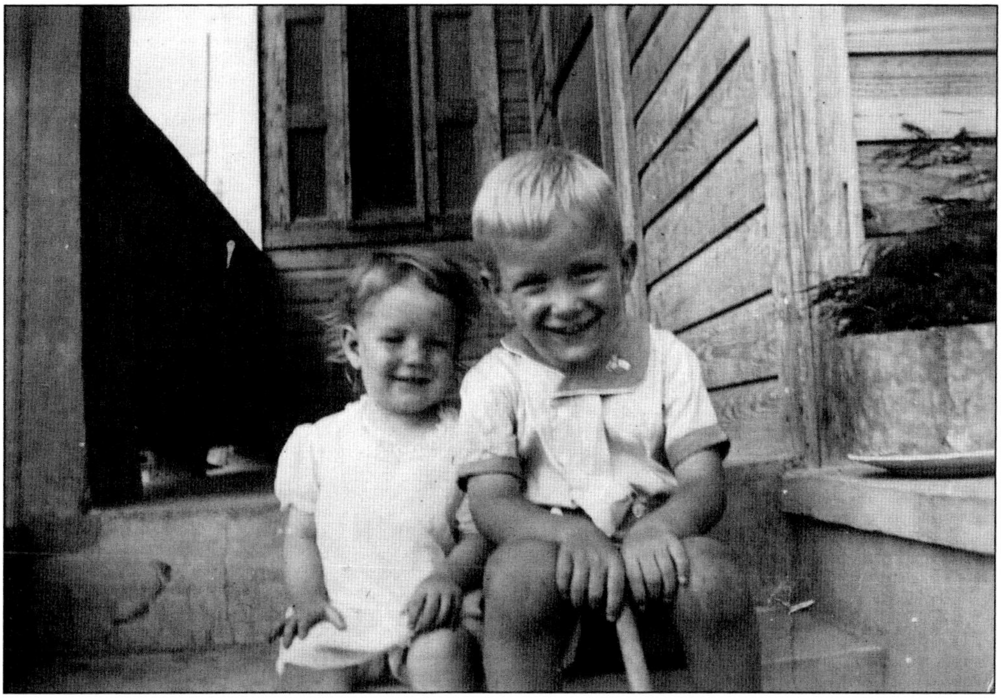

During the war, the Fiebrich family was based in Puerto Rico for about a year. Their daughter, Dorothy Jane (Dot), remembers playing with her big brother, Louie Jr. Everyone would come up to her parents when they were out shopping to see them because they had blonde hair and blue eyes. (Dorothy Tunstall.)

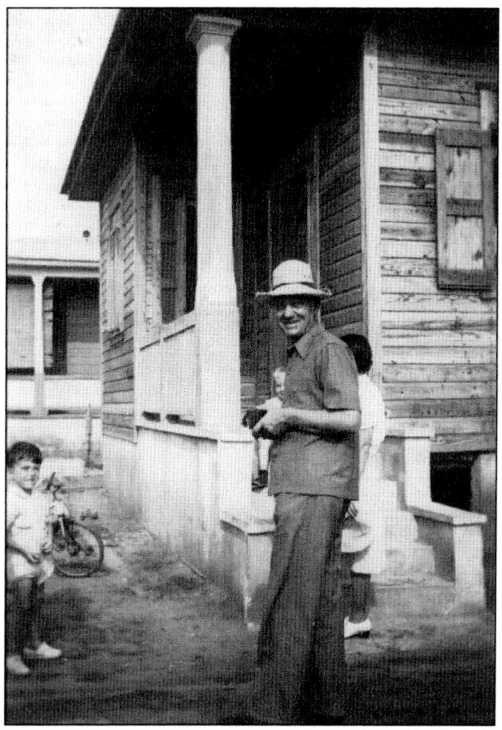

Dot Tunstall enjoyed the way her father was very quiet. She liked that he kept his culture and remembers he always said, "Vat's dis?" Her mom would cook mixed bread and liver nips for her dad. Julia Fiebrich loved to entertain and prepare feasts for friends. This explains why she enjoyed being the lunchroom supervisor for Lexington School District One. Julia and Louie had five grandchildren and six great-grandchildren. (Dorothy Tunstall.)

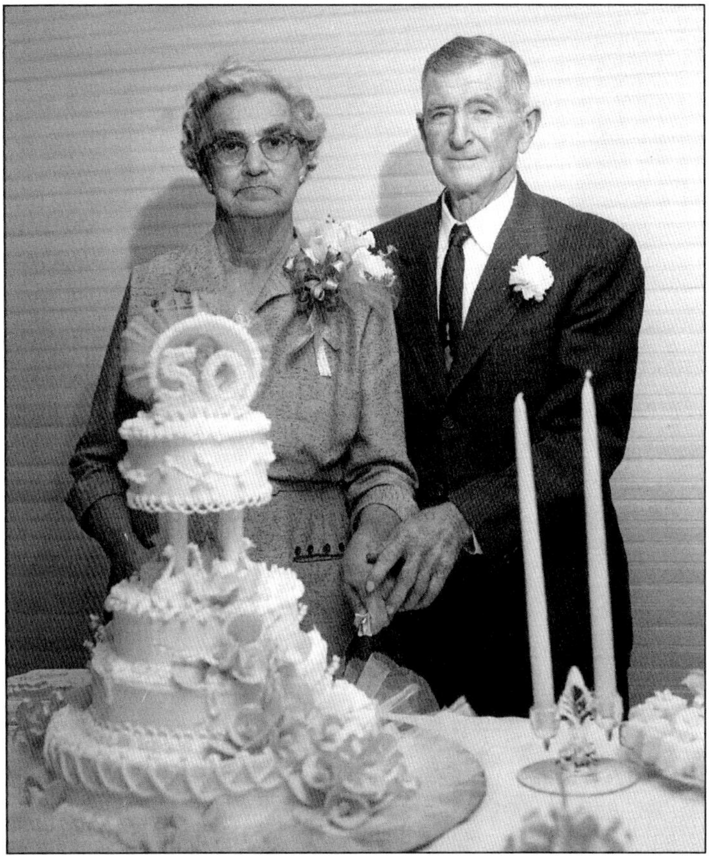

George Edwin Harmon and Ardella Kleckly Harmon, shown on the left at their 50th wedding anniversary celebration, had eight children. They lived in Lexington in a two-story house located where Windsor Crossing is now. George was a farmer and worked the land to provide for his family. He and Ardella and many others from their generation saw the rise of electricity, telephones, television, movies, wars, and transportation. The group photograph was taken during George's 90th birthday party. The Harmons were blessed with 10 grandchildren and many great-grandchildren. (Both, Ron Redd.)

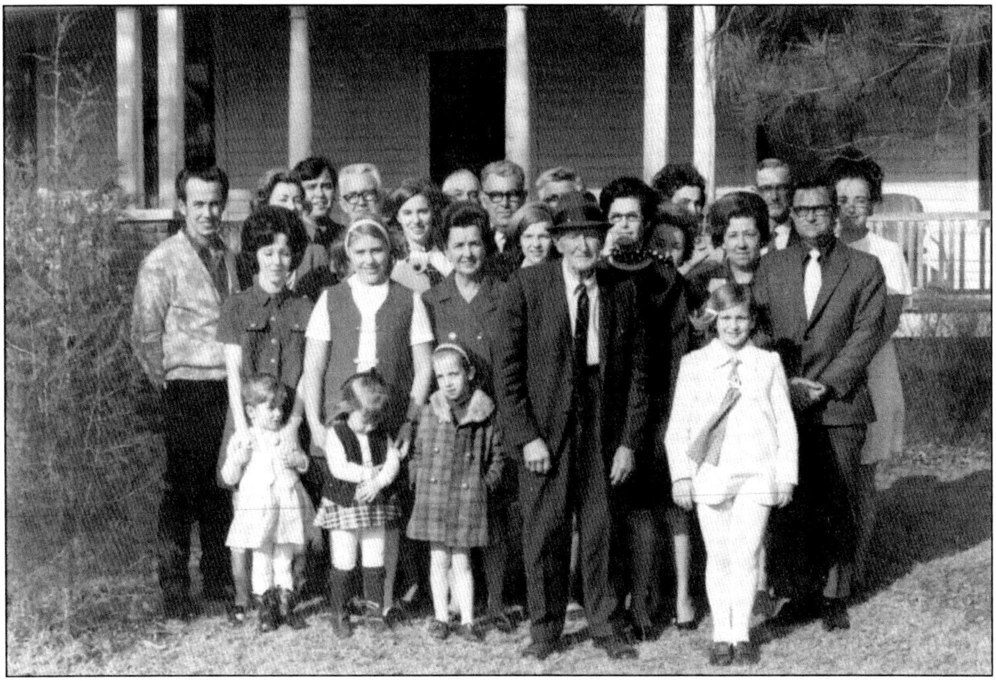

Dr. Homer Mathias was a family doctor who made house calls and delivered babies. He started practicing medicine in 1913 and was living above the drugstore when the town burned in 1916. Dr. Mathias was secretary of the Lexington County medical society and a member of the Lions Club. The switchboard always knew where he could be found for help. Dr. Mathias married Ernestine Barre in 1923, and they had three children, four grandchildren, and two great-grandchildren. (Mathias family.)

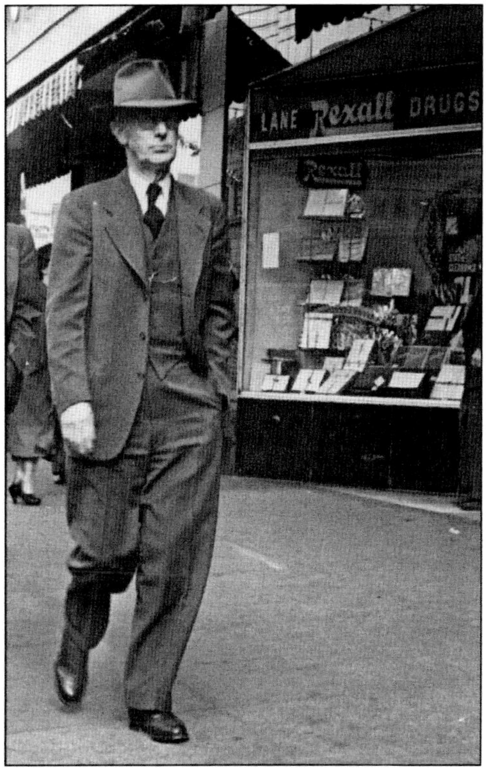

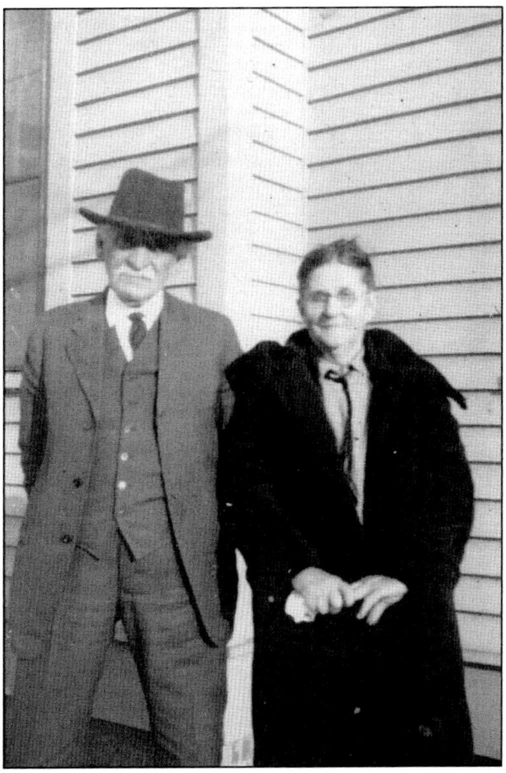

Bill Mathias learned to drive going on house calls with his father along the county's sandy roads. He remembers when office visits cost $2 and home visits $4. A member of the Methodist church, Dr. Mathias would sometimes get chickens, rabbits, or baked items as payment. Bill remembers only one vacation to the mountains with his family: they had to come back the next day after someone broke his leg. (Mathias family.)

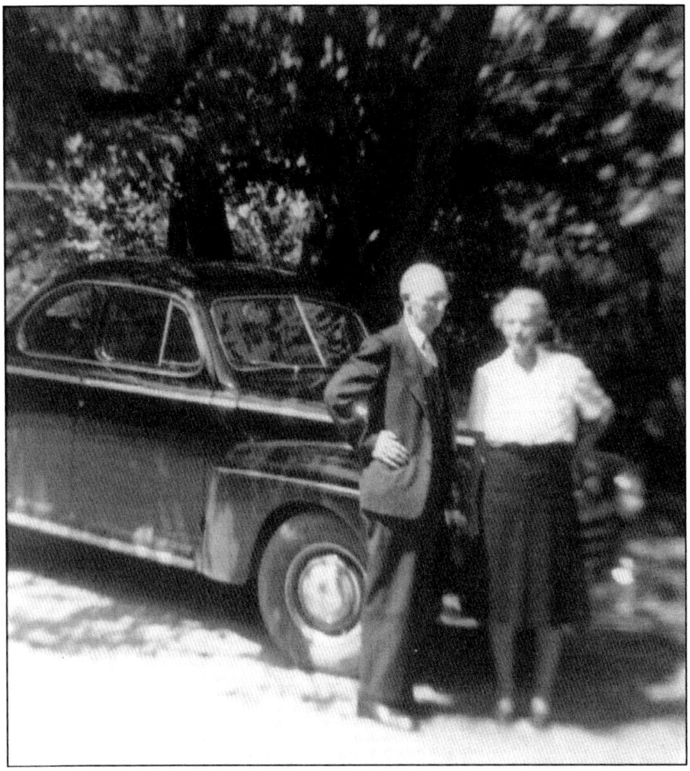

As a country doctor's wife, Ernestine was very busy. She was very active in the Athena club, an original women's club started in Lexington. Other clubs that women were involved with during these times were home demonstration clubs, bridge clubs, Lexington Women's Club, and the Lexington Literary Club. Ernestine was also very active in all activities at St. Stephen's Lutheran Church. (Mathias family.)

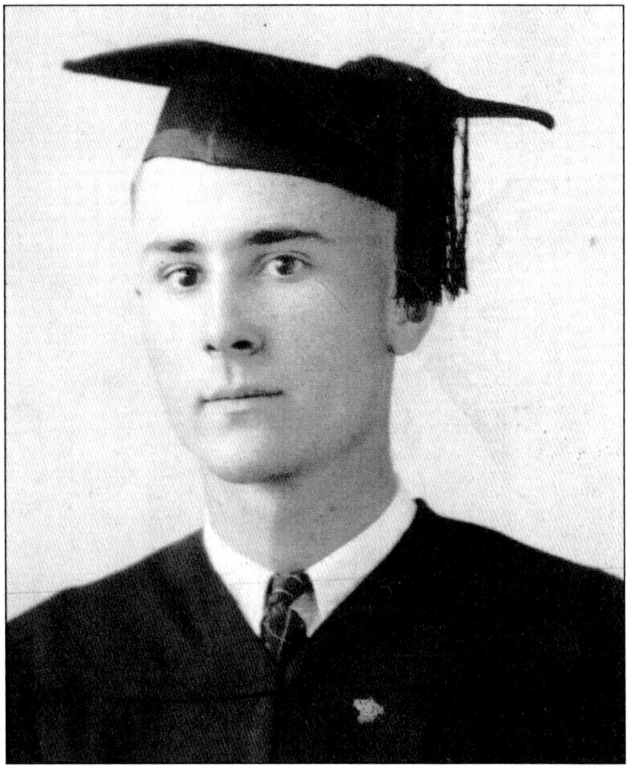

Harry Odelle Harman (1906–1969) was a student at the University of South Carolina (USC). After graduating, he became a teacher and principal at Red Bank Elementary School from 1929 to 1933. In 1933, he was elected Lexington County superintendent of education, a position he held until 1939. He resigned in the middle of his second term to become superintendent of Lexington Public Schools, which consisted of Lexington Elementary and Lexington High Schools. This new position was created to meet the division of school zones as growth began making division by districts an eventual outcome 14 years later. (Harman family.)

Harman received a master's in education from USC in 1936 and was awarded an honorary doctor of laws degree from Newberry College in 1955. In 1951, when a statewide school consolidation movement promised to offer better educational opportunities for South Carolina students, Lexington County was divided into five school districts. Harman became superintendent of Lexington County School District One and served until his death in 1969. His policies were always aimed at better education. (Harman family.)

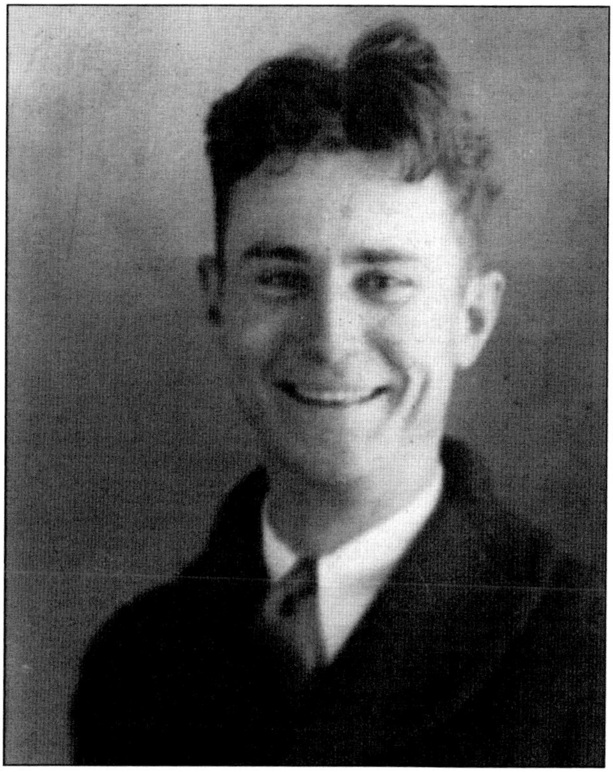

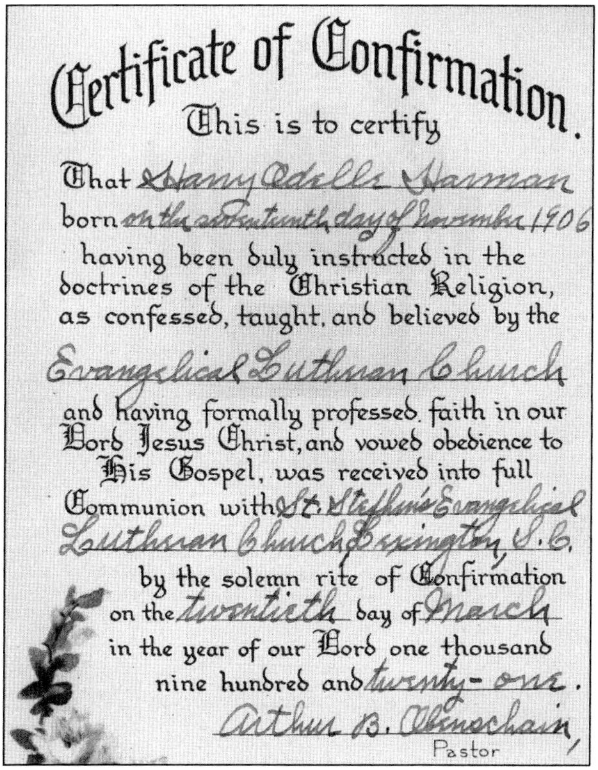

Certificate of Confirmation.

This is to certify

That Harry Odell Harman

born on the seventeenth day of November 1906

having been duly instructed in the doctrines of the Christian Religion, as confessed, taught, and believed by the Evangelical Lutheran Church

and having formally professed faith in our Lord Jesus Christ, and vowed obedience to His Gospel, was received into full Communion with St. Stephen's Evangelical Lutheran Church Lexington, S.C.

by the solemn rite of Confirmation on the twentieth day of March in the year of our Lord one thousand nine hundred and twenty-one.

Arthur B. Obenschain

Pastor

This certificate of confirmation was presented to Dr. Harman upon completion of his confirmation class. Dr. Harman was a lifelong member of St. Stephen's Lutheran Church, where he taught the men's Sunday school class and served on the council. He also served as a member of the executive board of the South Carolina Lutheran Synod, chairman of the board of trustees at Newberry College, chairman of the Lowman Home, and was a member of the board of publication of the United Lutheran Church of America. (Harman family.)

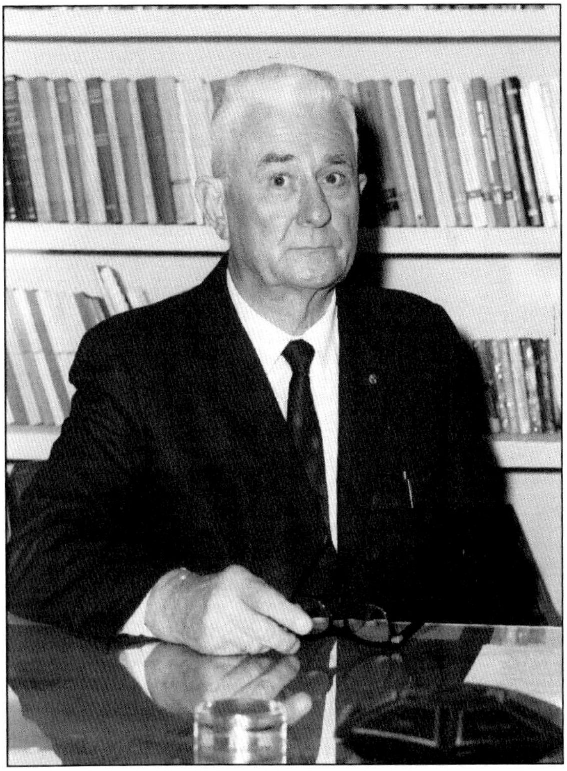

In the summers of the late 1940s and early 1950s, Dr. Harman taught education courses at USC, where he served on the board of trustees from 1945 to 1950. He was a member of Lexington Lions Club and was elected a district governor of Lions Club of America. Harman established the Lexington Chamber of Commerce and served as its first chairman. One of his strengths was building public support through local government. His last and most loved project was the Lexington County Medical Center. He traveled, met with committees, and served as the first chairman of the board. Fate prevented him from seeing its completion. Dr. Harman's peers admired his ability to work with people. He would open doors for his students through letters of recommendation and networking. (Harman family.)

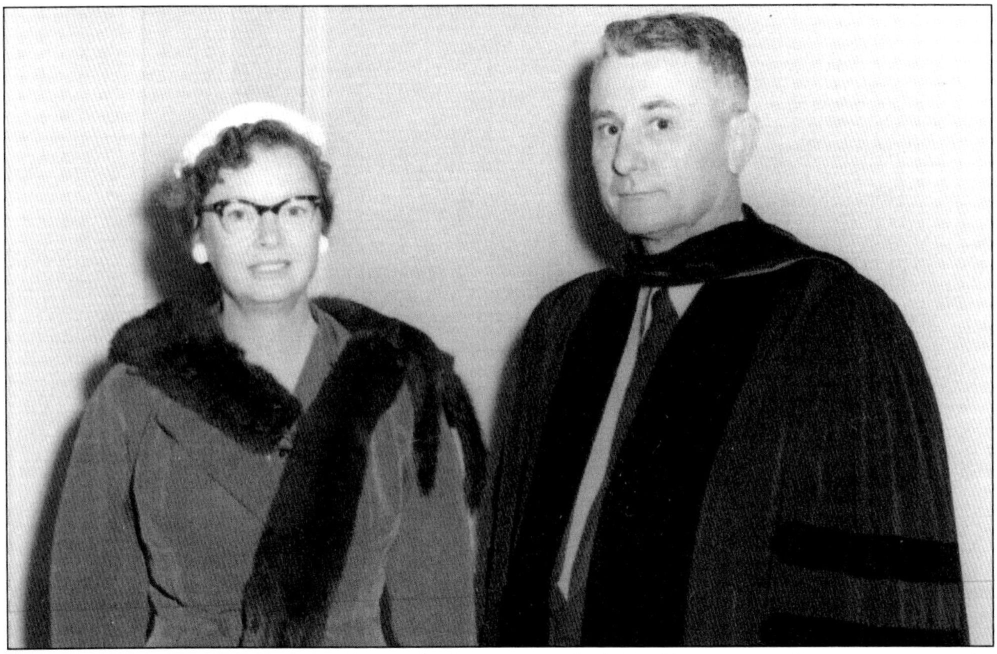

Harman was a forward thinker who made decisions to help build a strong education system. As district superintendent, he visited each of his schools weekly. He also met with staff and students in the classrooms. Dr. Harman built high expectations communicated by a staff handbook, which was one of the first of its kind in the Lexington educational system. (Harman family.)

Harman married Sarah Clark, who was always by his side supporting him in all of his endeavors. She was active in both church and community. They had 4 children, 7 grandchildren, and 13 great-grandchildren. His children remember their father as active in, supportive of, and dedicated to contributing to his community. (Harman family.)

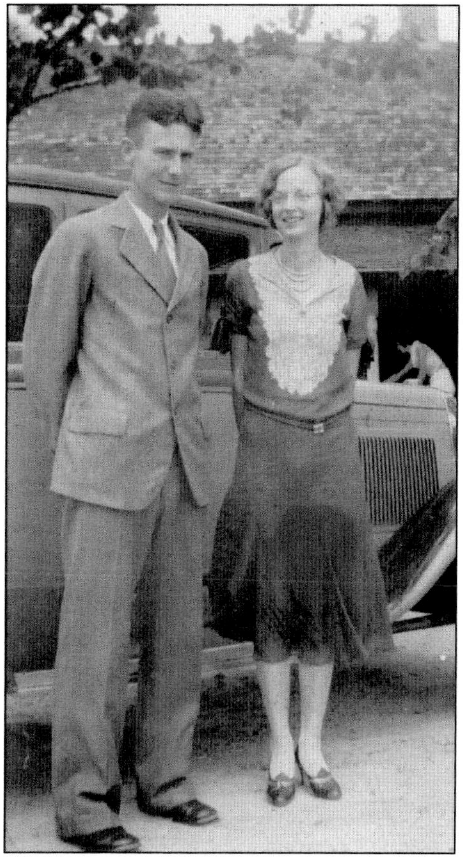

Pictured here are Harry and Sarah Harman's four children. They are, from left to right, Arthur (died 2007), who owned and operated Xerographic Efficiency Corporation in Charlotte, North Carolina; Paul, a former vice president and general manager of BellSouth Corporation (retired 1999) and brigade commander in the South Carolina Army National Guard (retired 2001); Beth Caddell, who retired in 1992 after 40.5 years of service in education; and Harry, who owned and operated Harman Funeral Home (now Caughman-Harman Funeral Home) and served as Lexington County coroner since 1977. Harry Harman's children remember their father as a warm and caring person who made his family feel important and supported his children's decisions and choices. He was busy, but he always made time for them. (Harman family.)

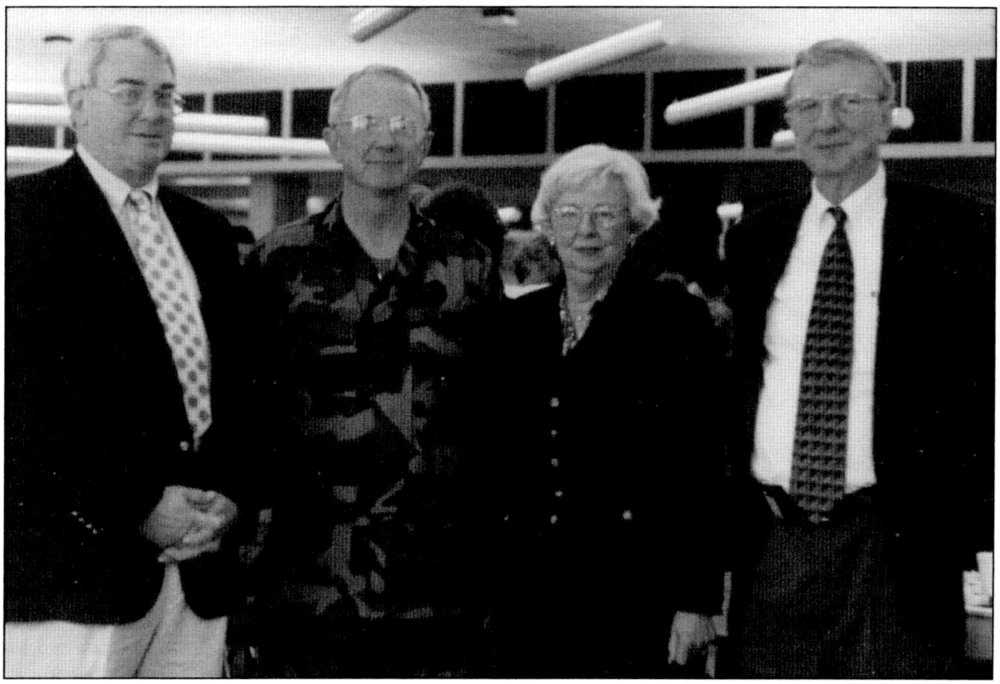

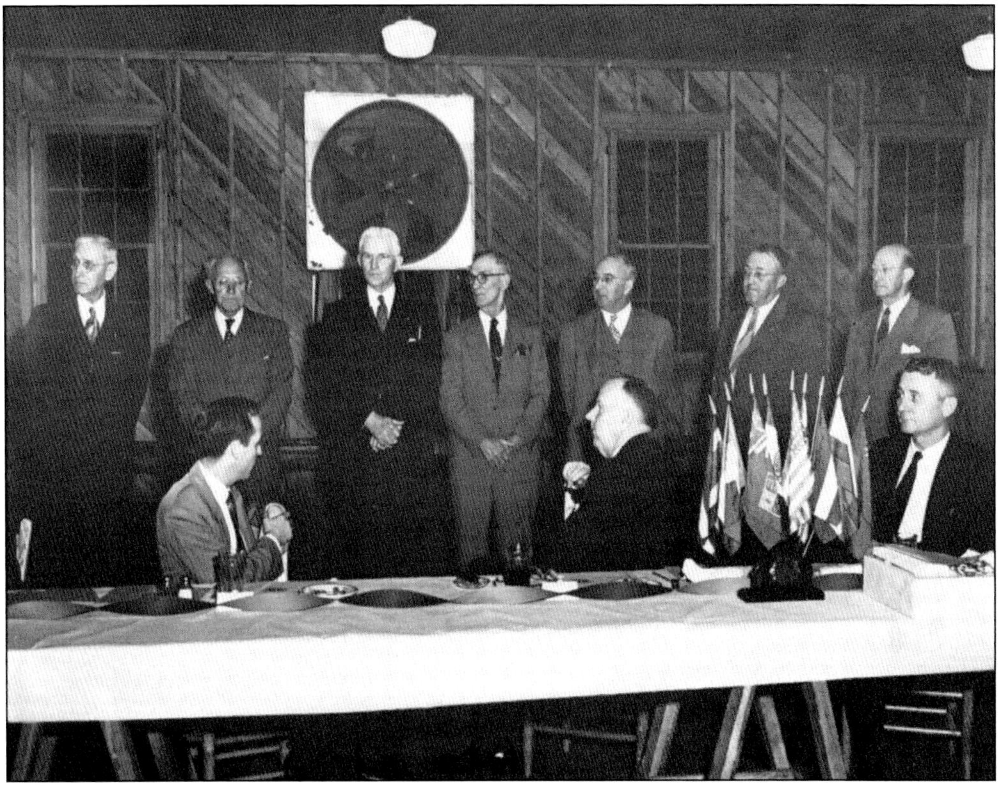

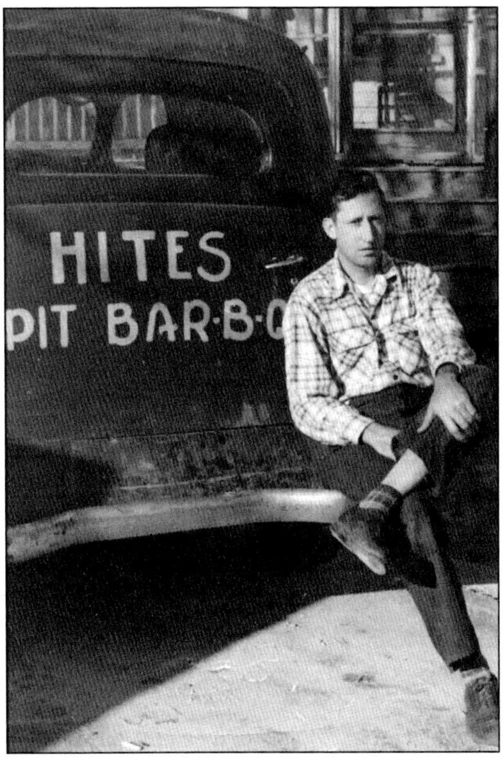

Among the civic leaders and charter members of the Lions Club pictured here are Heber Barre, Gus Barre, former attorney general T. C. Callison, Lexington County sheriff Cromer Oswald, W. W. Lorick, Holley Harmon, attorney Jack Carroll, and Harry Odelle Harman. The Lexington Lions Club is still very active in the community today. (Harman family.)

The youngest of nine children born to Sally Mathias Hite and John Henry Hite Sr., John Henry "Harry" Hite Jr. was born in Ridgeway, South Carolina, on July 31, 1917. His family moved to Lexington just after he was born. Before quitting school to help on the family farm, Harry finished fifth grade at the original White Knoll School, a two-room schoolhouse. (Susan Hite Wade.)

After serving in World War II, Harry Hite built and opened the 10 to 1, with hours from 10 a.m. until 1:00 a.m., in 1947. The 15-foot-by-18-foot building had a wooden floor. He said, "I had a counter with five stools and two booths. It started with a two-burner kerosene stove, and I put a piece of iron on top of one of the burners for a grill. That's how I grilled my first hamburger." (Susan Hite Wade.)

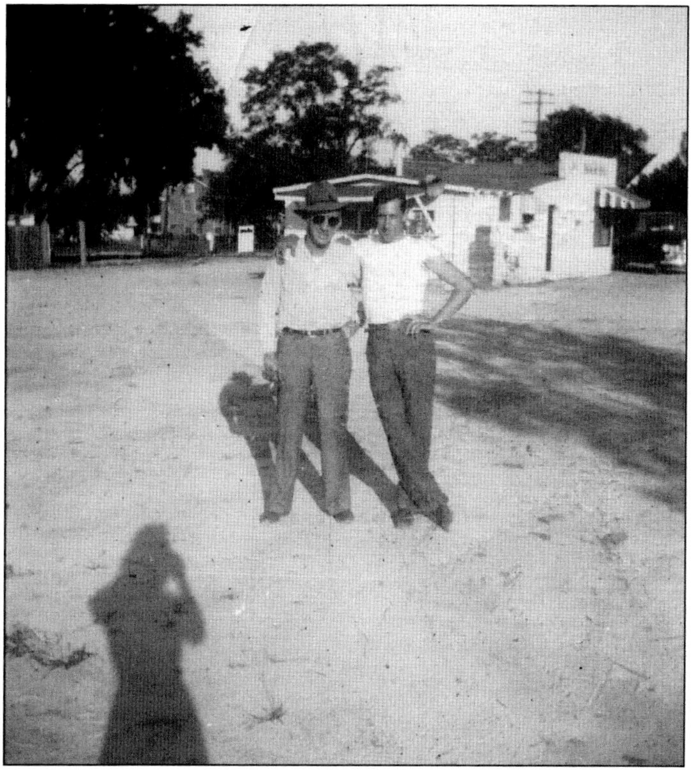

HITE'S DRIVE IN RESTAURANT

NIBBLE A BITE WHILE YOU SIT

JUICES

Tomato	10¢	Grapefruit	10¢
Orange	10¢	Prune	10¢

SOUPS

Chicken Noodle	30¢	Vegetable Beef	30¢
Chicken and Rice	30¢	Clam Chowder	30¢
Vegetable	30¢	Mushroom	30¢

Chile Con Carne 40¢

APPETIZERS

Tossed Salad	30¢	Shrimp Cocktail	50¢
Potato Salad	35¢	Celery Hearts	25¢
Lettuce and Tomato	25¢	Cole Slaw	15¢

SANDWICHES

Barbecue Pork	30¢	Ham and Egg	35¢
Hamburger	30¢	Bacon and Egg	35¢
Cheeseburger	35¢	Cheese Grilled or Toasted	25¢
Roast Pork or Beef	35¢	Pimiento Cheese	25¢
Ham, Boiled	30¢	Fried Egg	25¢
Ham, Fried	35¢	Chicken Salad	35¢
Ham and Cheese	35.	Bacon, Lettuce and Tomato	30¢
Lettuce and Tomato	20¢	Hot Dog Deluxe	20¢

BREAKFAST MENU

Sausage, 2 Eggs, Buttered Toast	65¢
2 Eggs, With Ham, Buttered Toast	75¢
2 Eggs, With Bacon, Buttered Toast	70¢
2 Eggs, Any Style, Buttered Toast	40¢
Cheese Omelette, With Buttered Toast	60¢
Hot Cakes, With Ham, Bacon, or Sausage	65¢

Hite's original menu consisted of a hamburger, a hot dog and a barbecue sandwich. The 10 to 1 was a popular hangout. "The customers were the most fun," Harry said. "Our restaurant was the town meeting place. Clemson boys would meet there before driving back to college on Sunday." Many people have fond memories of going to Hite's after church on Sundays. (Susan Hite Wade.)

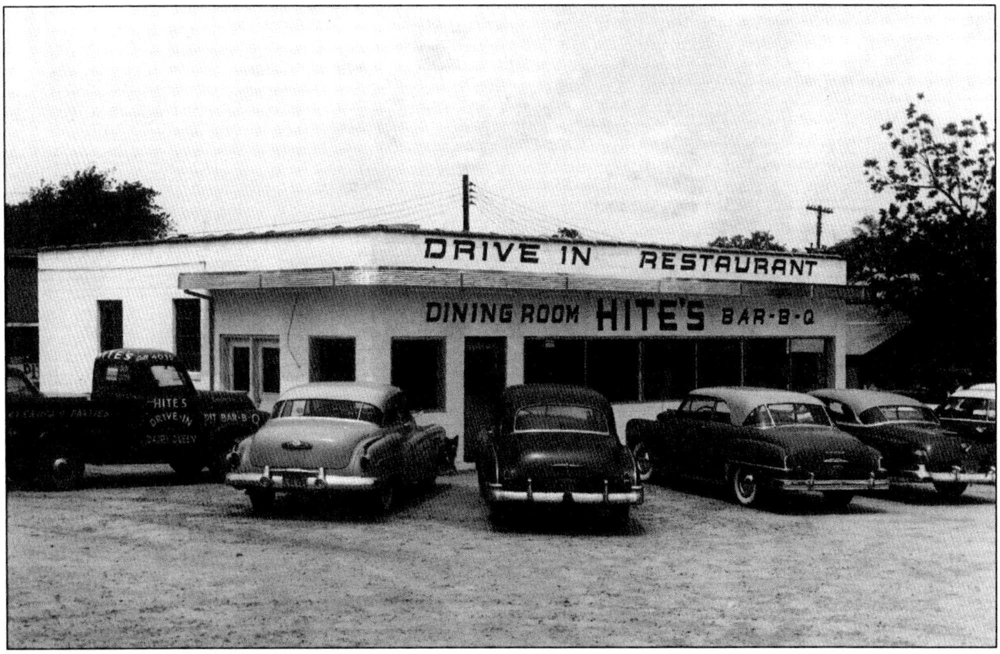

In 1948, Harry built the Dairy Bar next to the 10 to 1. The driveway that surrounded the Dairy Bar became a popular cruising site and hangout as well. Lexington natives remember some of their best times were evenings with friends at the Dairy Bar. U.S. representative Floyd D. Spence recalled his first job working the soda counter at Hite's. A new drive-in opened in 1953. (Susan Hite Wade.)

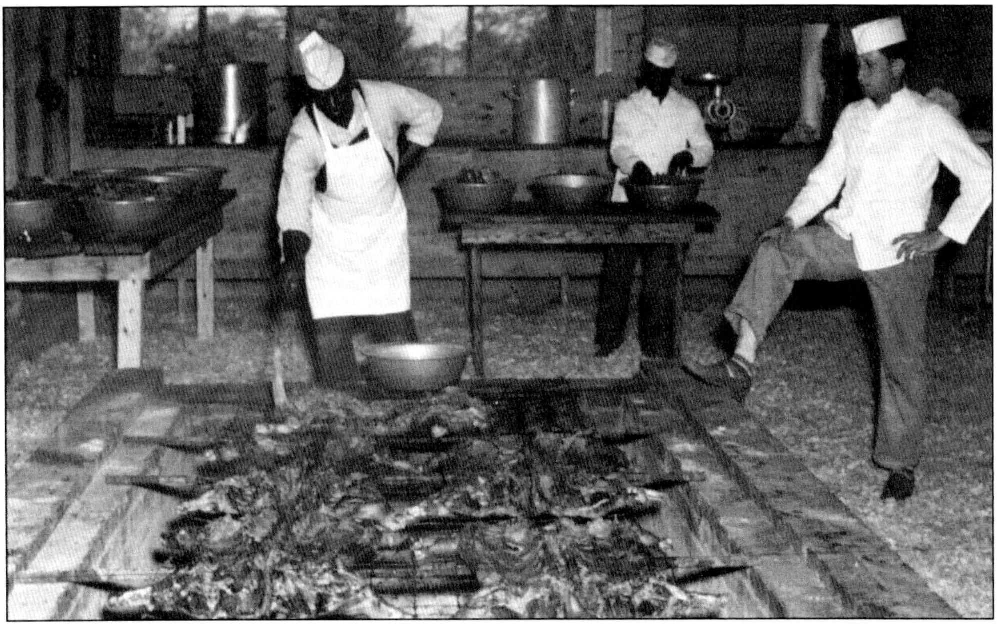

Harry Hite expanded his business by catering to local building sites. He also had a concession stand at the South Carolina State Fair. Susan Hite Wade remembers her father "never knowing what he will do next." She also recalls many fun times golfing with her dad, whose love for the sport eventually led to the creation of the Lexington Country Club. (Susan Hite Wade.)

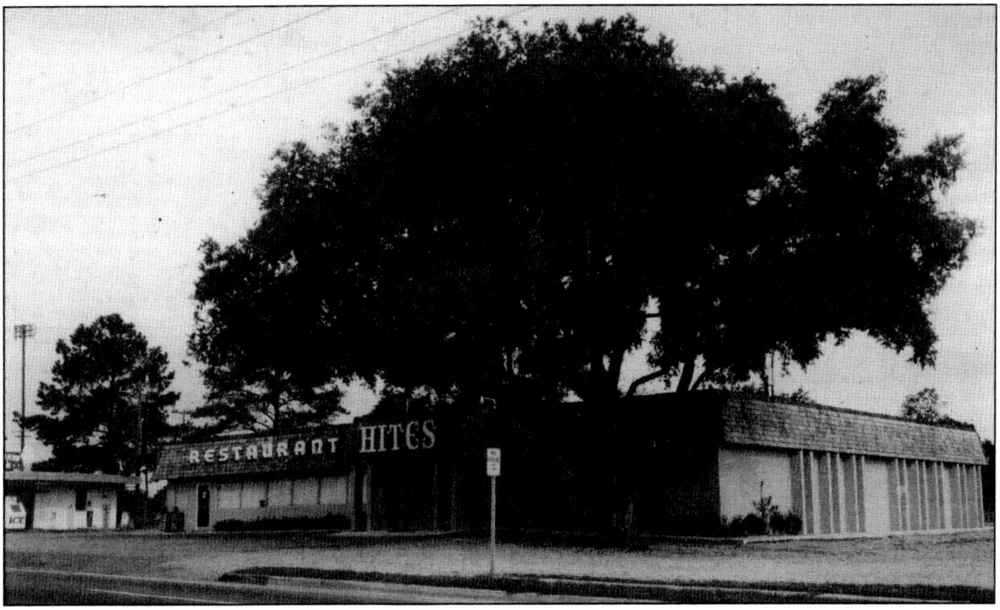

Hite's became the fastest-growing restaurant in the Midlands. He began with a single cook and ended with a staff of 45 by 1977, and he expanded his menu each year. In 1980, Harry Hite sold the business to the Maghans, and they kept the restaurant open until 1996. A mulberry tree out front was a place where people proposed, met, and relaxed over the years. (Susan Hite Wade.)

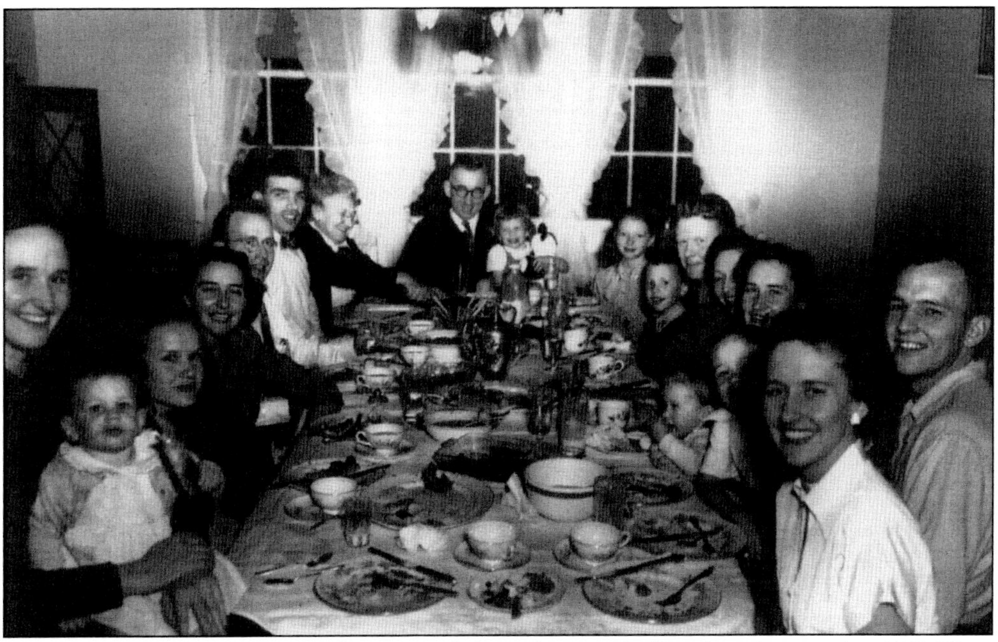

Emanuel Taylor and Nettie Goodwin met while working in Red Bank and married in 1913. They had 6 children and 16 grandchildren. They opened Taylor Hardware in 1918 in Red Bank, SC, near the mill. The Taylors attended Lexington Baptist Church. Their granddaughter Ann Sessions fondly remembers both her grandfather enjoying the beach and her grandmother's beautiful plants. Nettie even had a hothouse to grow plants year-round. This holiday family gathering was a usual sight for the Taylor family. (Ann Sessions.)

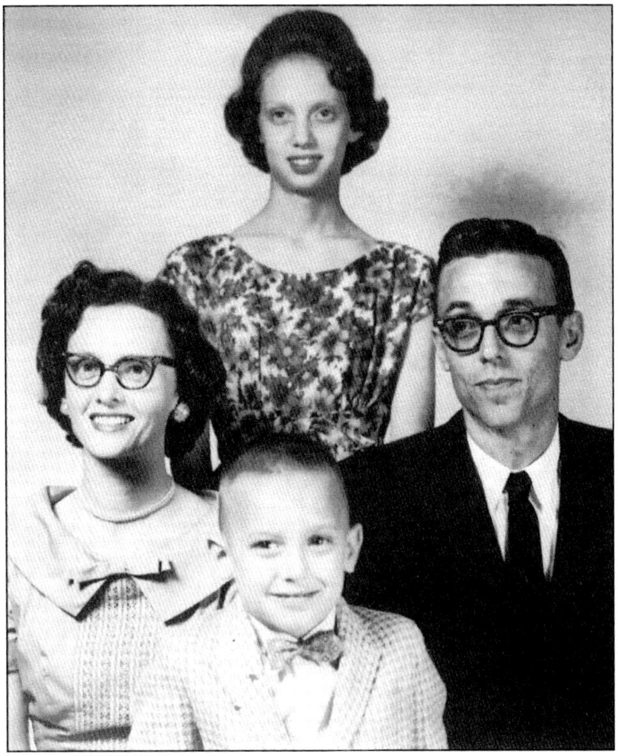

Joseph Bedenbaugh has been married to Edna Mills Bedenbaugh for 65 years, since 1945. They moved to Lexington in 1947 and have two children, four grandchildren, and one great-grandchild. Bedenbaugh became principal of Lexington Elementary School and joined the administration of Lexington District One when it was consolidated in 1951. Bedenbaugh feels that his two most important career events were helping families and staff through the district consolidation process and school desegregation. He is proud of the smooth and peaceful transitions made by parents, teachers, students, and staff. Joseph Bedenbaugh has also contributed to the community through Lions Club and Lexington United Methodist Church. (Bedenbaugh family.)

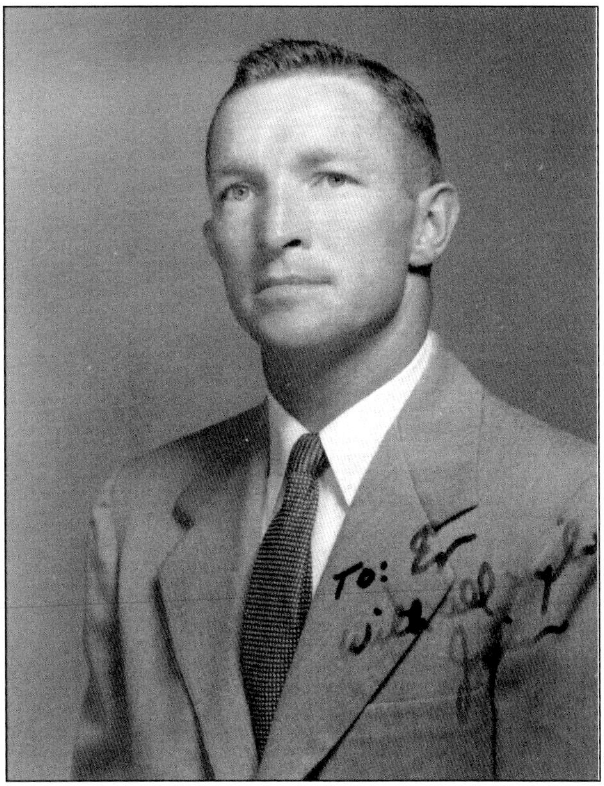

Jim Brittingham was serving in the Marine Corps at Parris Island when he met Evelyn Schnieder, from a farm family in Lexington. Jim and Evelyn were married and settled in Lexington, and he began working for an accounting firm in Columbia. Jim later began his own firm in West Columbia and was instrumental in organizing the Lexington State Bank with other local businesspeople. A member of the Lions Club and St. Stephen's Lutheran Church, he worked with several local business leaders to create the Lexington Country Club. Always a giving person, Jim is remembered by many for helping them when they really needed it. He and Evelyn had 4 children and 12 grandchildren. (Brittingham family.)

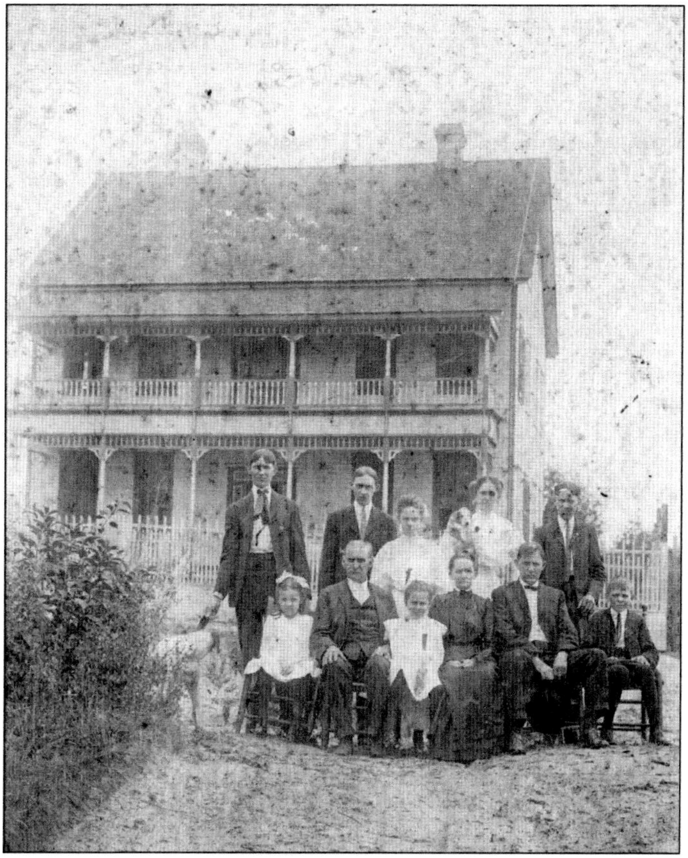

William Walter Barre and his wife, Elizabeth, had nine children. The family lived in this home on Hendrix Street. One of their sons, Heber, is pictured here (top left) with his family. After growing up on a family farm in Lexington, Heber graduated from Clemson University. After school, he returned home and began creating an electrical power plant on Barre Pond by Barr Road. Heber and his brother M. L. spent their summers wiring homes so people could get electricity. Electricity was only available at night; it was also cut off after a certain time, so people could not have lights all night. Barre sold the plant to South Carolina Electric and Gas in the 1930s. (Both, Mathias family.)

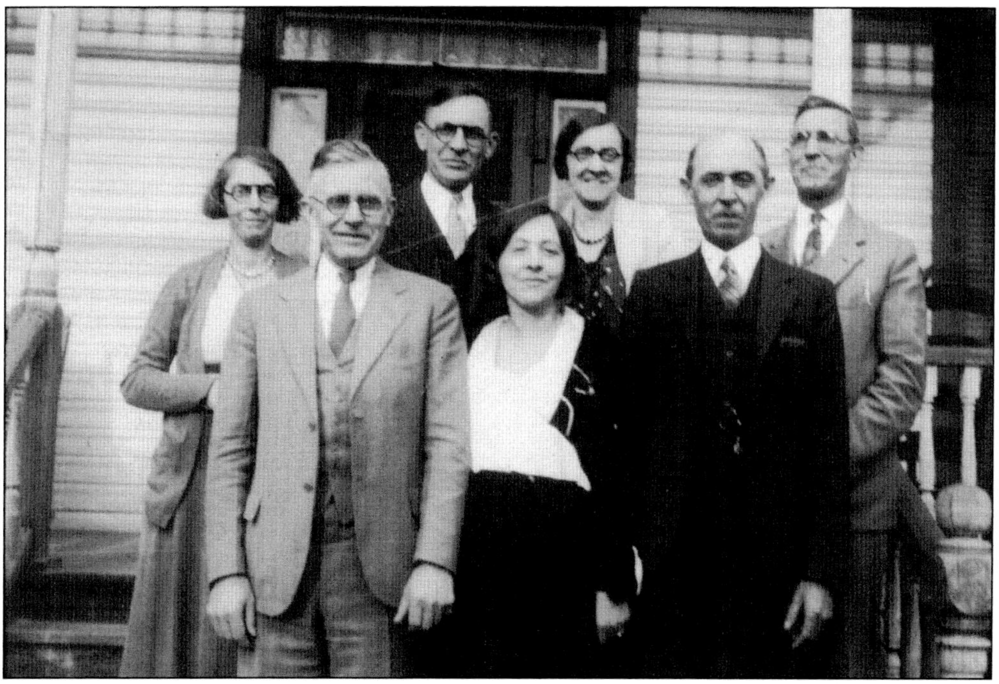

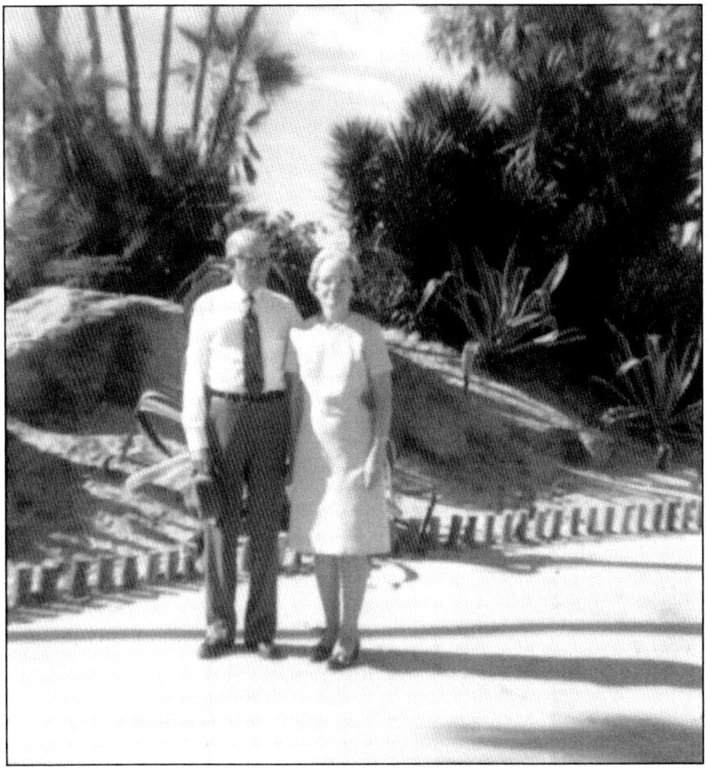

Sam A. George married Annie Laurie Kennerly from Swansea in 1935. At that time, some school districts required teachers to be unmarried. Annie Laurie taught for 18 years at Red Bank Elementary, which allowed married teachers. She was very involved in the Lexington Medical Center foundation and worked to make the hospital a reality for the people of Lexington. Sam and Annie Laurie had three children—Olga, Sam Jr., and Lynn. (Annie Laurie George.)

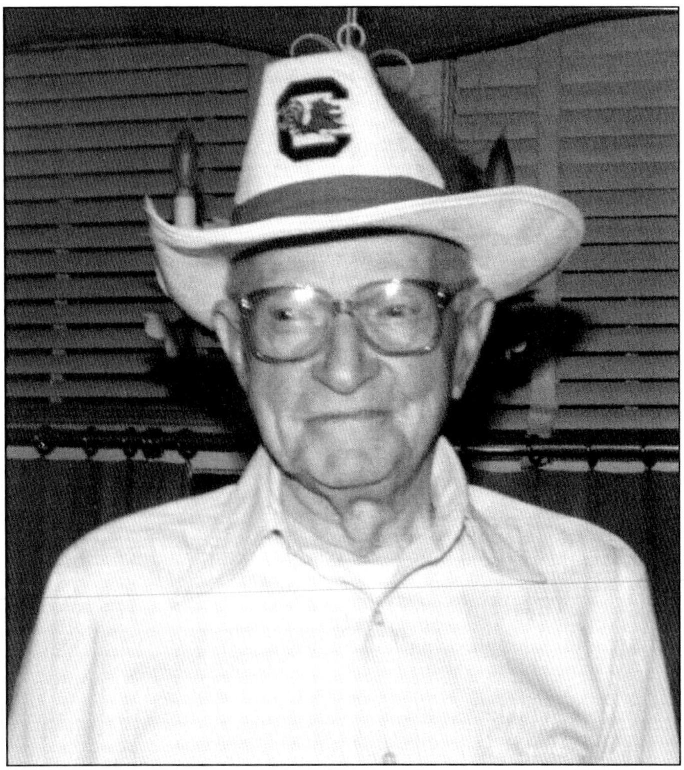

An active member of his community, Sam A. George spent countless hours attending meetings and events for the organizations he represented. A member of the Masonic lodge for over 50 years, Sam A. also achieved the high honor of becoming a Shriner. Sam belonged to the chamber of commerce, Lexington Methodist Church, and Lexington Country Club. Sam A. George continued his father's legacy and helped Lexington County become one of the first areas to have advanced telephone capabilities. (Annie Laurie George.)

Dr. James Liverman was born in North Carolina. A graduate of the Medical College of Virginia, he practiced in North Carolina before moving to Lexington in 1940 and opening an office on Main Street. Dr. Liverman was an obstetrician and delivered many of Lexington's residents. He saw a need for a community hospital and built one on Church Street in January 1951. (Kathryn Liverman.)

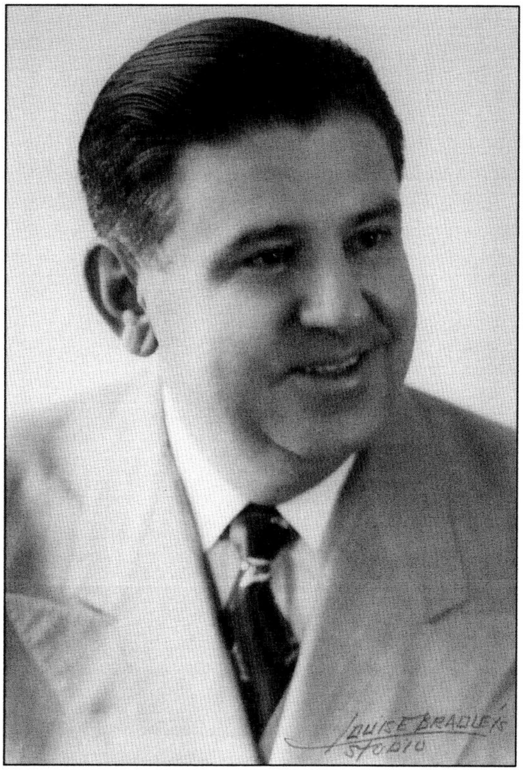

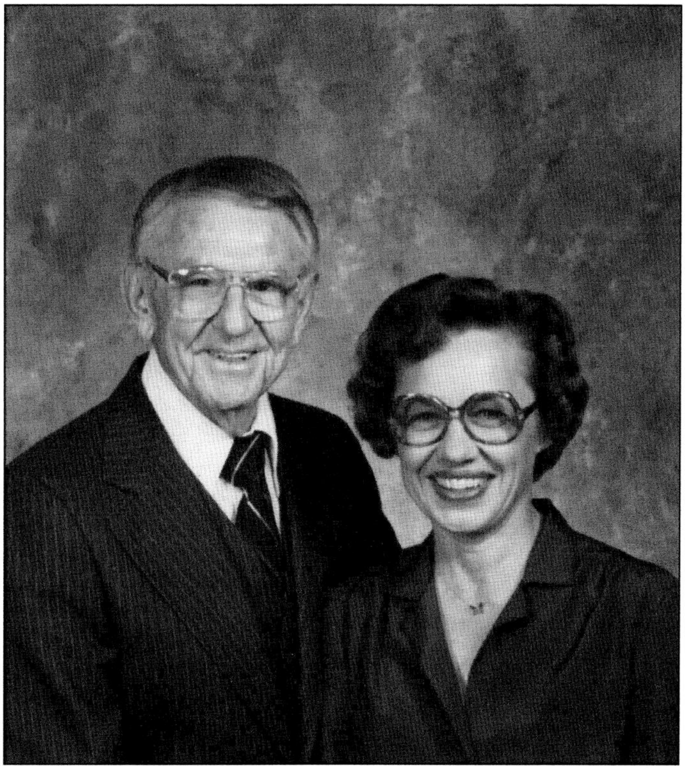

Dr. Liverman and his wife, Kathryn, helped many people in Lexington. Kathryn was the nurse by his side and remembers riding along on house calls. They had three daughters, including twins. Kathryn recalls how she and the girls would sing, tell stories, sew, and read while they waited. The doctor always kept his medical bag with him, even on vacation. He would say, "Any good doctor always has his bag." (Kathryn Liverman.)

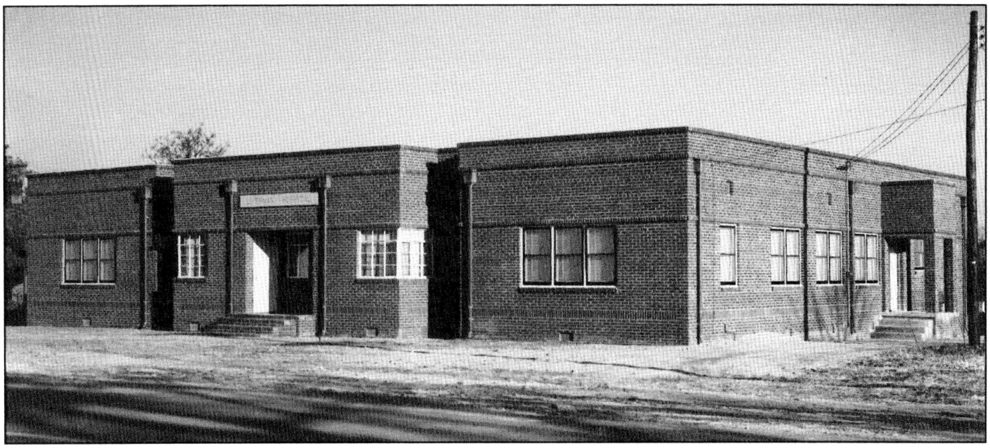

Between family life and the busy life of a country doctor, Dr. Liverman amazingly found time to care for and support the Lexington High School football team, the Wildcats. Michael Aun remembers how coach James Ingram and E. T. "Charge" Driggers recognized the doctor for not only taking care of the players when needed but also attending the games and cheering them on. Gincy Drayton says, "I remember my momma telling me that Dr. Liverman delivered me at Liverman's Hospital." Many people remember the kindhearted care at Liverman's Hospital in downtown Lexington. Before the Lexington Medical Center was ever needed, this small-town hospital run by local family members helped care for its people daily. (Kathryn Liverman.)

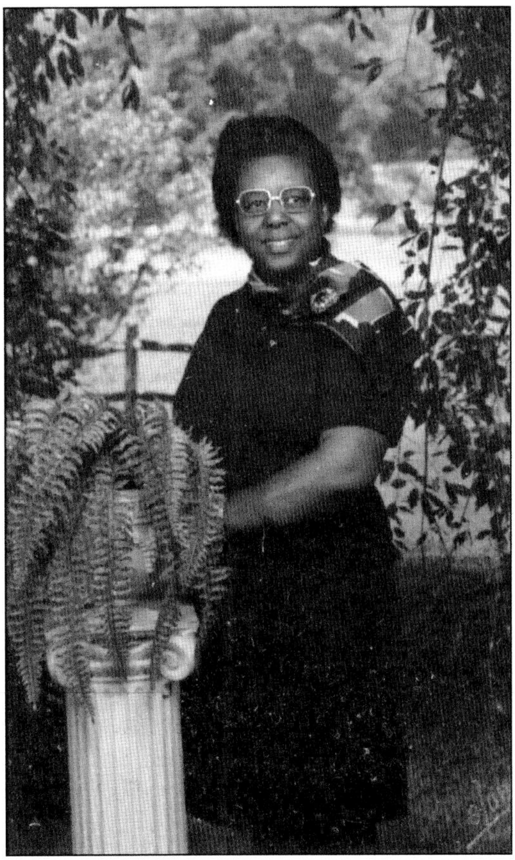

For more than 75 years, Ruth Sonley has been a member of St. Paul's Baptist, which she attended with her mother and her grandmother. Ruth was the organist and pianist for the church choir for 27 years. A graduate of Benedict College, she taught for over 30 years in Lexington School District One and also at one of the Rosenwald schools, which is now the intermediate school located on Hendrix Street in downtown Lexington. Rosenwald schools were funded by Julius Rosenwald, president of Sears, Roebuck and Company. Judge Lemuel Boozer, who believed in education for all, funded an African American school on West Main Street and Haygood Avenue between 1868 and 1929, prior to the Rosenwald School. After elementary school, all African American schoolchildren had to travel to West Columbia to attend high school at Lake View School. After the district integrated, Ruth Sonley taught at Gilbert for 12 years. Ruth walked to work before integration. When she began teaching in Gilbert, she learned to drive. Even though she is now over 80, Ruth is still an active member of the Lexington community. (Ruth Sonley.)

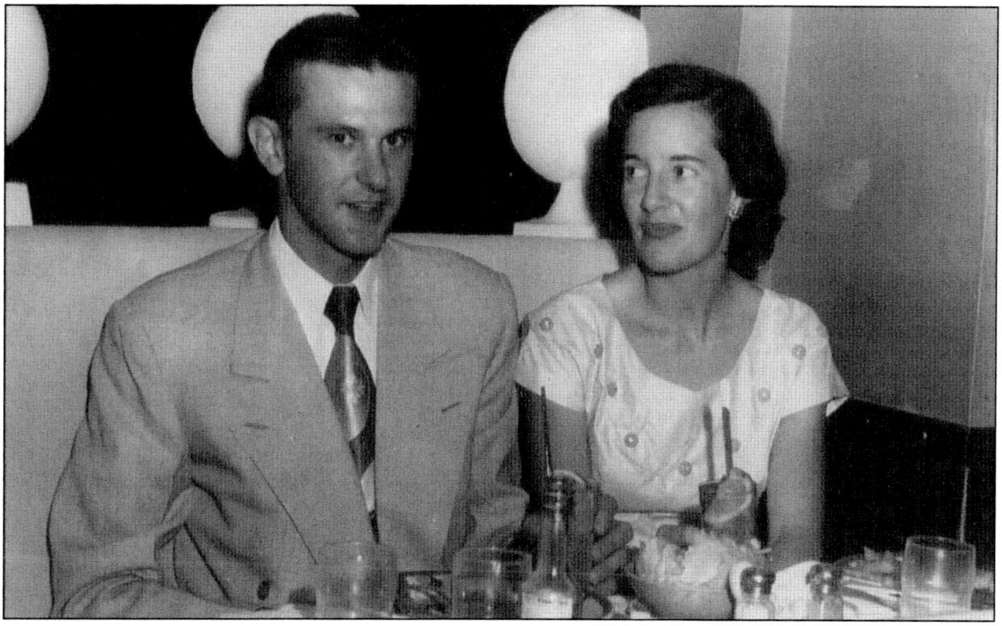

Dr. Gray Macaulay was the head of the Dorn Veterans Administration Hospital dental clinic in Columbia. He and his wife, Jane, lived on Crystal Lake in Red Bank since 1952. Before they wed, Jane was a schoolteacher at Schneider Elementary School. The Macaulays lived a very Christian life. They both attended St. Stephen's Lutheran Church and served in many volunteer roles. (Macaulay family.)

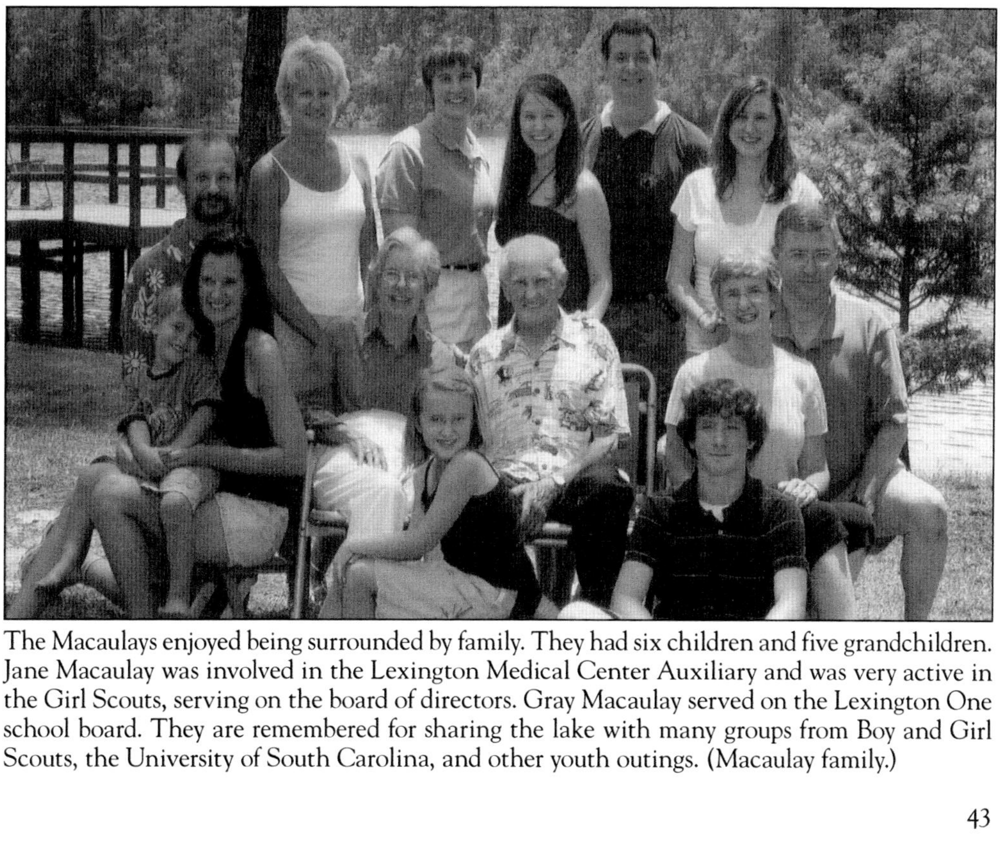

The Macaulays enjoyed being surrounded by family. They had six children and five grandchildren. Jane Macaulay was involved in the Lexington Medical Center Auxiliary and was very active in the Girl Scouts, serving on the board of directors. Gray Macaulay served on the Lexington One school board. They are remembered for sharing the lake with many groups from Boy and Girl Scouts, the University of South Carolina, and other youth outings. (Macaulay family.)

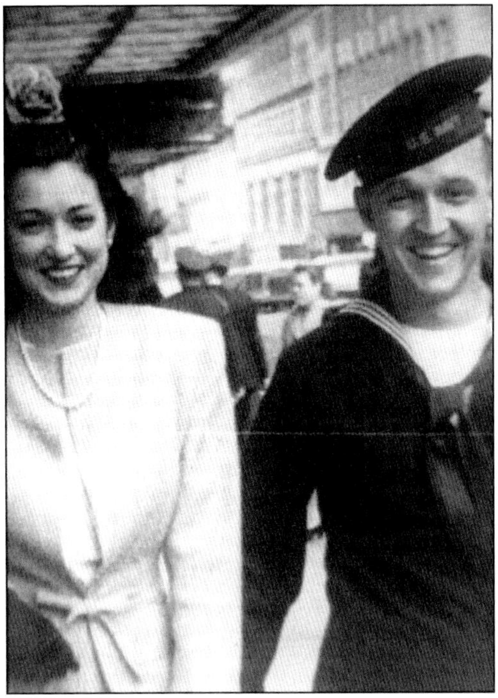

This happy couple represents many young people during World War II. While it was a time of great worry and stress for many, it was also a world full of opportunities to travel and celebrate life. Wallace and Doris Redd met one day when Doris came to town with some friends. Wallace was at the store when he saw her. They started dating and were married in 1946. (Ron Redd.)

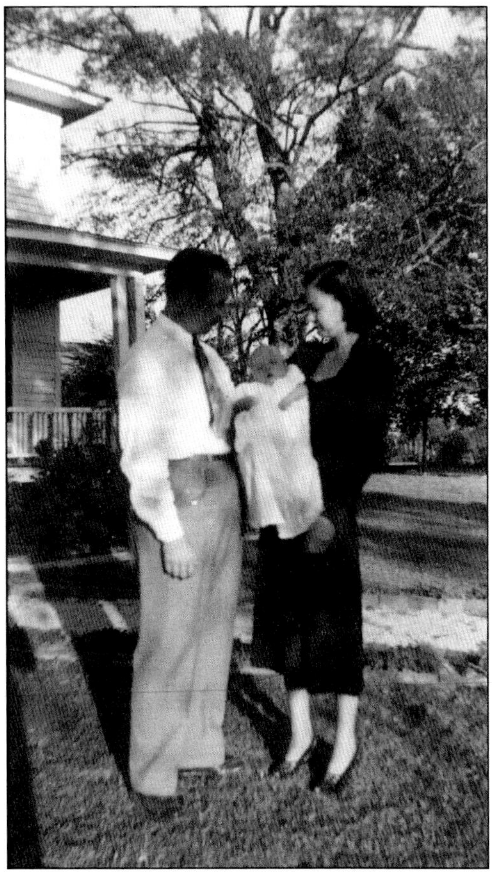

Wallace and Doris Redd lived in this small house on Elm Street until 1951, when they built the home on Third Avenue. Doris was best known for her ability to cook. All of her sisters and her grandmother Ardella Harmon were excellent cooks, and Doris made delicious mashed potatoes and loved to bake pies and fruitcake. Her homemade rolls were out of this world. The Redds were devoted to church, family, and friends. (Ron Redd.)

Beulah Fortune married Melvin "Jack" Glover in 1941. Beulah and her two sisters, Edna and Lillian, were raised in an upstairs apartment at 209 East Main Street, four doors from the old courthouse. Jack met Beulah when he was stationed in the finance department at Fort Jackson. He made a career of the army and retired in 1960. The Glovers had four children and were very active in St. Stephen's Lutheran Church. (Drew Glover Welch.)

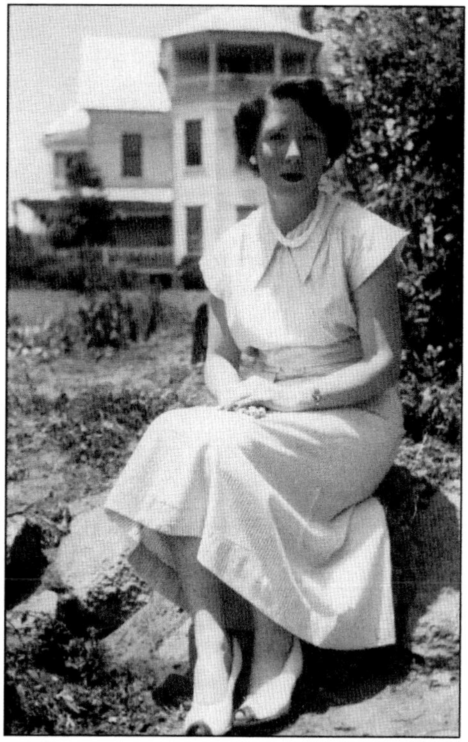

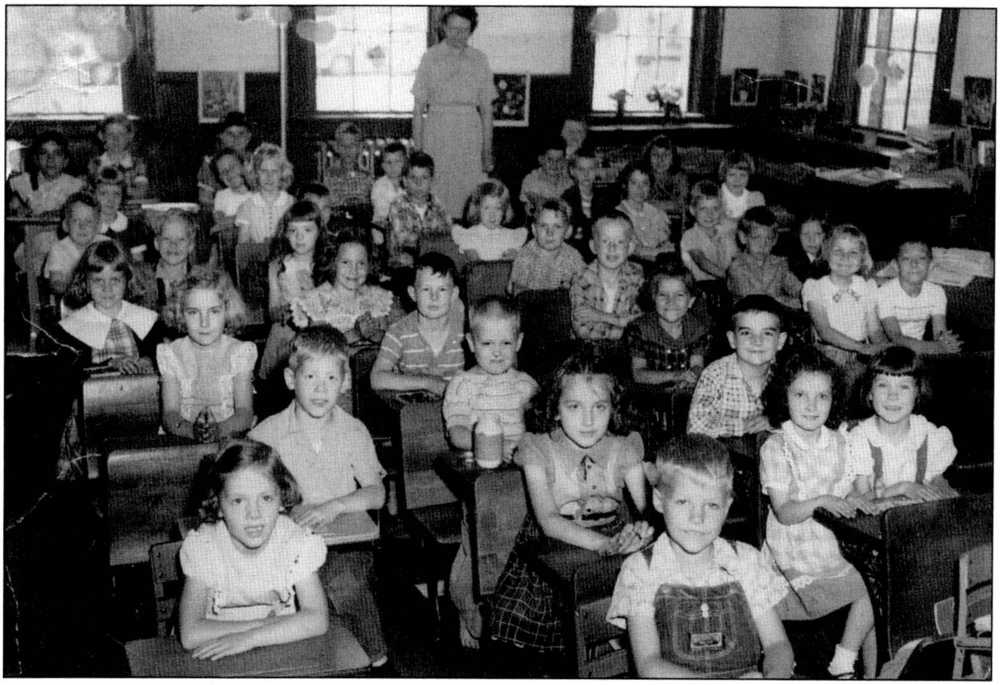

Louise Roberts taught at Lexington Elementary School for over 40 years. Drew Glover Welch is seated in the front left. Mary Dell Aun is seated at the back left corner. Also pictured in this 1953 class are Connie Jackson McNeil and Nolan Wessinger. A rite of passage for these students was to fall in the creek and have to go home and change their clothes. (Drew Glover Welch.)

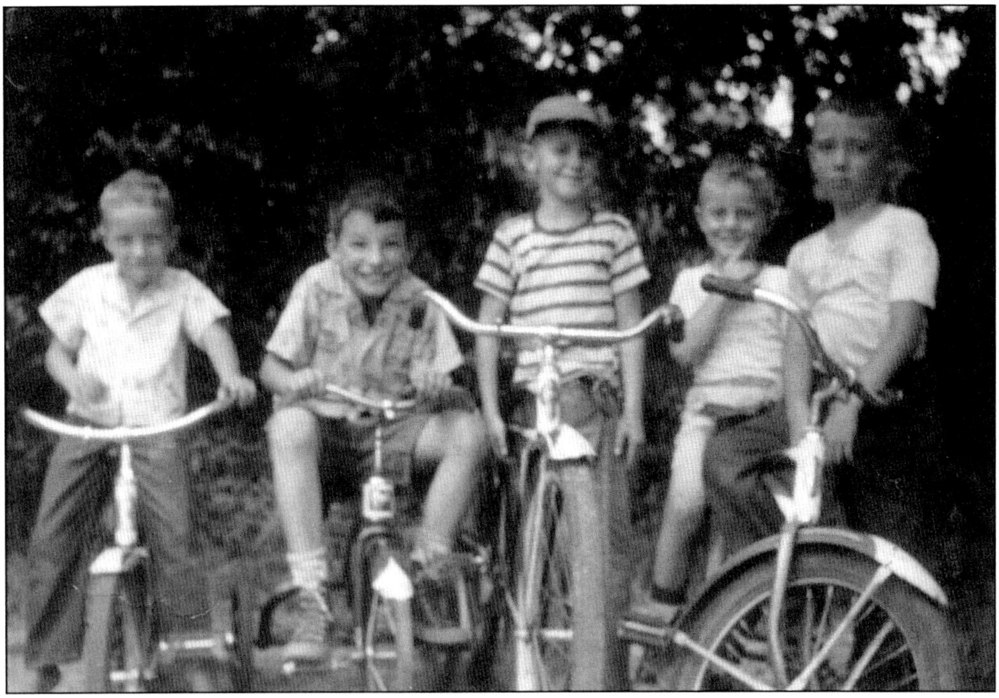

Election night was a big night in town. Beulah Fortune Glover remembers that all of the people from the surrounding areas would pile into cars and plan to spend the evening at the courthouse. A big white sheet was put up against the building, and as they were tallied, the results of the voting would be projected like at a movie theater. When the results were final, there would be big celebrations. Here is a picture of, from left to right, Mikey Wingard, Tommy Rawl, Arthur Harman, Paul Harman, and Butch Glover, who grew up on Main Street. (Drew Glover Welch.)

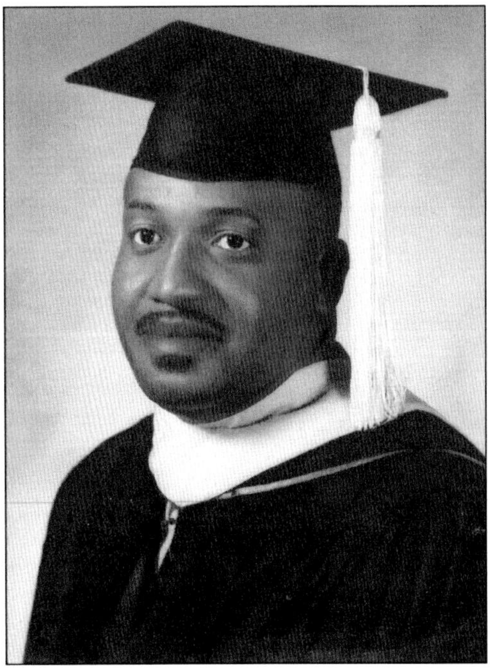

Willie Caractor taught sixth grade social studies at Batesburg-Leesville Elementary School for over 20 years. He had served for two years in the Pacific theater during World War II and was a graduate of both Benedict College and South Carolina State University. Respected in the Lexington community, Caractor worked to develop strong communications between different active civic groups that benefited all parties. (Mary Caractor.)

Caractor married Mary Sonley in 1952. Together they raised three daughters—Constance, Terry, and Bridie R. Willie was devoted to his family and to helping others in the community. He was known to have a friend to talk to in any part of town he visited. Mary Sonley Caractor recalls how many people would visit to get his advice. They were thankful because his advice was certain to be successful. (Mary Caractor.)

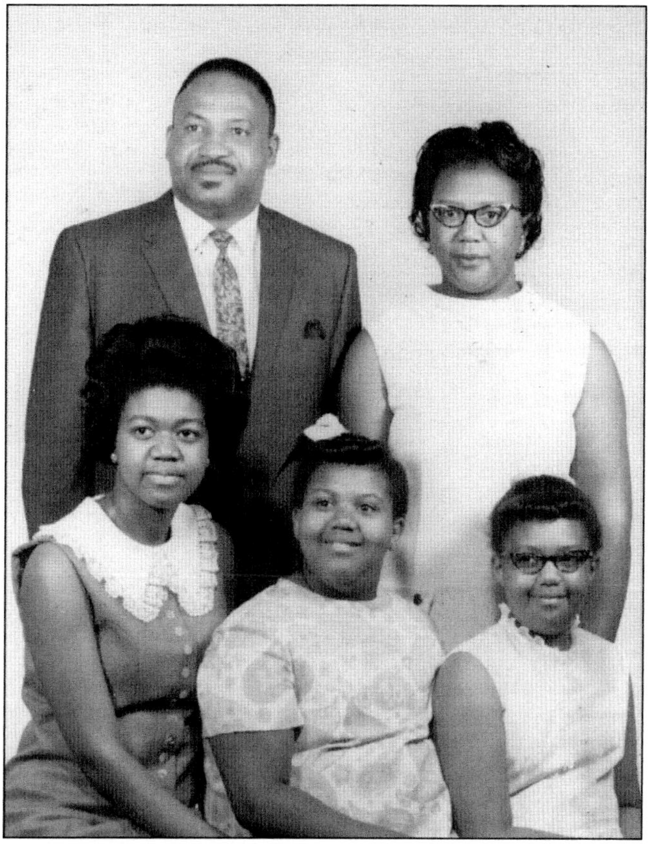

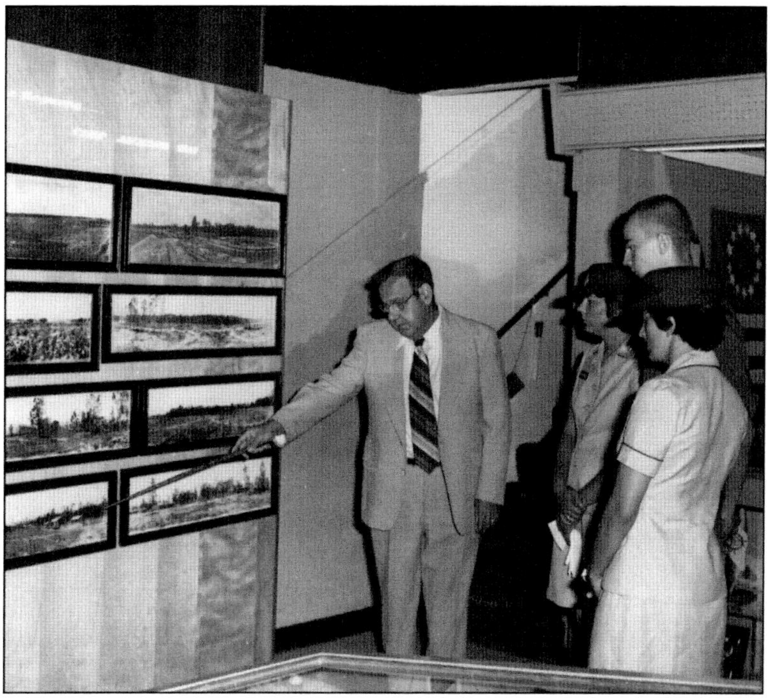

Clayton B. Kleckly has left a legacy for all of Lexington County. Known as a Lexington County historian, he was inspired to love history through a friendship with Uncle Tom, the son of a former slave. Clayton worked for the Internal Revenue Service and began a second career creating the Fort Jackson Military Museum after his retirement. (Nancy Kleckley Hughey.)

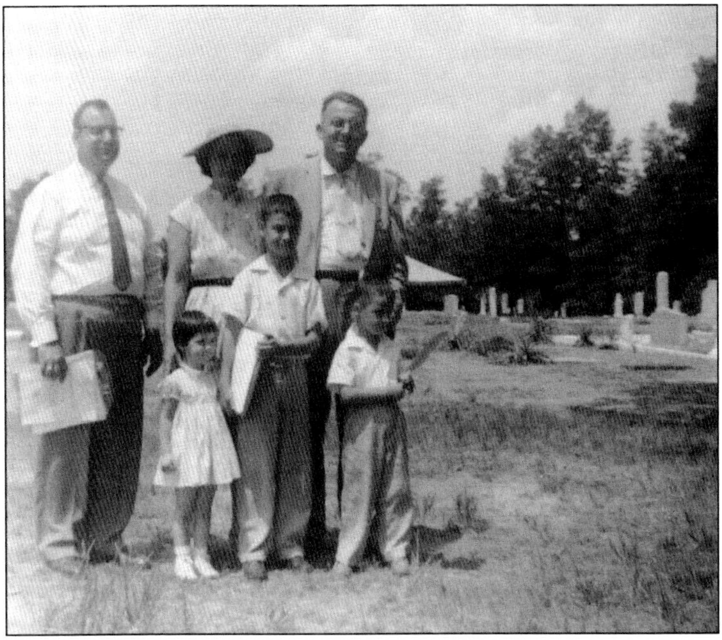

Kleckly was married to Esther "Peggy" Hagood. They had four children, three grandchildren, and three great-grandchildren. He belonged to many organizations and loved being a part of his community, and their daughter, Nancy, remembers her father sitting at the kitchen table designing the Lexington County seal. Peggy ran a flower shop, and the family helped deliver the altar flowers for many of the local churches. (Nancy Kleckley Hughey.)

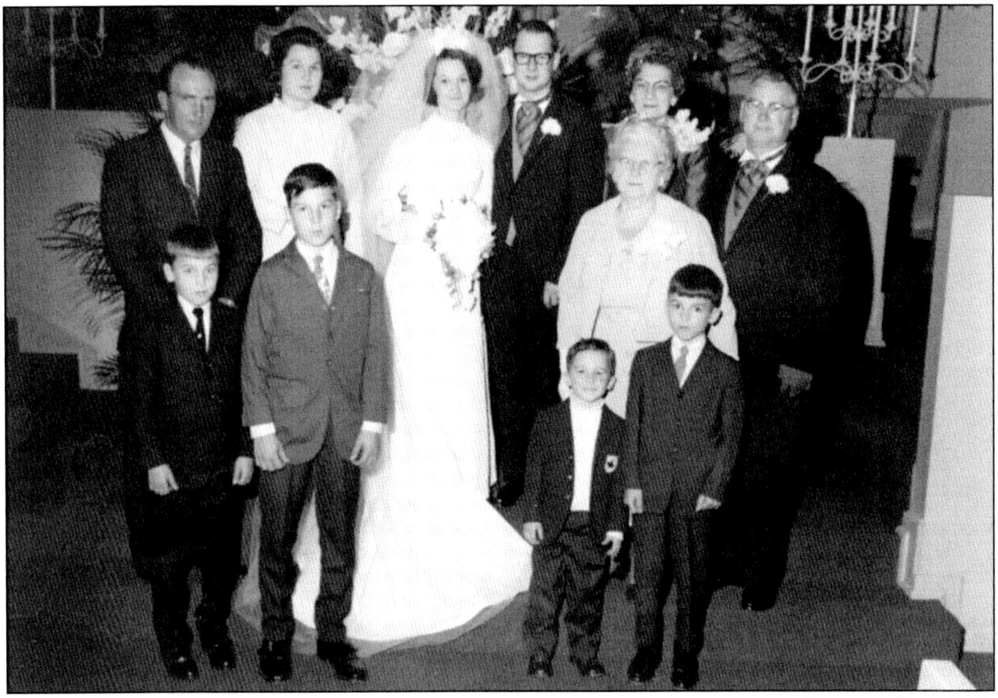

James Ingram hitchhiked with a friend, Olin Hearn, from Alabama to Newberry College and, while there, was asked to fill in at a football scrimmage. He was so impressive that the college offered him a four-year scholarship, and that is how he came to stay in South Carolina. Ingram arrived in Lexington during the 1930s with his first wife, Christine Bedenbaugh from Prosperity. They had 2 children, 7 grandchildren, 11 great-grandchildren, and 2 great-great-grandchildren. Christine Bedenbaugh Ingram died on January 28, 1986, the day of the Challenger disaster. (Jim and Sarah Ingram.)

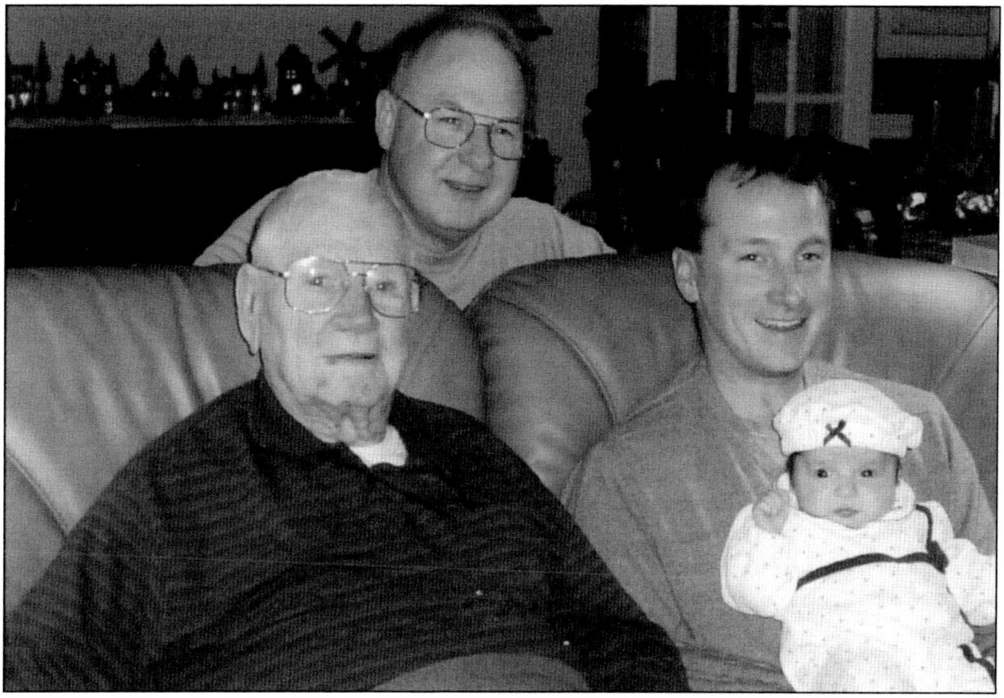

Pictured here are, from left to right, coach James Ingram, his son Jim, grandson Jaye, and great-granddaughter Annalisa Riley Ingram. Annalisa is the first girl born to the Ingram family in three generations. James Ingram was an active participant at St. Stephen's Lutheran Church. His passion was to help the Shriners Hospital for Children, and he enjoyed fishing and especially speedboating. (Jim and Sarah Ingram.)

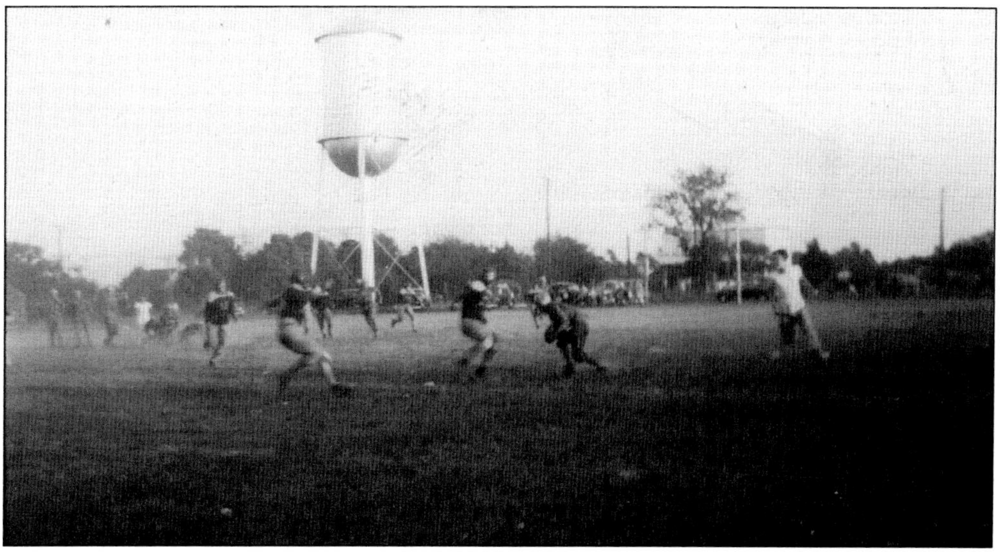

James Ingram was coach and athletic director for 40 years at Lexington High School. His son Jim remembers him telling a story about creating the famous "cross-blocking" style of playing football. Ingram devised this style while serving in the Navy during World War II with the legendary Paul Brown of the Cleveland Browns. Cross-blocking was the cornerstone of success for the Lexington Wildcats during Ingram's career and is still used today. (Mathias family.)

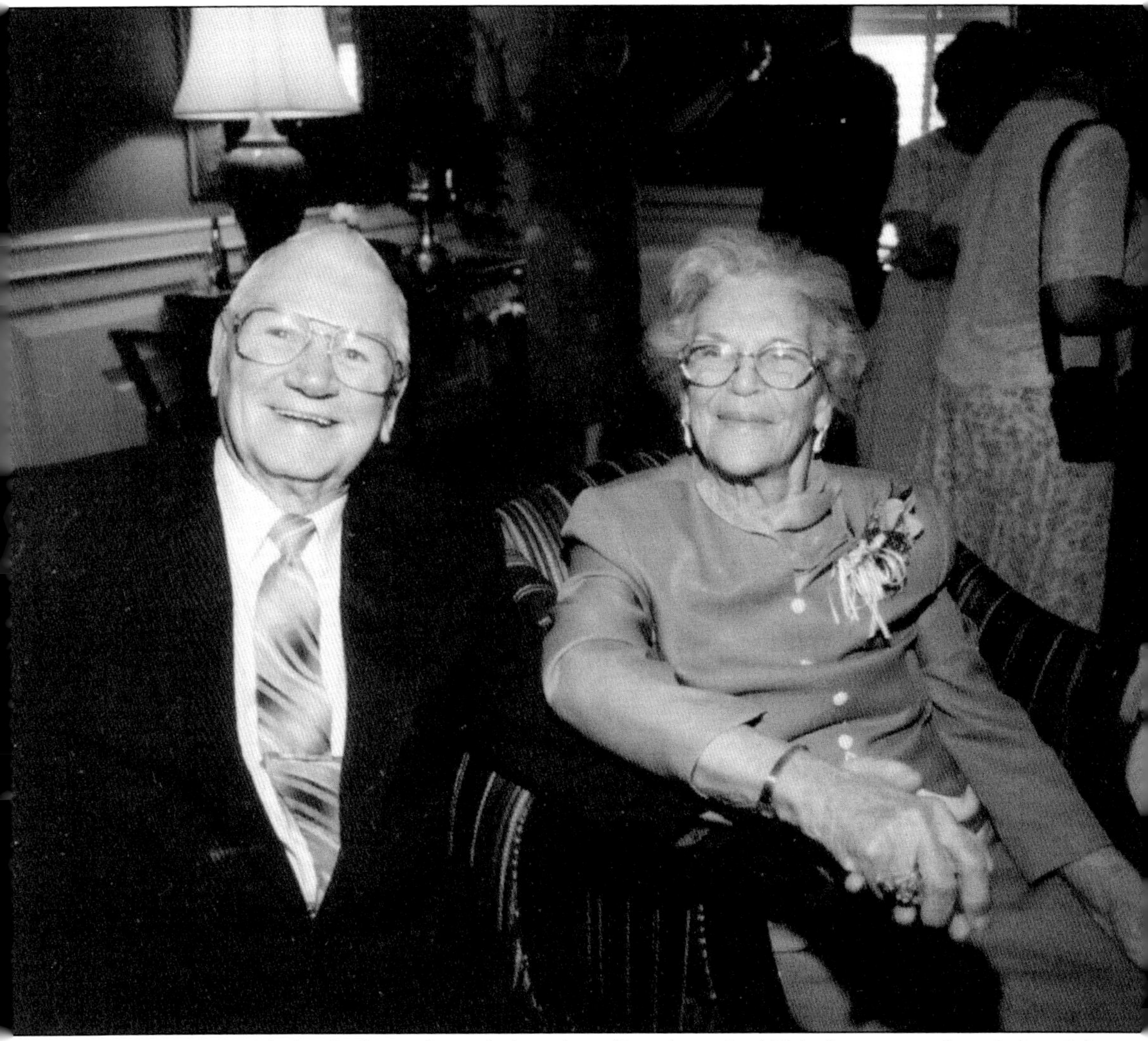

Ingram met Ethelyn Jackson through friends in Batesburg. In 1986, they married, and their life together lasted 18 years. They enjoyed living on Lake Murray, fishing, and traveling the United States. Ingram was very thankful to find another special person in his life. Family members were glad to see that the couple was happy. (Jim and Sarah Ingram.)

Three

Lake Murray

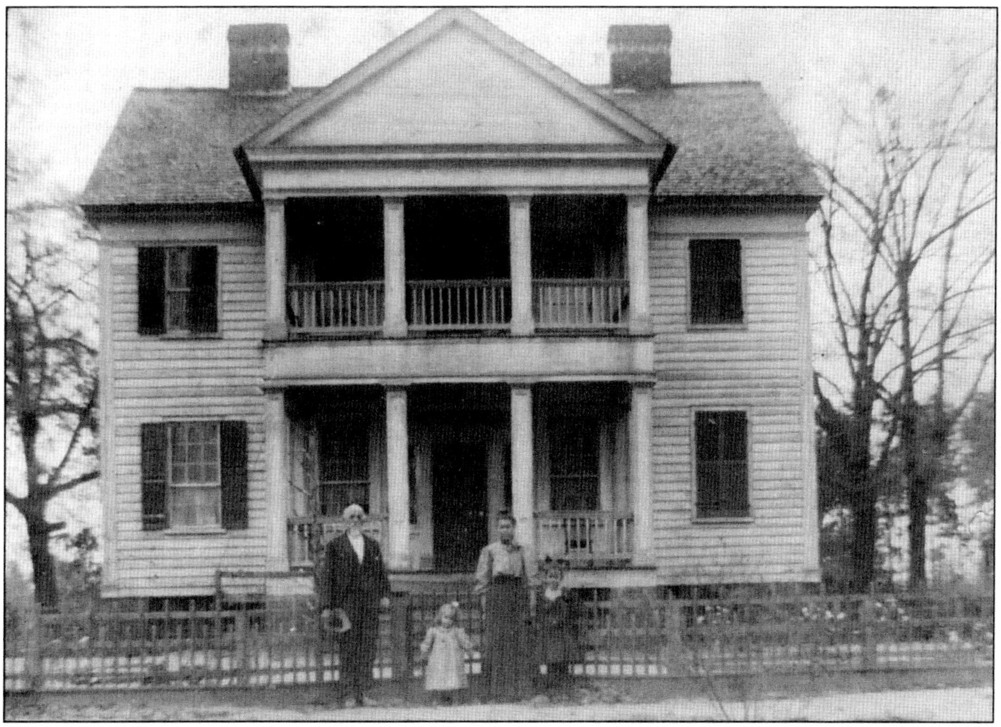

In 1927, five thousand people were relocated so the biggest earthen dam in the world at that time could be constructed to provide inexpensive electricity for people in Lexington and surrounding areas. Among the displaced farm families were the Wingards, who stand outside their home later covered by the waters of Lake Murray. They continued to farm after they moved to Lexington. Many homes, stores, churches, and schools given up for this endeavor at great personal cost sit underneath the lake. (Kathryn Liverman.)

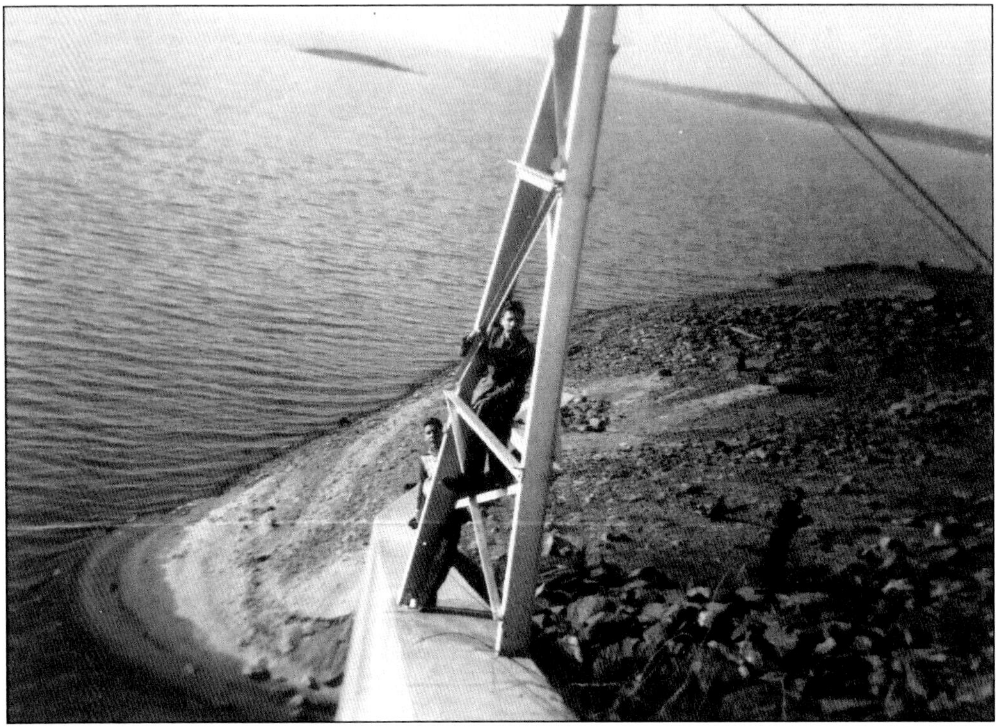

The new age of electricity arrived in Lexington in 1911. In 1924, a plan was submitted to the Army Corps of Engineers for the world's largest earthen dam to be built in Lexington County. Engineer William S. Murray of Utica, New York, successfully proposed this project, and construction began in 1927. The first step was to convince 5,000 residents to relocate, and 6 schools, 3 churches, and 2,323 graves were moved. While the project cost $20.1 million to build, its larger price was a lifetime of history and memories for those whose communities were buried forever under the lake. Even though 2,000 people were able to work daily during the Great Depression, local residents did not embrace the new resource. William S. Murray is now remembered with respect by some and with sadness by others. (Both, Mathias family.)

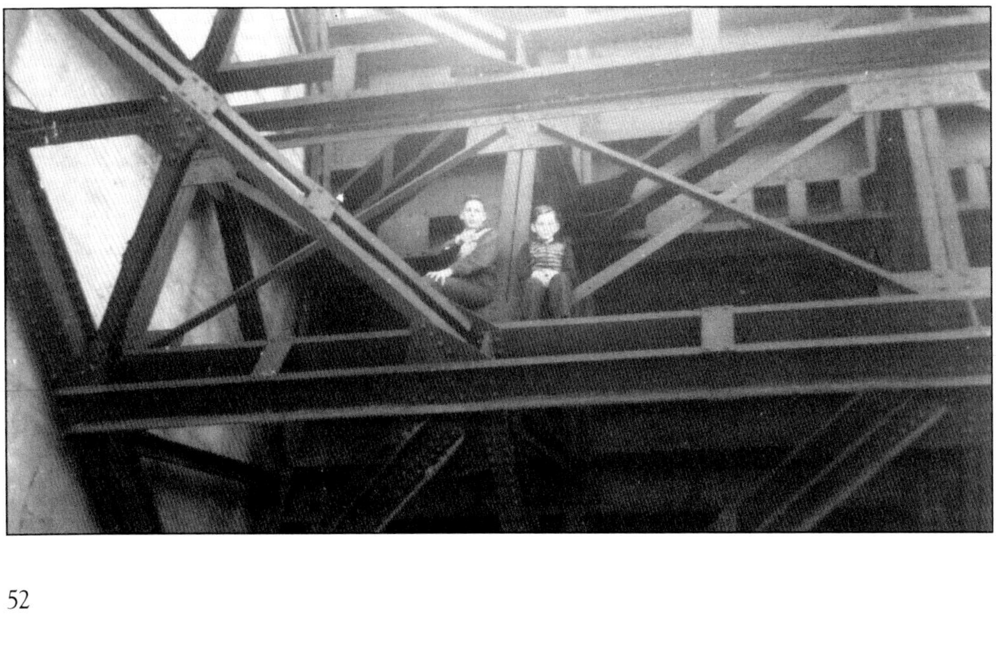

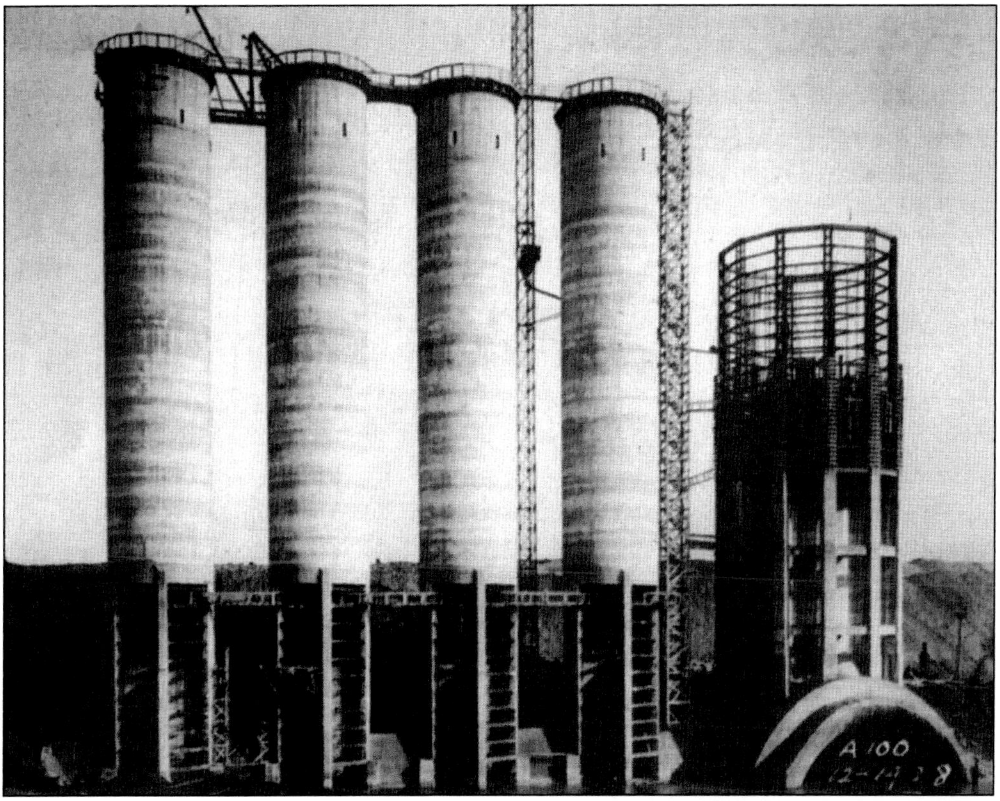

Although resources say that the community worked together to make the dam a reality, many residents say that families regretted selling their property and moving to a different location. When the Saluda River was dammed, the 50,000-acre reservoir created had 500 miles of shoreline. Ed Fettner, of the Irmo area, completed the mapping of the lake and provided copies of the maps to the people of Lexington County. It took another 20 years for people to want to move to the lake region. In the 1940s, people began purchasing lakefront land for $1 per acre. Lake Murray is now a haven for boaters, fishermen, tourists, and recreation. As a result, that same land that was $1 per acre is now selling for thousands of dollars per acre! (Both, Mathias family.)

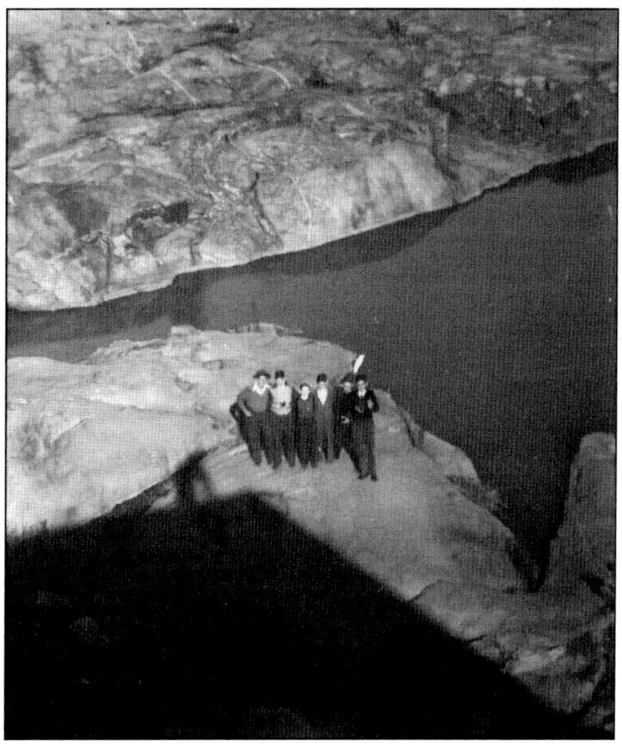

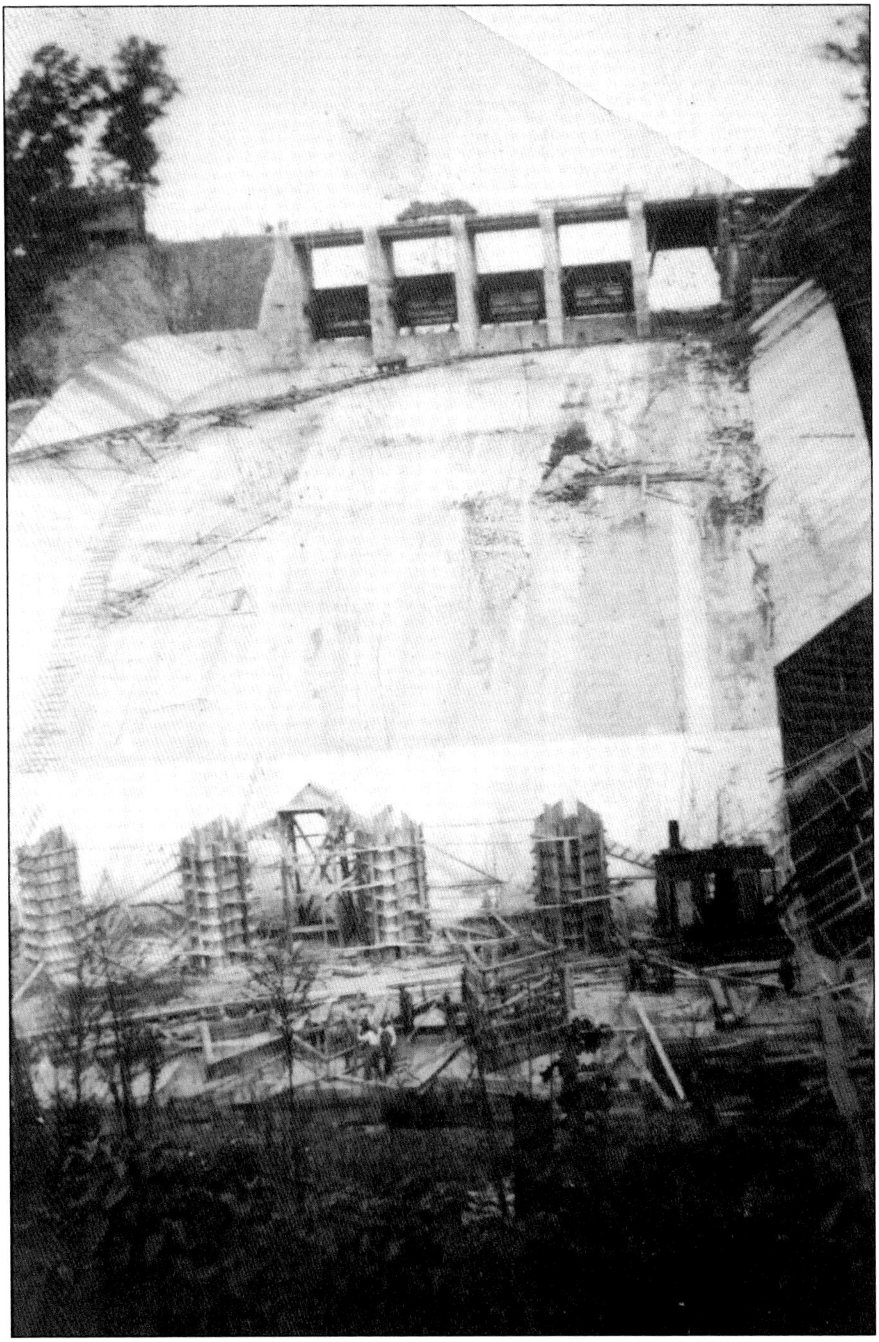

Some families will say that it was the lake that brought them to Lexington. Pearl Fortune Seay and John D. Fortune came to Lexington because John was working on the dam. They tell a story about a banner hanging in Lexington that said, "Lexington was the best little town by a dam site!" The Depression hit as the dam was being built, and Pearl worked in a sewing room at that time. The couple had 3 daughters, 9 grandchildren, and 12 great-grandchildren. Pictured here is the building of the dam wall looking from the bottom up. Without the machines of today, this was an enormous task completed by sheer will, sweat, and man power. (Drew Glover Welch.)

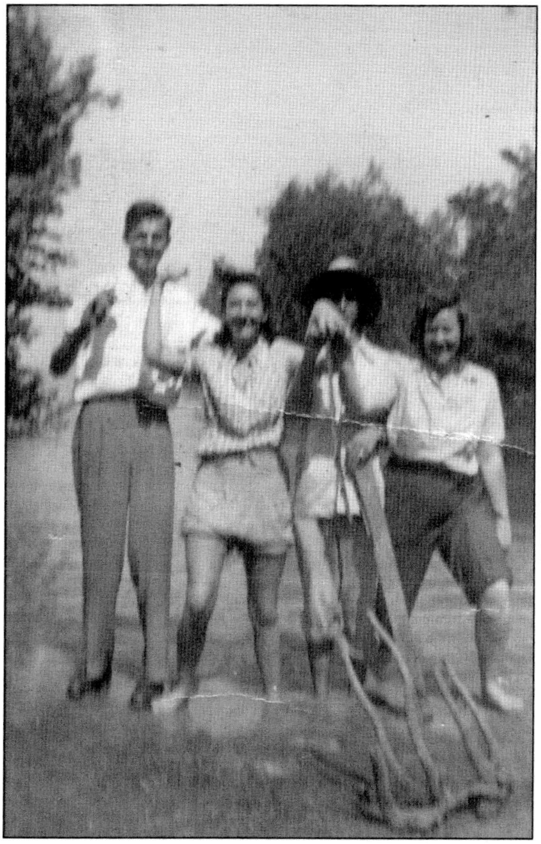

From the 1940s, the lake became a place for families to retreat and spend time relaxing. Due to World War II, everything was being rationed. Doris Rawl Reynolds remembers that sugar, gasoline, and many other things were not easy to find. Since the usual senior class trip to Washington, D.C., was out of the question, the 1944 senior class at Lexington High School arranged a visit to Lake Murray. Seniors Sonny Smith, Freddie Taylor, Melba McCartha, and others enjoy a day of picnicking and wading during a turbulent time in history. (Both, Doris Rawl Reynolds.)

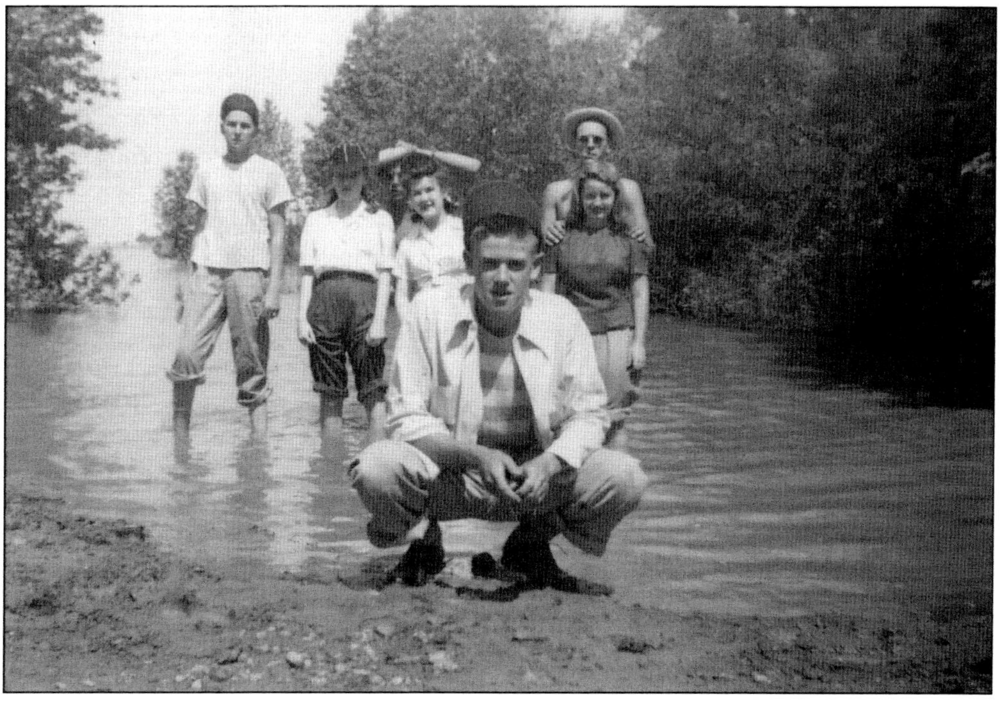

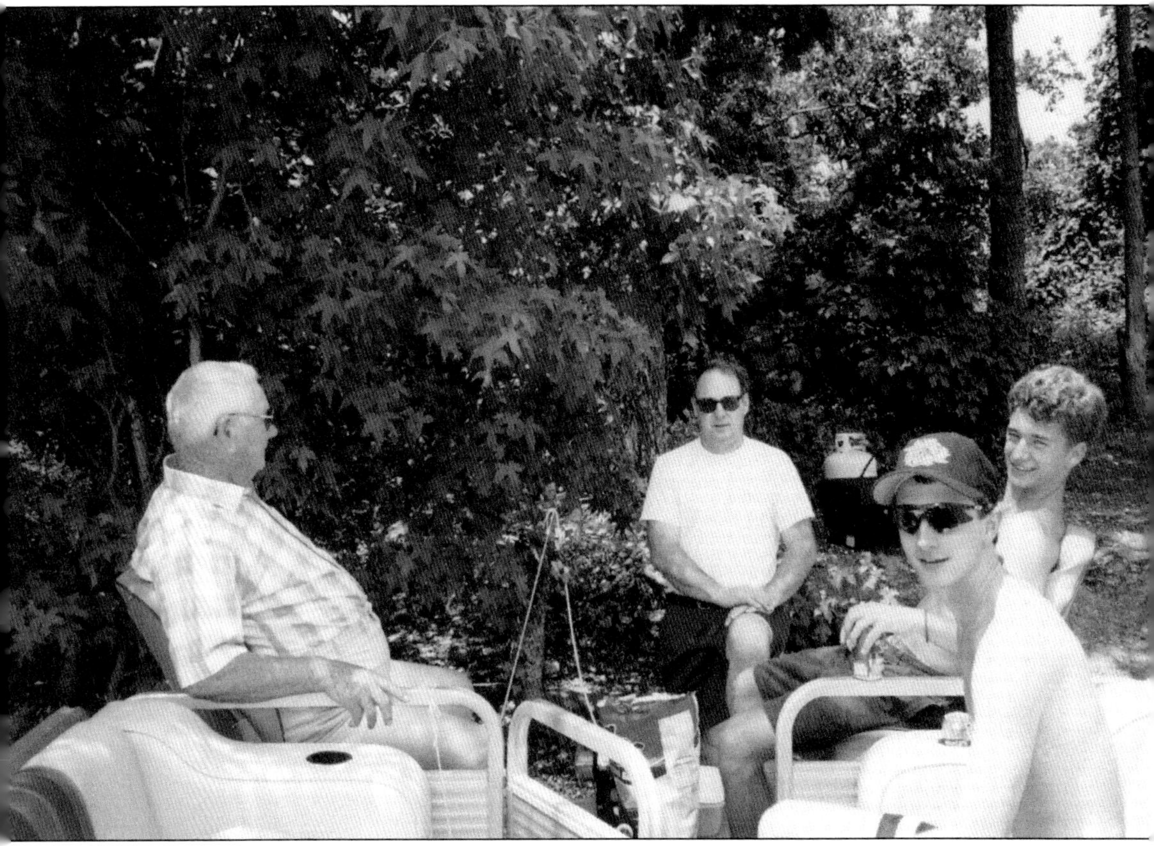

Three generations of Ingrams are enjoying the beauty of the lake area. Pictured here are, from left to right, James, his son Jim, his grandson Blake, and his grandson Jaye. Once things began to settle down and people began to realize how wonderful it was to have a cool swimming and boating spot, more began to find lakefront places to call their own. Some owned family property that became lakeshore property, while others bought land from people sure that it was "no good." Old buses were often pulled out to these properties to be used as changing cabins or storage for chairs and equipment. During this time period, boats were not easily purchased. James Ingram taught students how to build boats in shop class. Skills such as welding and woodworking made boatbuilding possible. (Jim and Sarah Ingram.)

Four

Outlying Areas

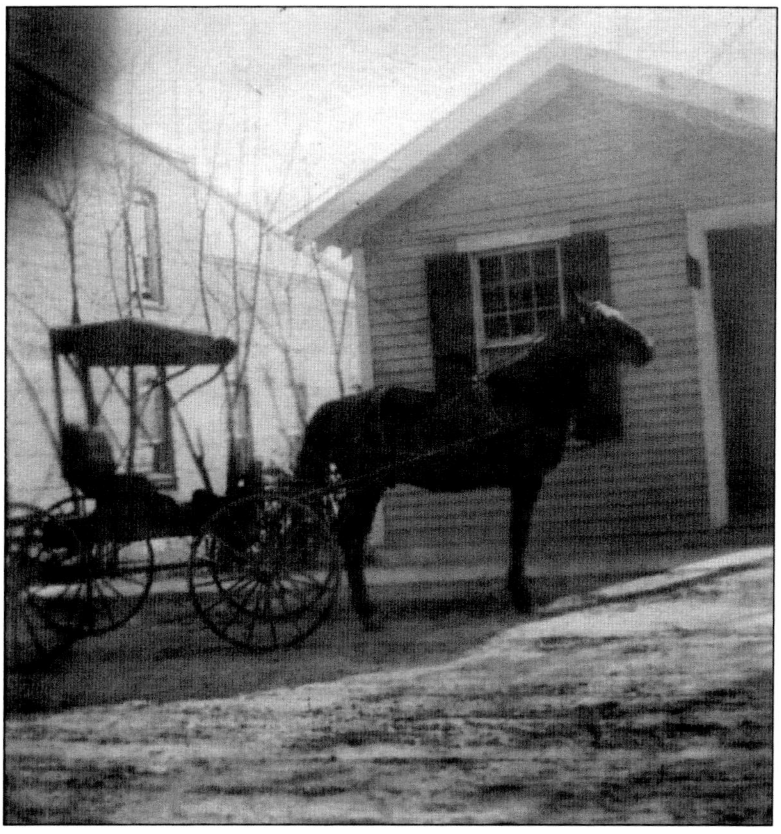

Horses and buggies like this one, which belonged to Dr. Mathias, were not an uncommon site at any home in the early 1900s. Transportation was evolving before the eyes of a generation. Outlying areas grew with the railroad as it emerged from the coast. Along with passengers, the railroad transported goods to and from the coast and other areas. (Mathias family.)

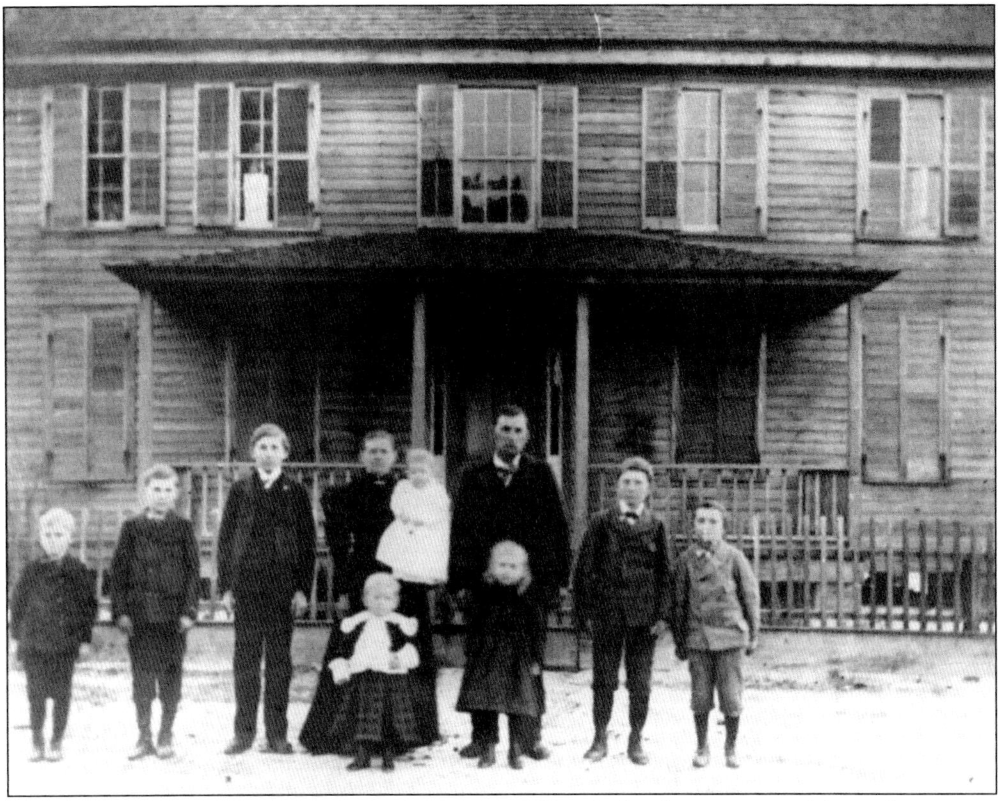

West Columbia was one of the early stops on the railroad. This area is close to both the old county seat in Granby and the capital in Columbia. It became part of the Columbia suburbs over time. Many prominent families, such as the Shulls, settled this area as farmers and later continued on as mill and factory workers. (Shull family.)

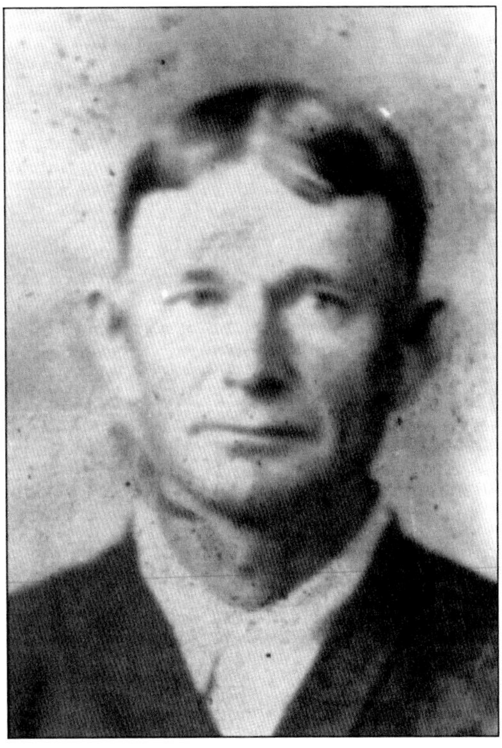

Houston Oliver Shull lived in West Columbia. He was a hardworking farmer and builder. Shull grew a variety of vegetables and raised pigs for barbecue, constructed homes and churches in the area, and enjoyed playing checkers. He married Emily Arine Shull, and they had seven children. (Shull family.)

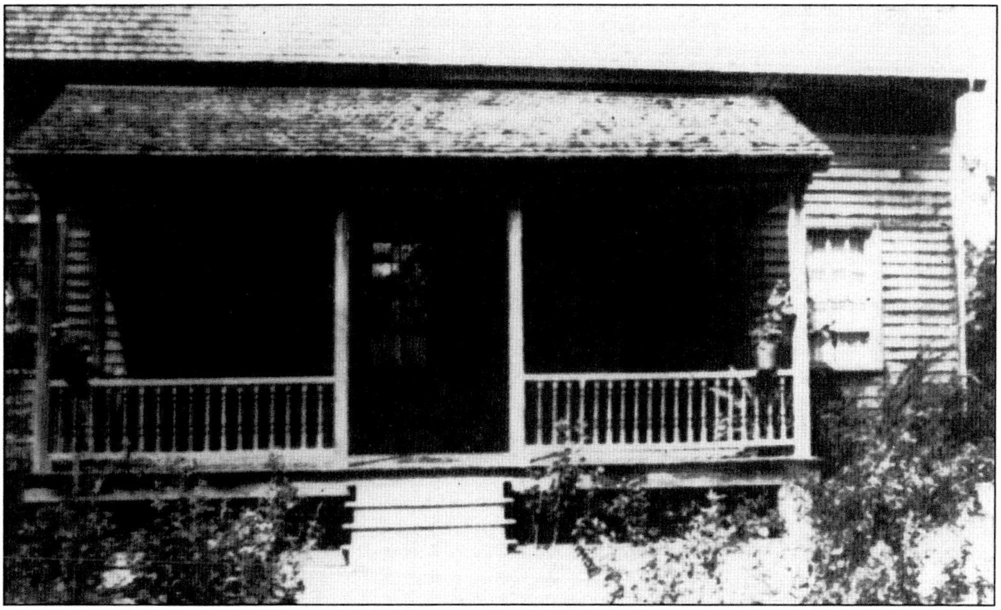

Typical of the type of homestead early settlers would construct with help from friends and neighbors, this house was the home of Fannie Roof Shull. Her descendants have been helping to build Lexington County as farmers, teachers, administrators, and a variety of other professions. The lumber mills in the area made purchasing wooden planks reasonable, so many homes were built out of wood. (Roof family.)

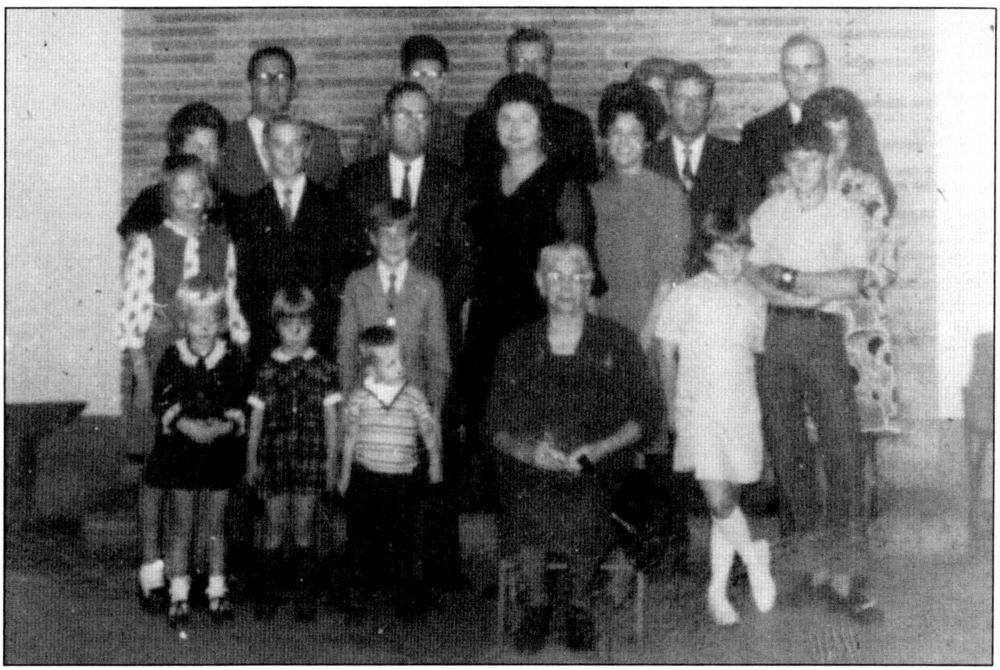

Four generations of the Shull family are in this photograph. The Shulls originated from Germany. Many families who came to the United States to participate in the Township Act of 1733 were pleasantly surprised to receive land they had been promised. Each family was given 100 acres per man of the household plus 50 acres each to his wife and each child over age 12. (Shull family.)

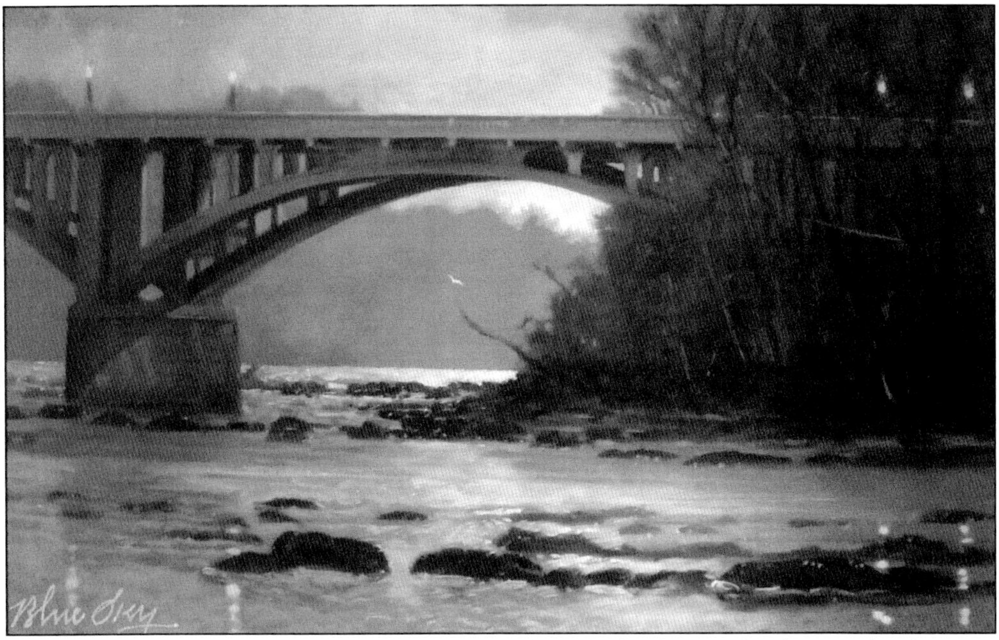

Cayce was another outlying area. The Cayce family had a land grant for this area by the river. The site of the former county seat, Granby, lies in what is now Cayce. The area grew up with warehouses and riverfront traffic as well as other activities. Cayce people were known as "river rats" and have spent many years overcoming that distinction. There was very little growth in residences until fairly recently as a result of this perception. (Artist Blue Sky.)

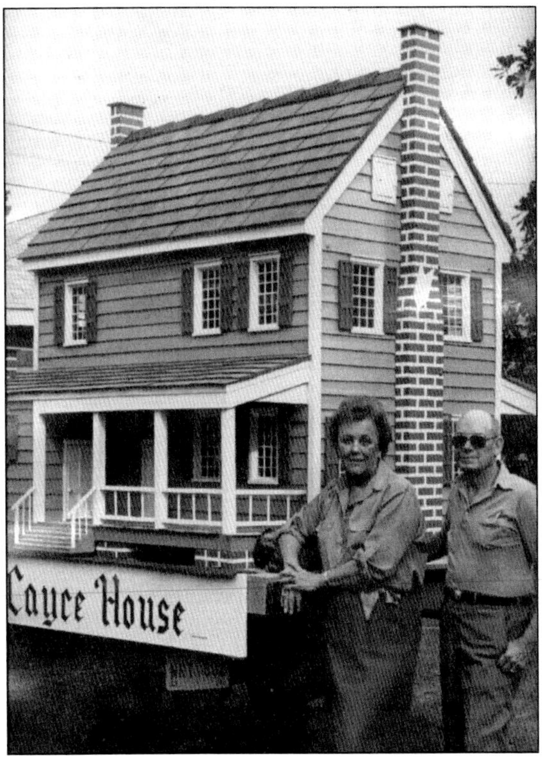

John Ellisor and Betty Abbott McKissick stand in front of a model of a 1765 trading post—which became the Cayce family home in 1817—that Ellisor created for the bicentennial celebration of the city of Columbia. The model was included in the parade to promote the idea of creating a historical museum. In 1989, Ellisor's dream became a reality when the Cayce Historical Museum opened in a full-scale replica of the 1765 building. Ellisor also promoted Scouting for over 50 years and was a Mason, a Shriner, a lifetime member of the Lexington County Law Enforcement Association, and an active member of Main Street Methodist Church. (Cayce Historical Museum.)

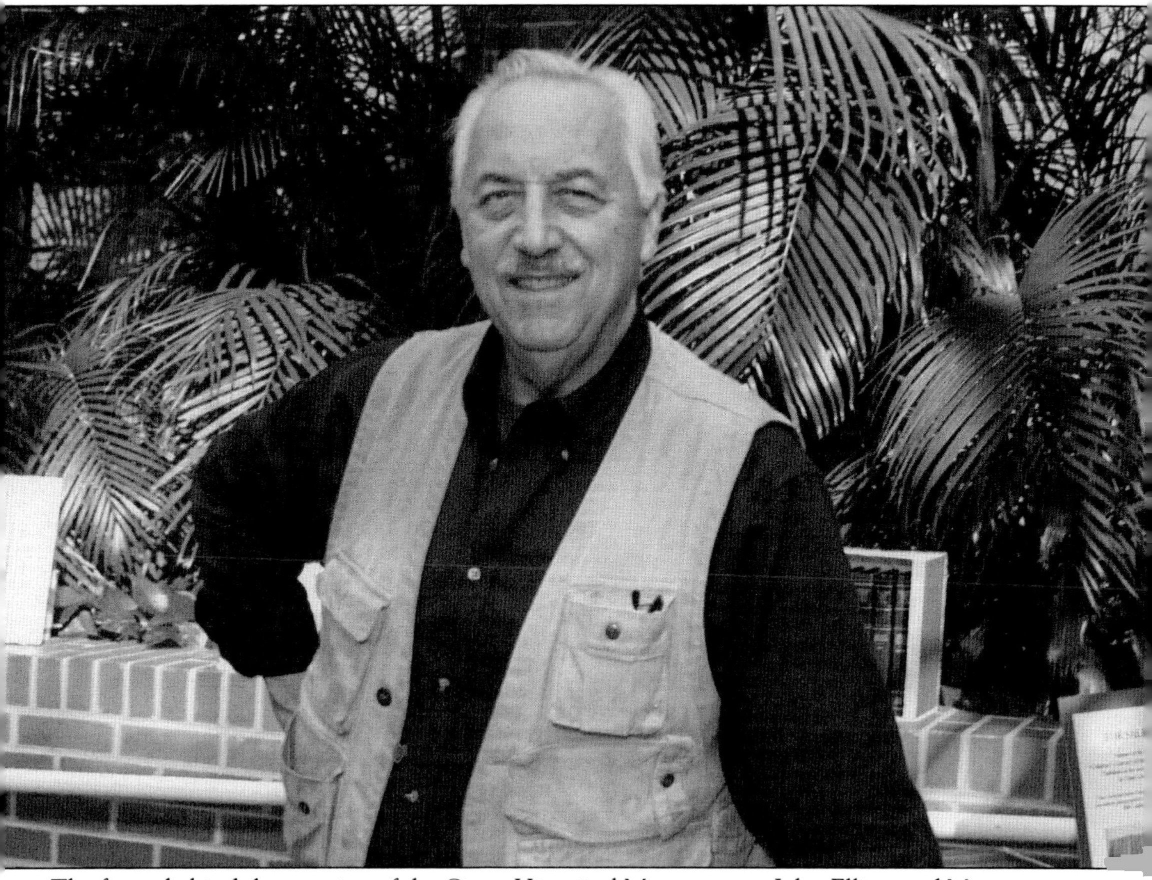

The forces behind the creation of the Cayce Historical Museum were John Ellisor and Margaret Harbin. They brought together the team who built the museum and donated it to the city. The team included Eloise Lee, Lowell Spires Sr., Margaret Spires, Herbert Wood, Ann Diamond, Leo Redmond, and Robert Malpass. Funding came from grants and local donations and was supported by local politicians. Many people pulled together to help make this project work. Ground was broken in 1986 and work completed in 1989. Museum director Leo Redmond remembers how amazing it was to see people come forward to share their time, money, and skills. For 20 years, the museum has sponsored a Christmas tradition that consists of a free open house, music, homemade goodies, trees decorated from the period, and docents dressed in costumes of the early 1800s. The museum is now supported by the city of Cayce. (Cayce Historical Museum.)

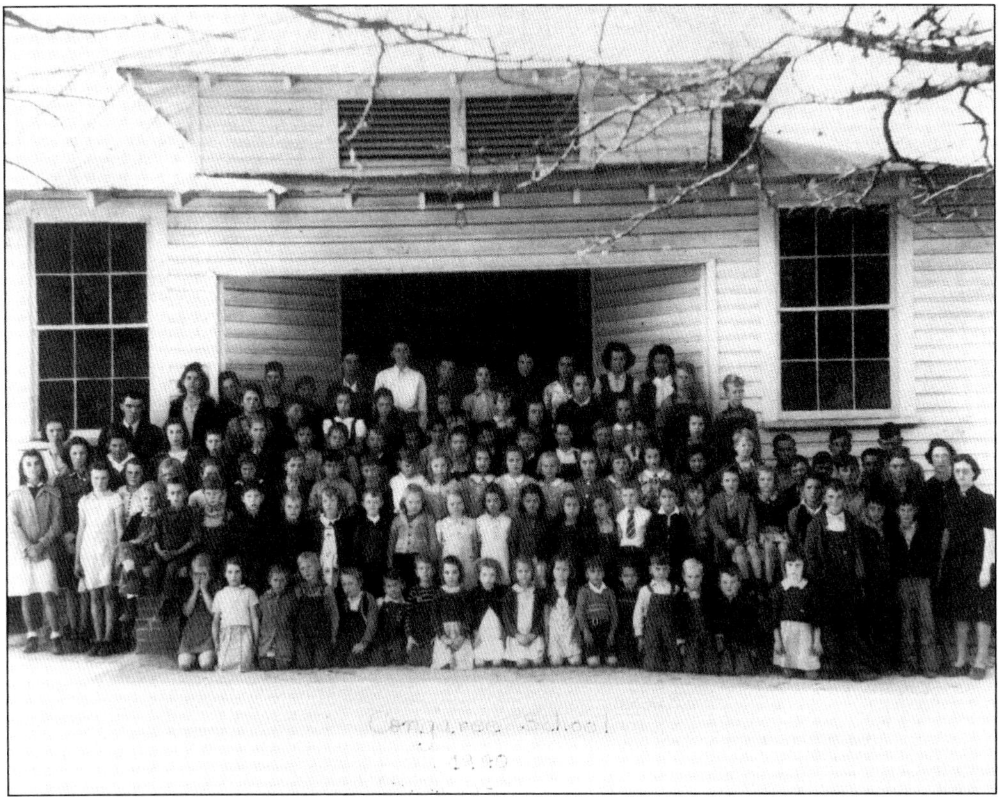

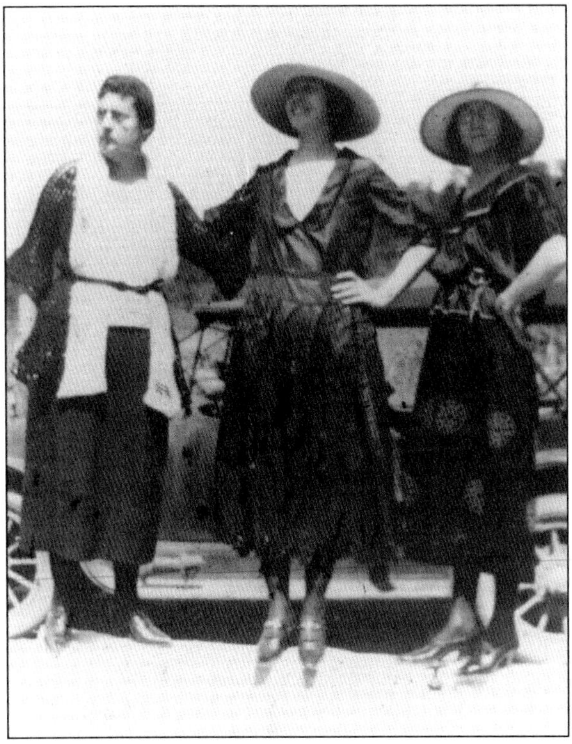

The town of South Congaree began in the early 1900s. Like other areas of the Saxe Gotha Township, this area was settled through land grants. This one-room schoolhouse was similar to other schoolhouses in the region. It served children of varying ages until 1940. Mayor Bobby Vining tells an interesting story told to him by his grandfather, "Big Daddy," who worked in the Olympia Mill in Columbia as a child. According to the tale, when Sherman marched through the area, he had to cross the River Styx. Sherman unloaded gold and silver from two big wagons and buried it until he could come back for it. Bobby said that his granddaddy told him about city folks who had heard the tale and would come wandering down the creek bed looking for that hidden treasure. People in South Congaree still wonder if there is gold down there somewhere. (Both, Town of South Congaree.)

The community of Ossa decided to change its name to Edmund to honor state senator W. H. Sharpe's eldest son, Julius Edmund Sharpe. Senator Sharpe was the railroad's lawyer, a general store owner, and a member of the local school board. He served in the South Carolina State Senate for the 64th, 65th, 70th, and 71st General Assemblies. Pictured at right are Senator Sharpe's six sons. Julius is in the middle of the back row. (Herb and Catherine Sharpe.)

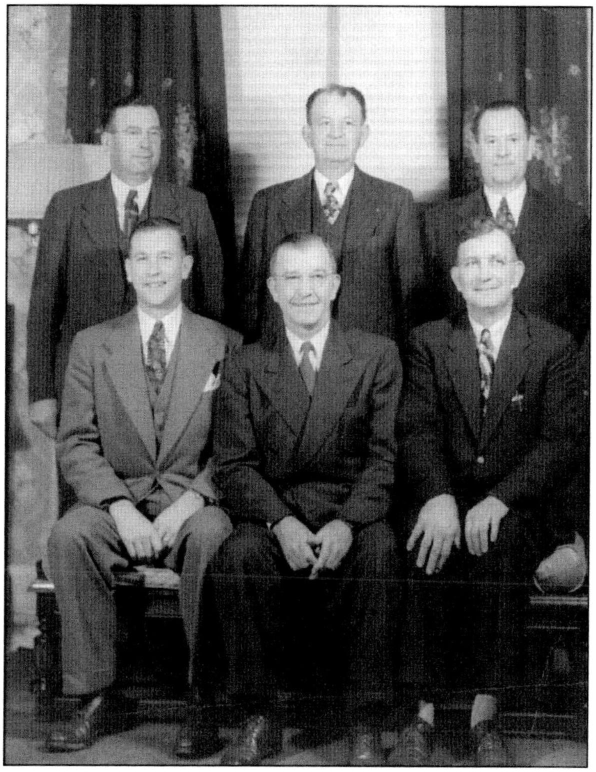

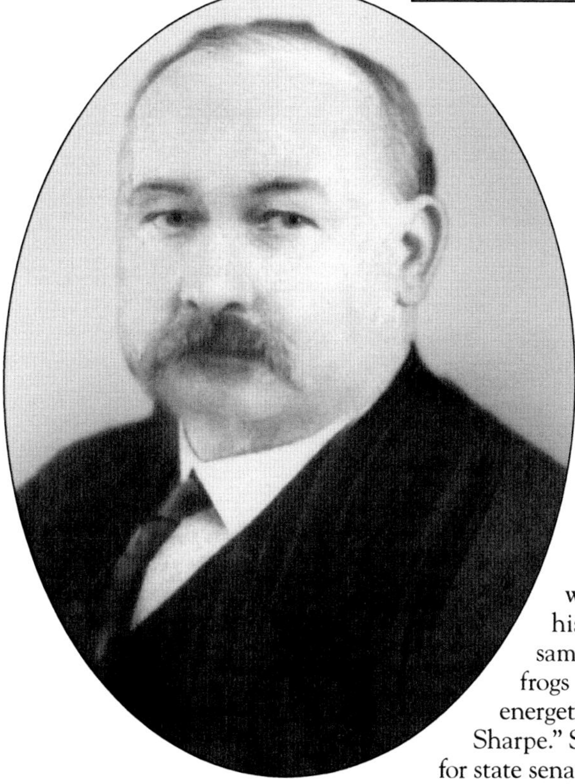

Senator Sharpe was married to Alice Eugenia Goodwin. He was a member of Bethel Methodist Church, a dedicated Democratic Party member, and a lawyer. Herb Sharpe remembers this family story about his grandfather: Courson was attending a stump meeting in Red Bank in 1912 to debate against Will Sharpe. James Courson said he drove by a pond on his way there and all the frogs were chanting, "Courson, Courson." In his speech, Sharpe said, "I rode by that same pond, and I heard all those tired old frogs saying Courson, but I heard all the energetic young frogs saying Sharpe, Sharpe, Sharpe." Sharpe won the election that year for state senator. (Herb and Catherine Sharpe.)

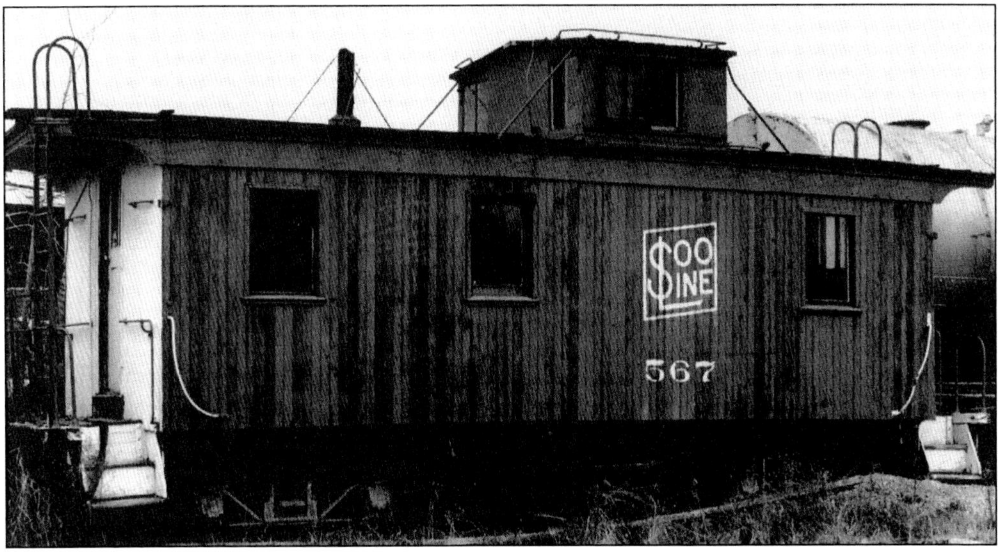

For years, the train was the favored way to move around from town to town, but with the advent of the automobile came the Greyhound bus. Frances Price remembers taking Greyhound to Columbia to go to business school and work before everyone had his or her own automobile and the roads were paved. Murray Price remembers watching the men pave Highway 6 using mules to pull the machine with tar. (Lexington Main Library.)

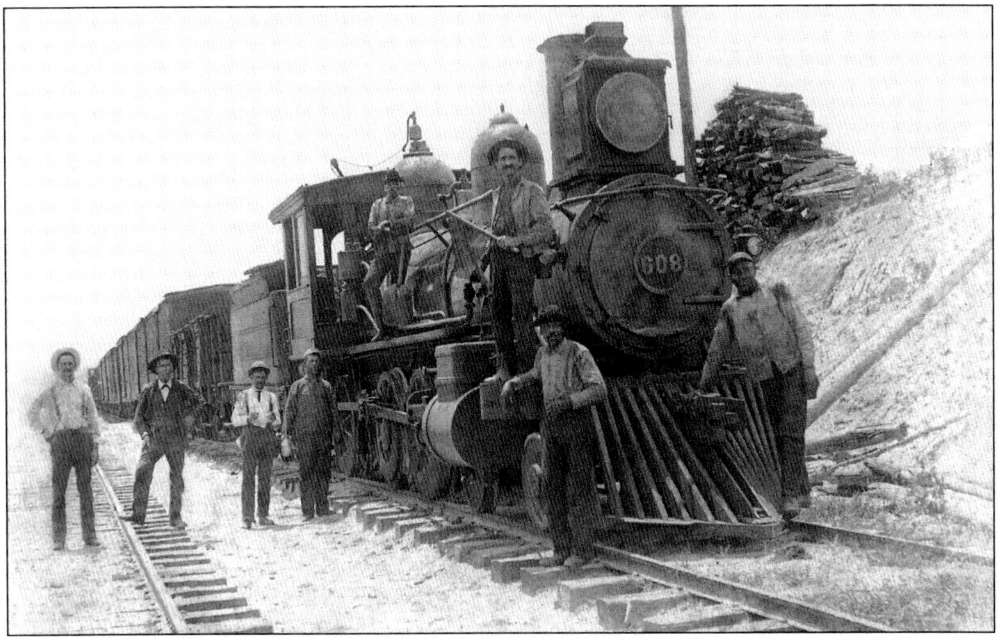

In 1900, the Southern Railroad built a line connecting Columbia and Savannah. Today Pelion is the only old railroad stop in Lexington County on this line that is an incorporated town. The location chosen for the town of Pelion was due to the ponds in the area that provided quality water for the steam locomotives. The name Pelion was taken from a mountain in northern Greece, because Pelion was one of the high hills in the roadbed. Lessie Haltiwanger Fort, owner of the land surrounding the railroad line, paid Percy S. Norris $5 a day to survey the acreage and lay out the town. She also provided land for churches and a school. (Vernon Romans.)

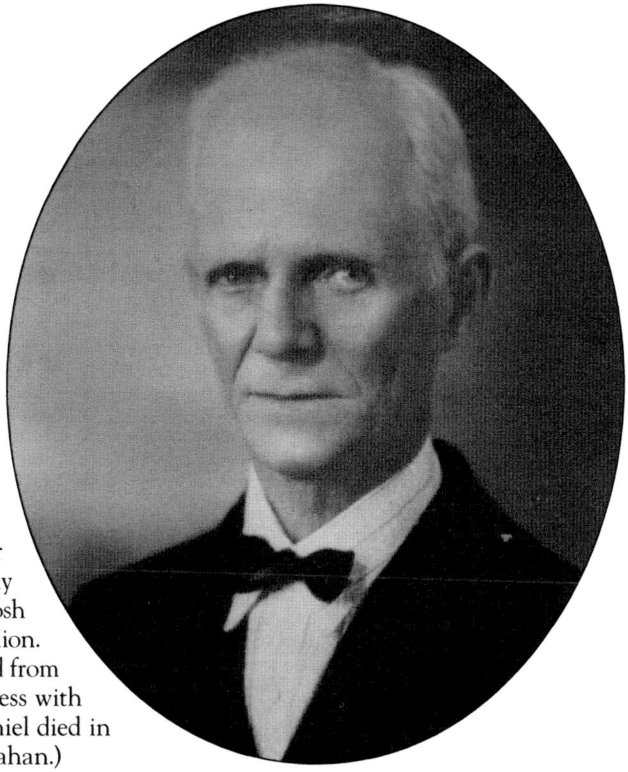

Daniel Shumpert's great-grandfather, Jacob Shumpert, came from Germany in the late 1700s. In the early 1900s, Daniel and Sarah (Sally) Shumpert relocated to Pelion from Rishton because of the railroad. They opened Shumpert's Store by the railroad tracks. It remains the main place in Pelion to purchase groceries and other items. Sally was known for her exceptionally fine meals "elegantly served," as remembered by "Uncle" Josh Harman when recalling a visit to Pelion. The Shumperts' son D. F. graduated from Newberry College, went into business with his father, and took over when Daniel died in 1937. (Both, Laura Shumpert McMahan.)

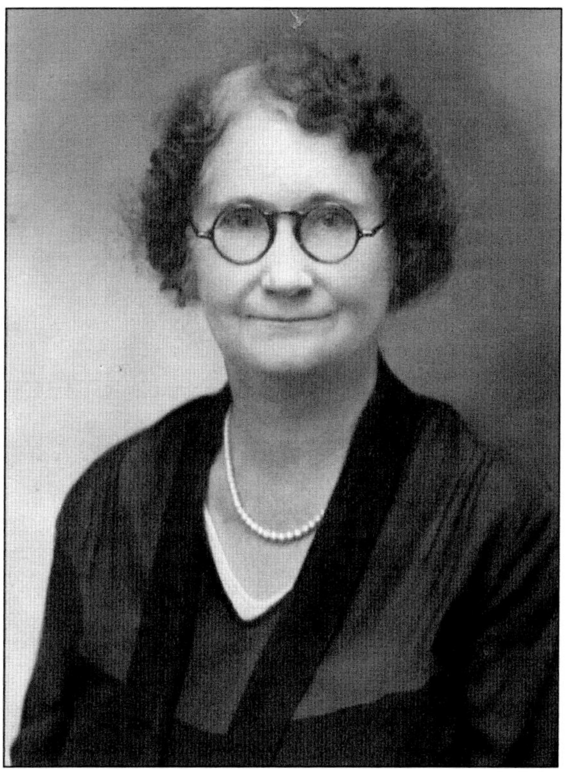

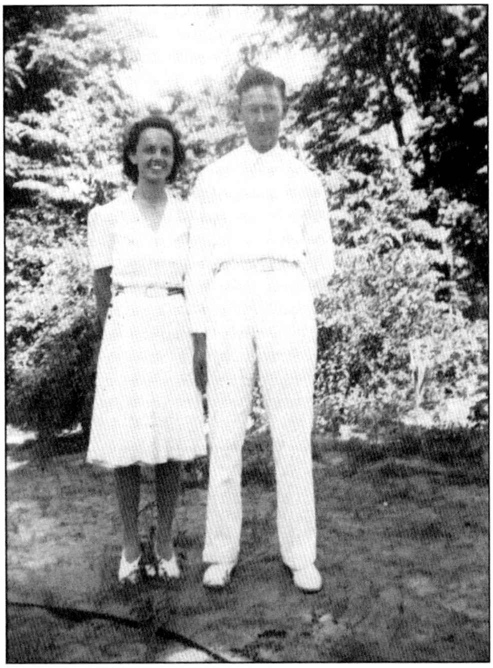

D. F. Shumpert was the youngest child of Daniel Franklin Sr. and Sarah (Sally) Camelie Lybrand Shumpert. In 1939, D. F. married Anna Lois Clark, who taught fourth grade at Pelion School. They had met at Holy Trinity Lutheran Church when he asked her to help teach Sunday school. The Shumperts had two children. (Laura Shumpert McMahan.)

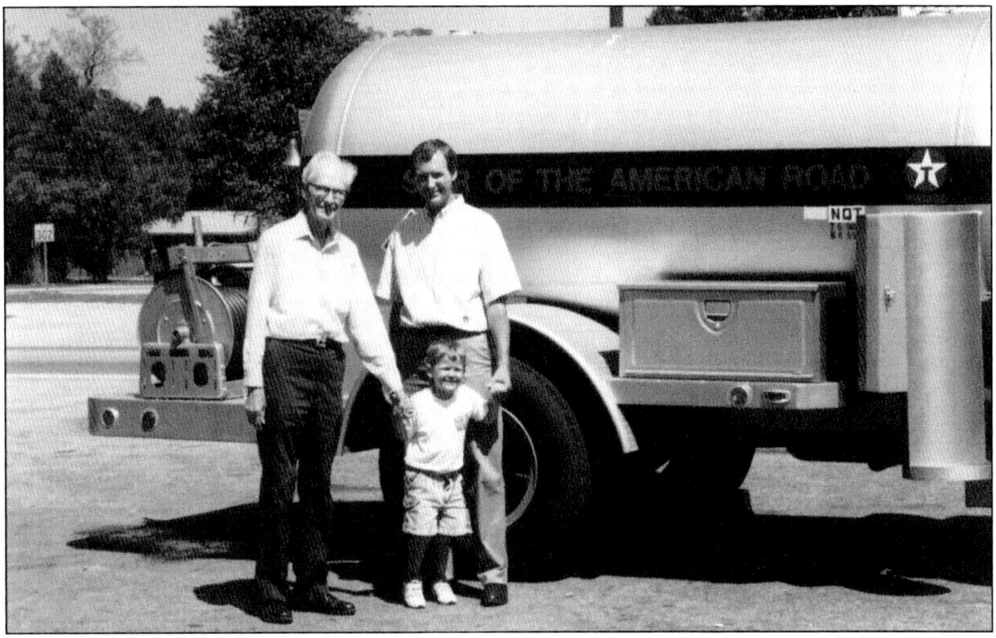

D. F. Shumpert was a firm believer that school and church were the backbone of a community. He served for 15 years as a member of the Lexington School District One board of trustees. Shumpert expanded the family business and added an oil company, gas station, Pelion Manufacturing Plant, and a movie theater. Many young people remember working at Shumpert's Store as their first job. Ruth Nichols said, "Most of the community depended on him in some way at some time. He wouldn't turn them away." Jean Haggard, principal of Pelion High School, stated that there was an unspoken partnership between the school and the business to support the student employees. Shumpert's son, D. F. III (Frank), still honors this today. (Laura Shumpert McMahan.)

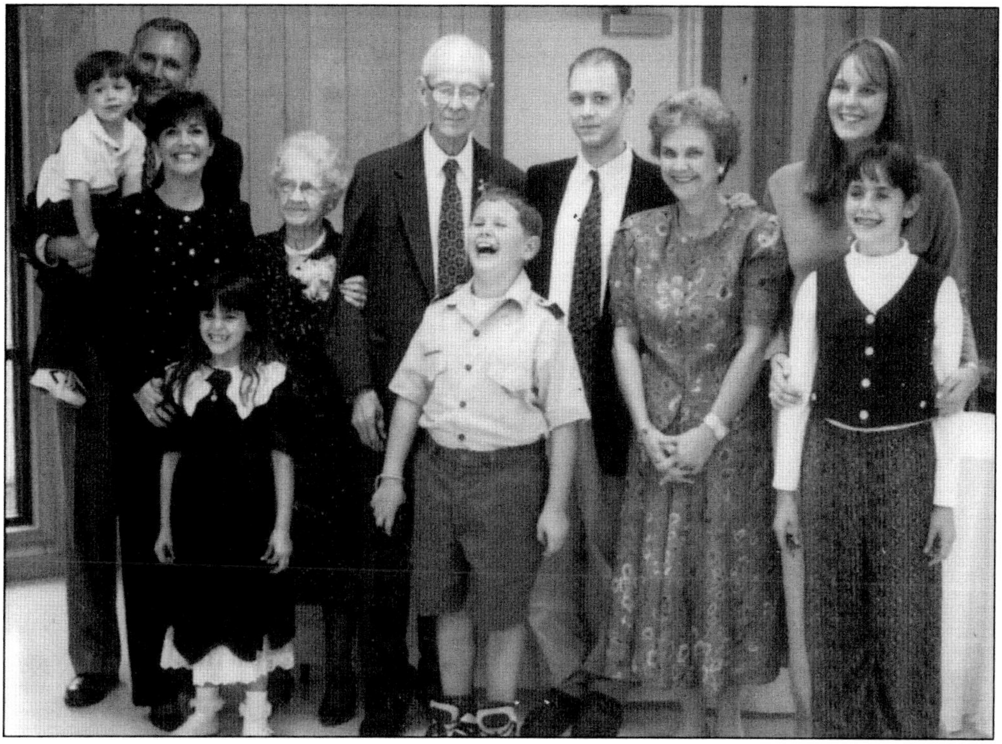

D. F. and Lois Shumpert had two children, six grandchildren, and one great-grandchild. The children and grandchildren have all stayed close to home. Laura Shumpert McMahan remembers being surrounded by family. D. F. always reminded his children that they could be whatever they wanted to be. Everyone was expected to go to college and to have a career. The family had a strong work ethic. The Shumperts were very generous in a quiet way. They would often help those who really needed it and did not expect payment in return. (Laura Shumpert McMahan.)

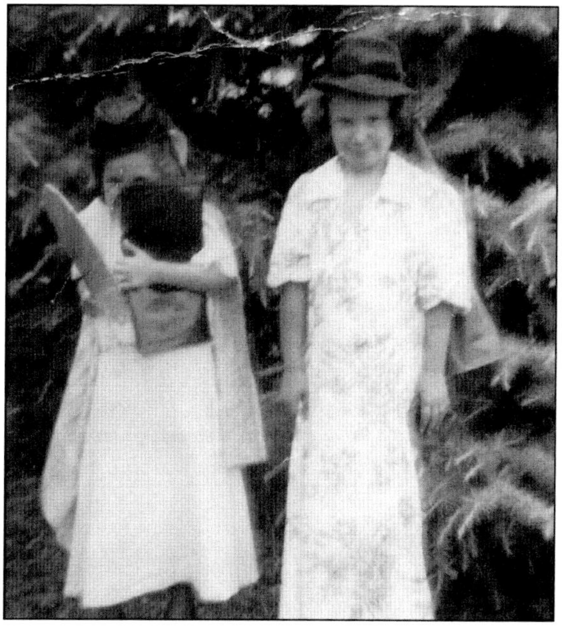

Laura Shumpert McMahan (left) and Jean Nichols Haggard grew up together in the 1950 and 1960s in Pelion. One of their favorite activities was to dress up in Shumpert's grandmother's old clothes. They also had fun attending school activities, events at all the Pelion churches, and going to the movies at the local theater in Pelion. (Jean Nichols Haggard.)

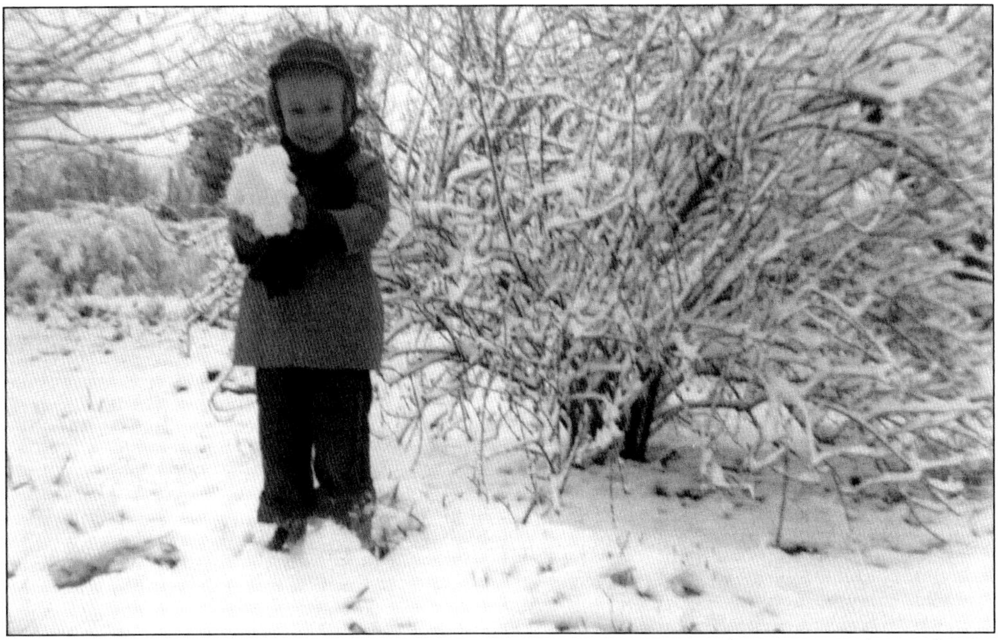

Pictured here is D. F. III (Frank) Shumpert on Christmas morning. Local German traditions began with Christmas Day and would run through Epiphany. Families would plan visits and meals and attend special church functions to celebrate the birth of Jesus. The 12 days of Christmas were a very important time for celebration. Frank Shumpert believed he was named the third because he was born three days after Christmas. Frank III plays in a highly unusual snow in Pelion on January 13, 1968. There was actually enough snow to make a snowman. Pictured below is D. F. Shumpert in front of his store and gas station. (Both, Laura Shumpert McMahan.)

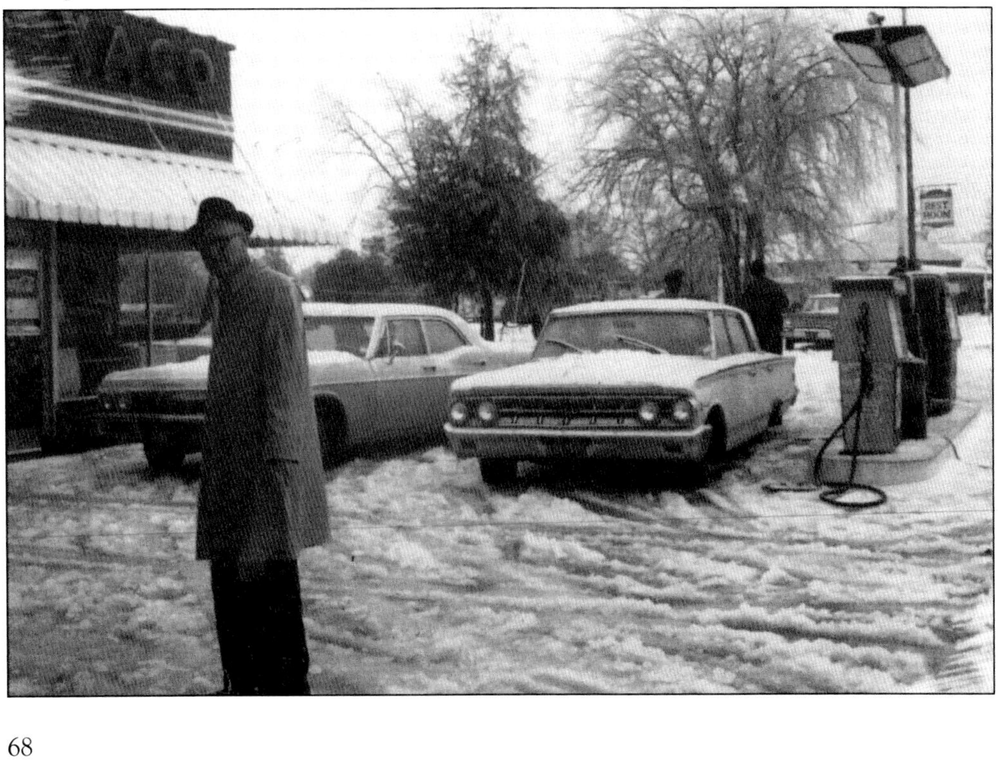

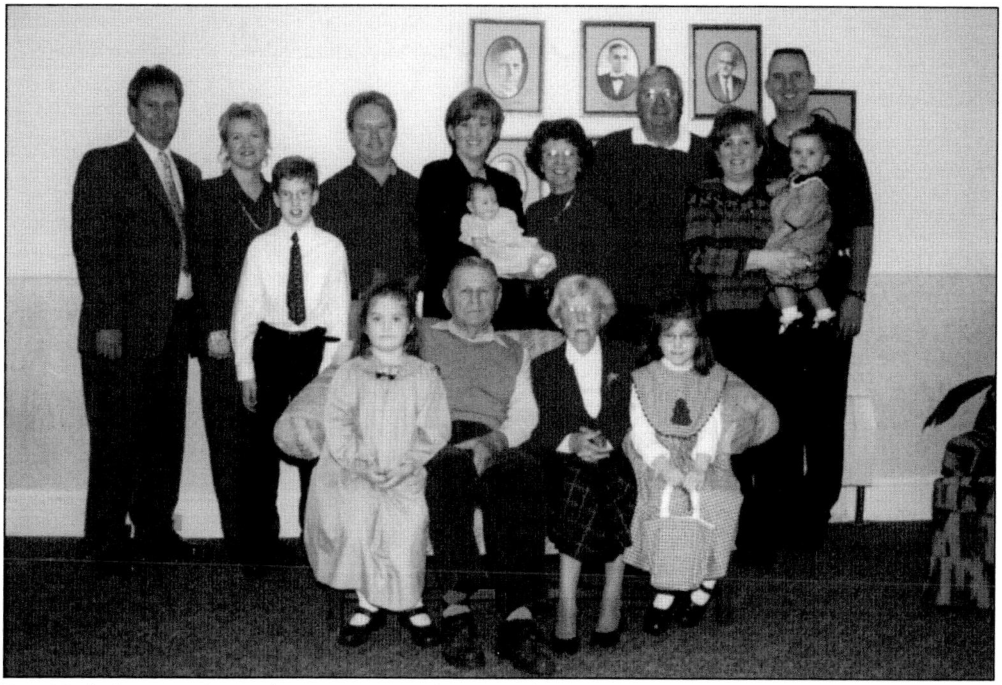

Roy Nichols moved to Pelion in 1949 to become the superintendent of Pelion School and was instrumental in the structure and continued success of the school until his retirement in 1974. From 1977 to 1981, his wife, Ruth, served as principal; following the family tradition, their daughter, Jean Nichols Haggard, became principal in 1992. The Nichols family has been devoted to education, to serving the community, and to leadership in the church. (Jean Nichols Haggard.)

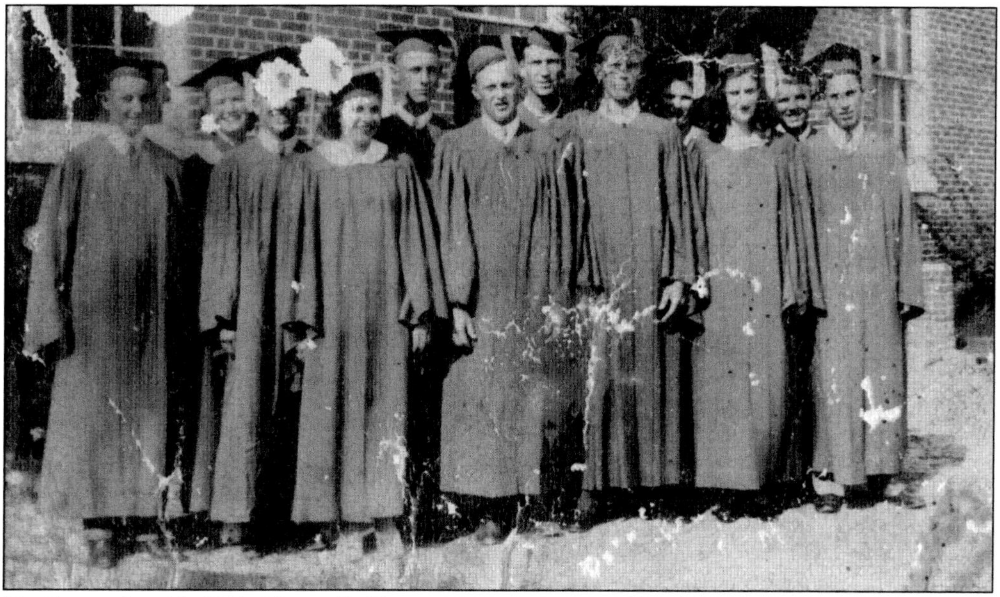

On September 15, 1922, Henry R. Shumpert gave 6 acres of land for a new school in Fairview. This new school consolidated students from Hoods Branch, Huffman Burnt Mill, and the old Fairview School. The school was the heart of the community, and residents remember its sports teams, teachers, and traditional functions. (Donna Padgett Smith.)

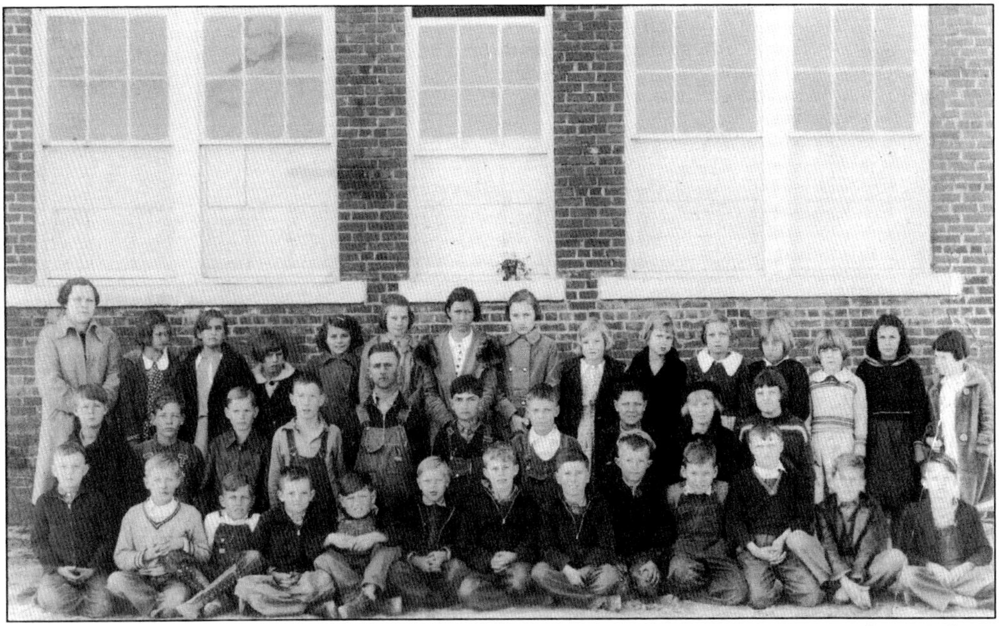

With the consolidation of schools in Lexington County in 1951, Fairview was merged into Pelion. A majority of the parents were understandably disturbed at the loss of the neighborhood school, and many tears were shed when the property was sold. (Donna Padgett Smith.)

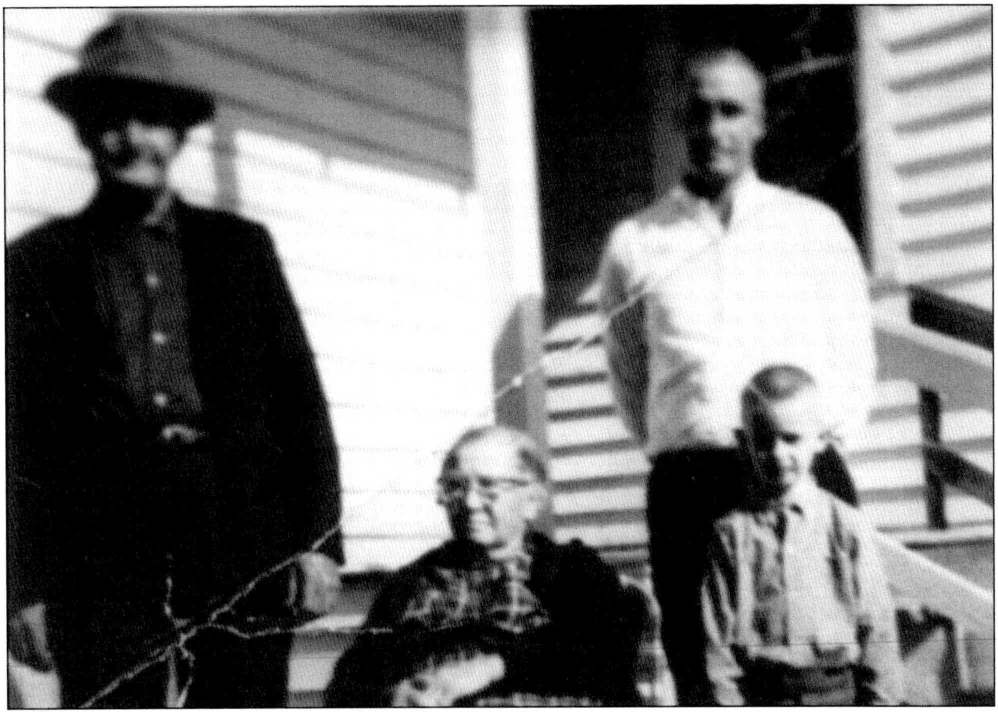

Family land kept families together. Four generations are in this picture. They are Eliza Williams, Cephus Coleman Shumpert, James Theo Shumpert, and James Doyal Shumpert. The Shumpert family grew and expanded, yet many of the children lived on family land and have therefore stayed connected with the family. (Wendy Shumpert West.)

On his way to church at New Hope Baptist, Hayden Yonce rides his mule. He was very glad to own the mule, since most people walked to church and town at this time. Hayden remembers attending Pelion Elementary School, a two-story building with the elementary on the first floor and upper grades on the second. Hayden and his dad farmed row crops and ran a produce stand where they sold their vegetables. They had to use the mule to plow the rows on approximately 25 acres. Today there are still a few farm families in the county with produce stands. Hayden also enjoys hunting and fishing and has passed his love on to his son and grandchildren. (Both, Hayden Yonce.)

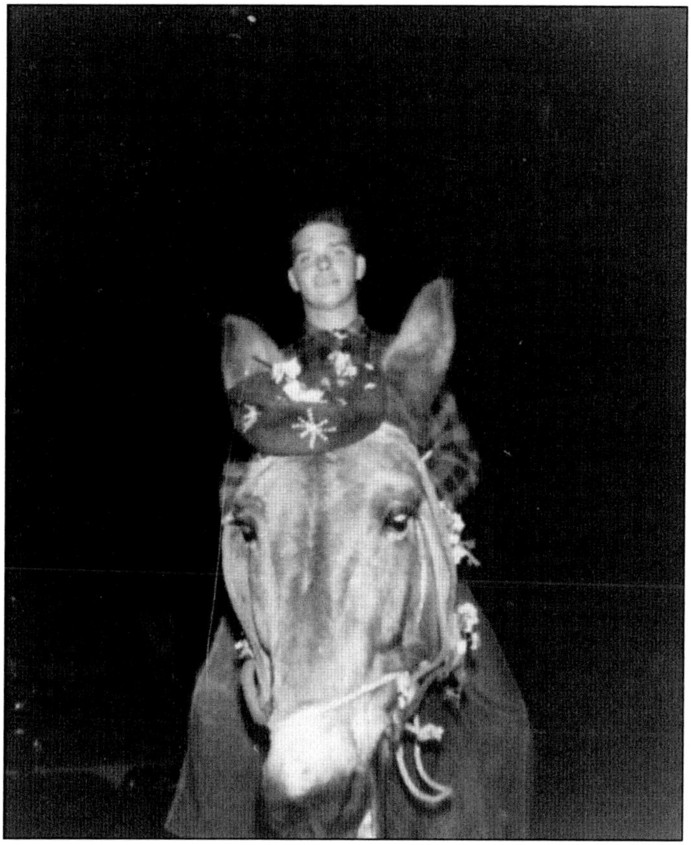

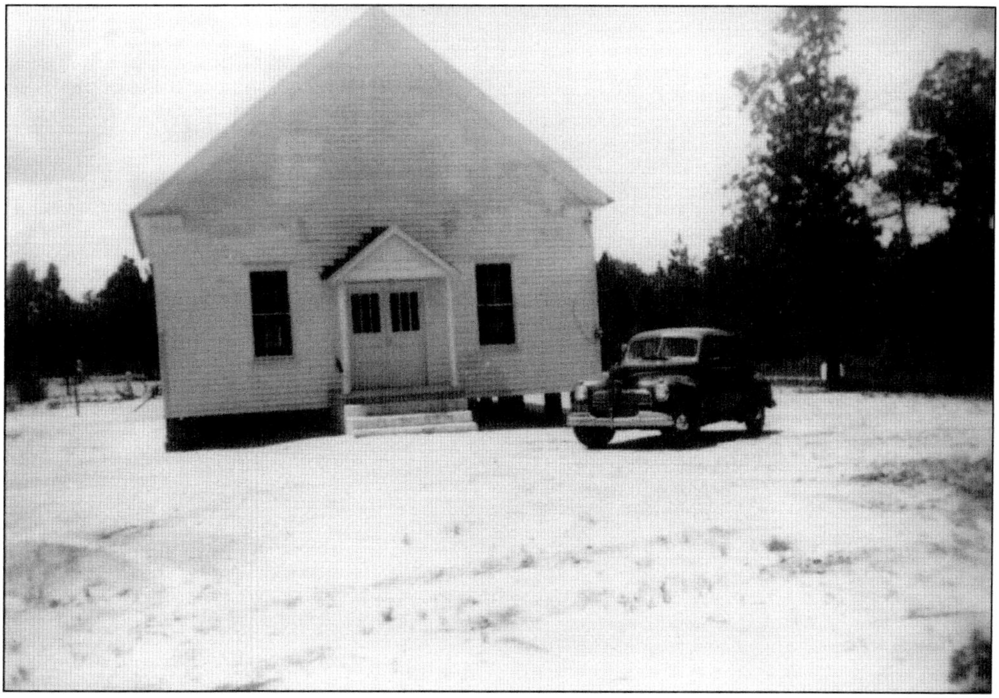

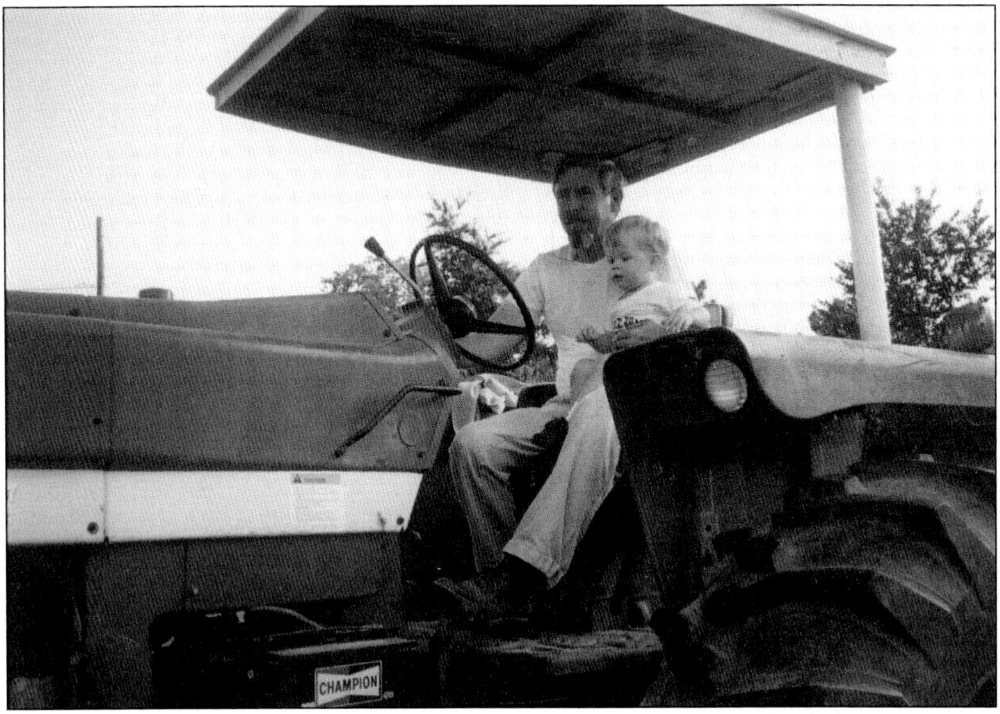

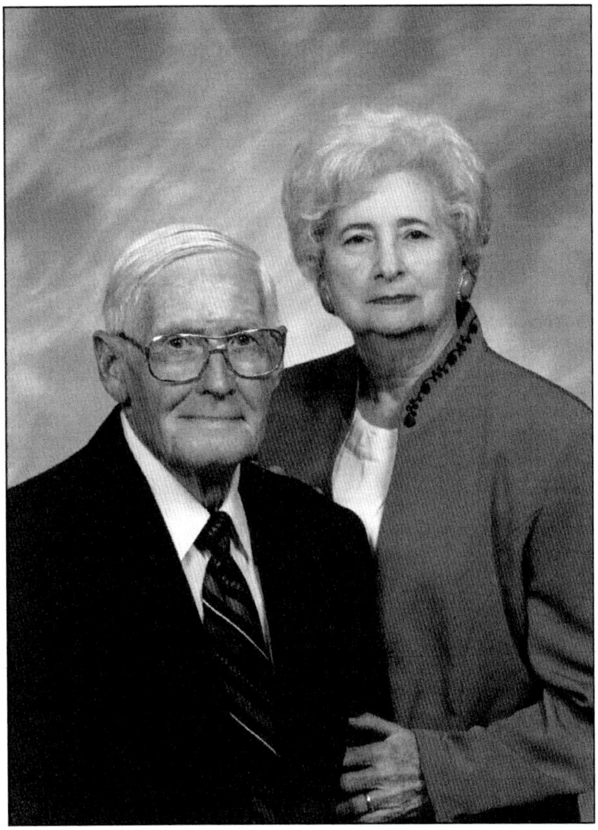

The Jackson family has four generations of farmers. Houston Jackson and Mattie Robbins Jackson farmed mostly cotton in the early years. Their son, Andrew, took over the family farm and changed over the years to corn, wheat, and rye. When the Depression came, a neighbor, Ruby Red, bought Jackson's land and sold it back to him for the same price years later. This act of kindness demonstrates the generosity of people during hard times in Lexington County. (Jackson family.)

Andrew Jackson married Eloise, and they had a son, Sam. After 20 years of farming, Andrew Jackson started working as a welder for Midlands Construction Company. When the company closed, he went to work welding for the state highway department. Andrew was a Mason, and both he and Eloise were members of the Order of the Eastern Star. (Jackson family.)

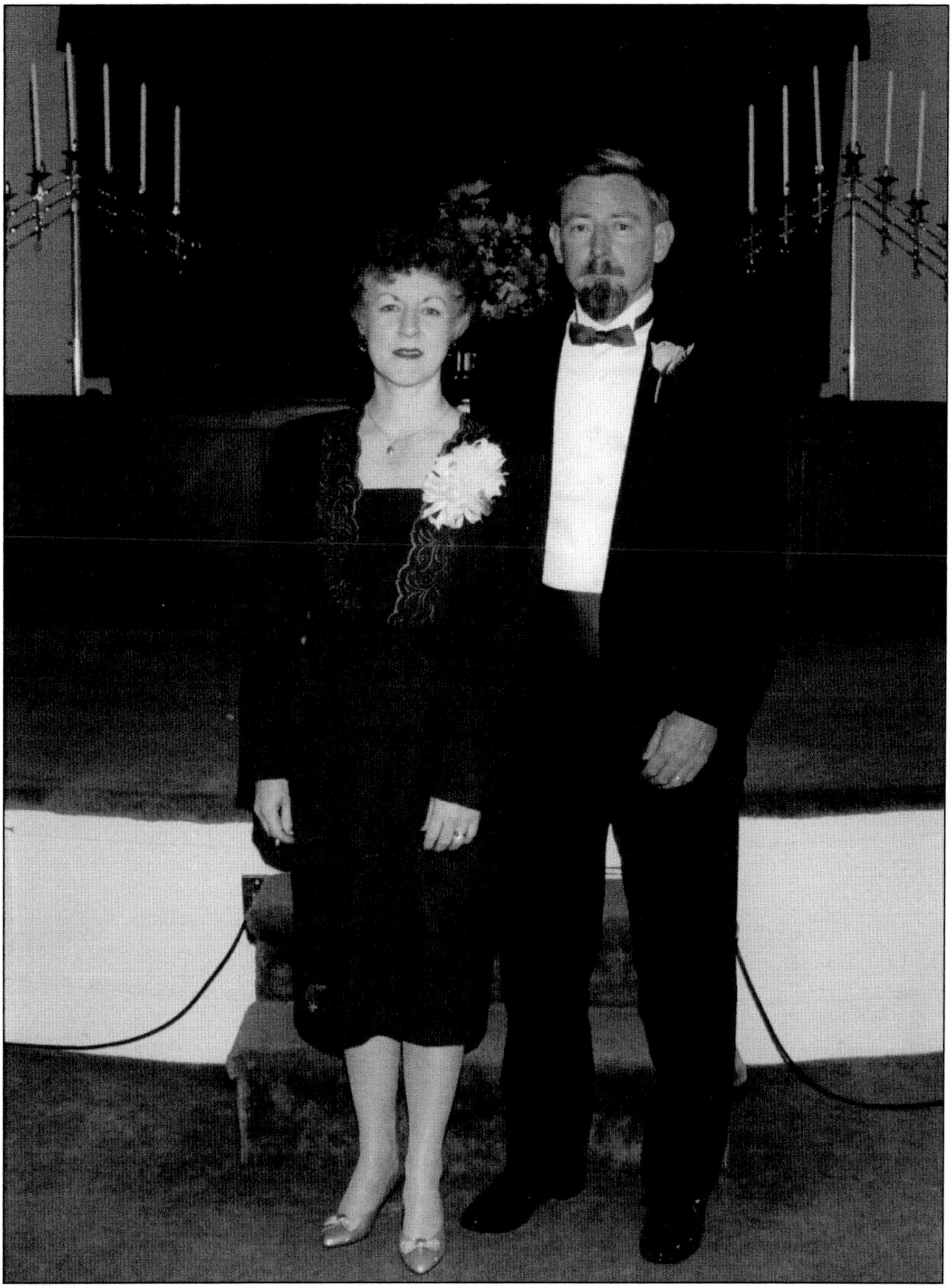

Sam Jackson married Beverly Bodie in 1969. He worked for 37 years with the South Carolina Highway Department as an engineer. Beverly worked for 22 years in finance with the South Carolina Department of Corrections. They have been very active in Florence Baptist Church near Pelion as well as the South Carolina, North Carolina, and Georgia Tractor Pull Associations. (Jackson family.)

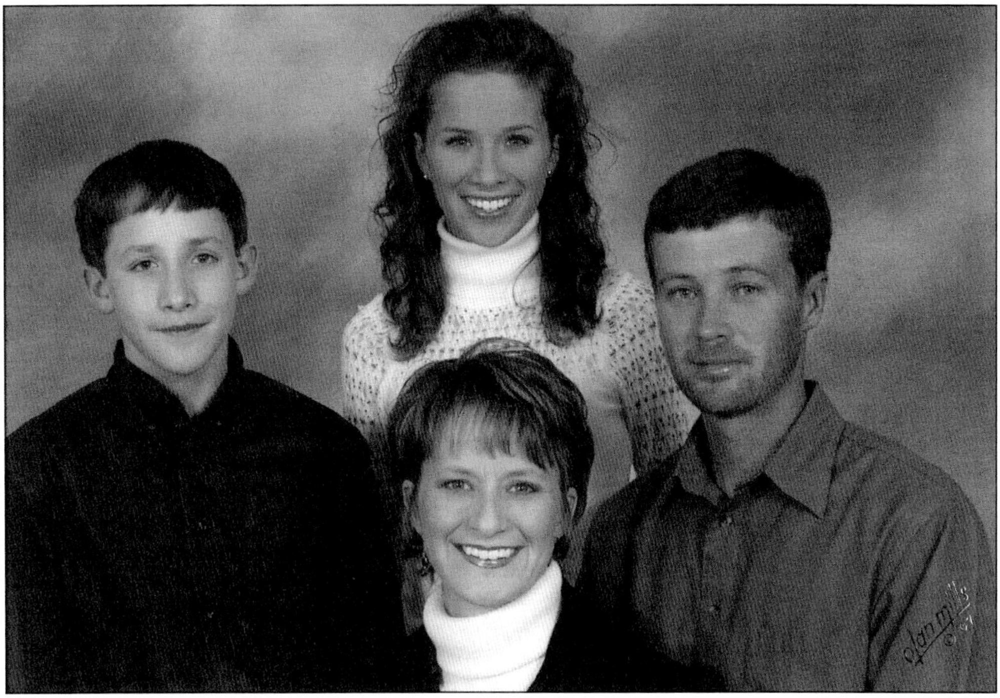

Beverly and Sam Jackson had two sons, Sam Jr. and Andy. The sons have expanded the family farming operation and sell wholesale to restaurants and stores. Sam Jr. married Heather Windham, and they have two children, Sam III and Tim. Andy married Valerie Windham, Heather's sister. They also have two children, Lyndsey and Aubrey. They enjoy supporting community events held by Pelion Peanut Party, Future Farmers of America, Town of Pelion, and Farm Bureau. Three generations participate in local tractor pulls. (Both, Jackson family.)

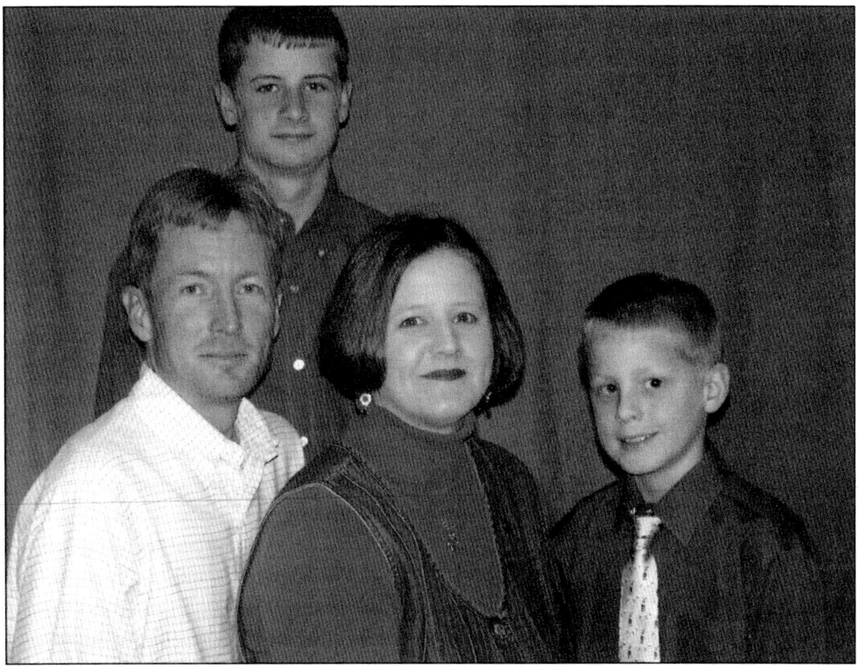

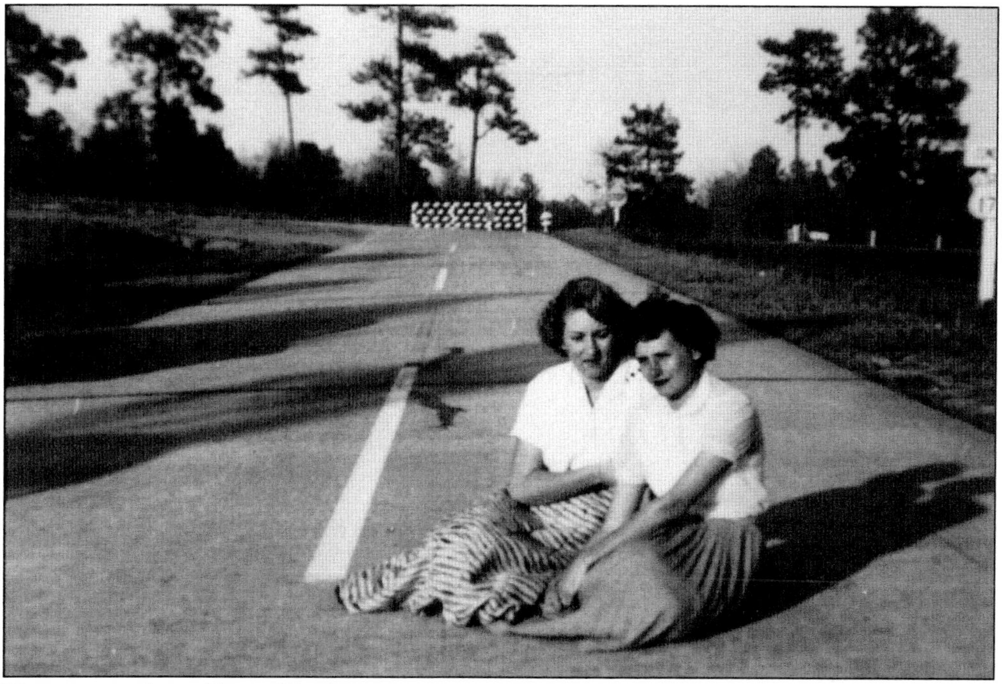

This picture shows Elaine Ward Shumpert (left) and Becky Day Shumpert in 1937 sitting on a section of newly paved Highway 215, present-day Fairview Road. No one in Pelion had ever seen a paved road before, and it was the talk of the town. This was just the beginning of a whole new world of transportation. (Wendy Shumpert West.)

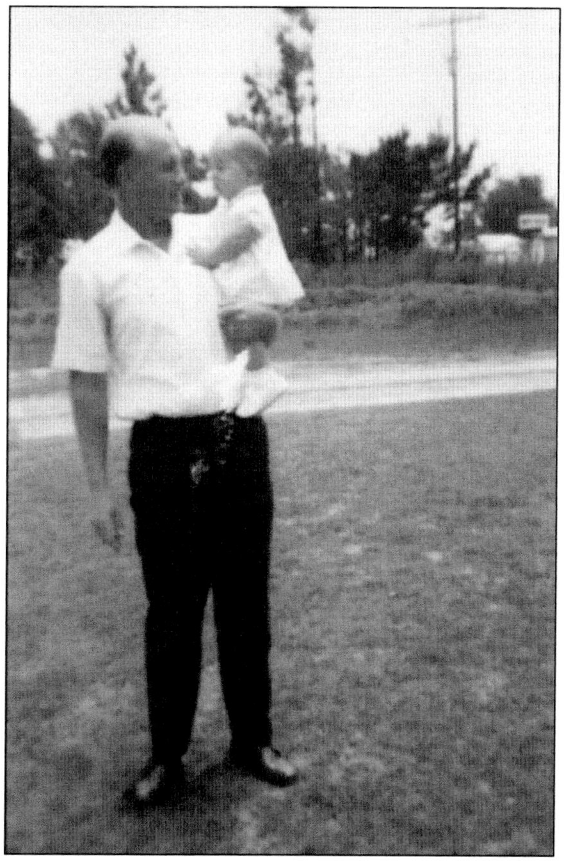

James T. Shumpert and Becky Ann Day met through a mutual friend. They were members of Convent Baptist Church in Fairview, South Carolina. Becky later stayed at home with their two children. James worked at the Savannah River Site and was a poultry farmer. Pictured here, James plays with their daughter, Wendy. (Wendy Shumpert West.)

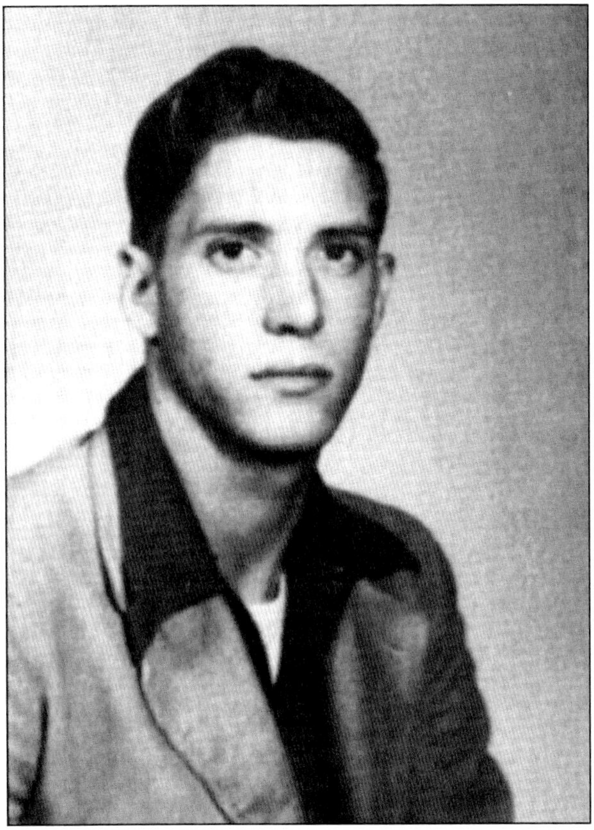

Billie Gene Stone returned to Pelion High School to teach and later became an administrator. One student defines Stone's special traits as character, devotion to the school, and devotion to the Pelion community. Billie Gene started the Pelion Rescue Squad, which has helped so many citizens. When Billie Gene worked with the rescue squad, injured townsfolk would often specifically ask him to travel with them to the hospital because they trusted him. He used to say, "A word to the wise is sufficient." He was an excellent role model and respected by many. (Jean Haggard.)

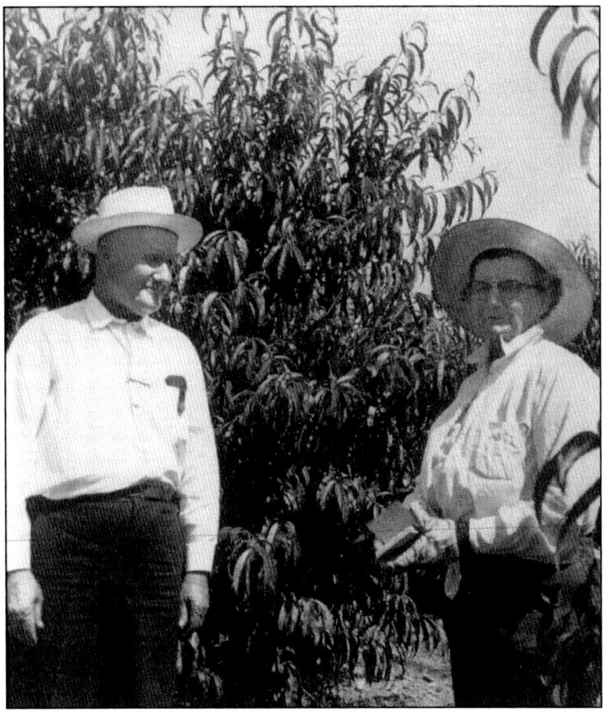

Walter P. Rawl had many loves—his family, God and church, friends, and education. He and his wife, Ernestine, had 7 children and 18 grandchildren. There was always work to do on the farm, but Walter never kept any of his children out of school. Although he received few years of formal education, in a one-room country school, he valued education highly. The land where Lexington High School and Lexington Technology Center are located was not for sale, but when Walter was approached about selling it for schools, he agreed. Doris Reynolds remembers her mother working in the fields or the orchard with a crew of her own helping her husband run the farm. Together, Walter and Ernestine Rawl were a terrific team. (Doris Rawl Reynolds.)

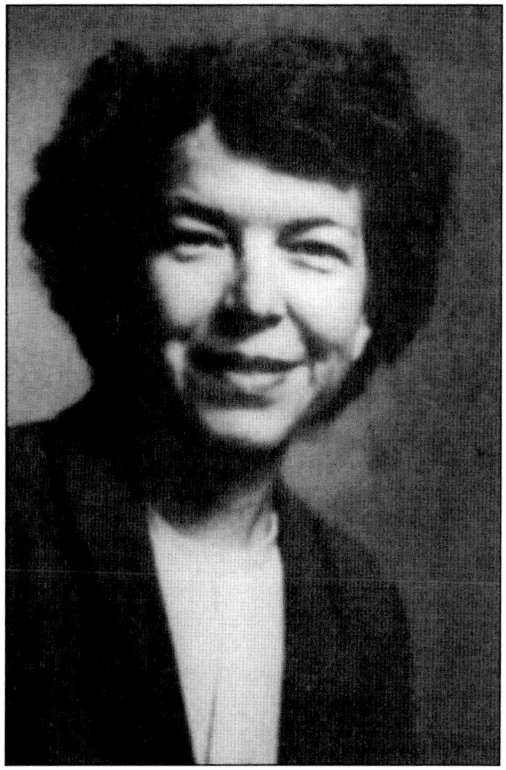

Pictured here are Miriam Dorn (right), a fourth-grade teacher, and Maudie Shumpert, a third-grade teacher, at the consolidated Pelion Elementary School. This two-story building served all of the students in the surrounding areas and was a central part of the community for news and events. Many people today still remember these two ladies fondly. Some mentioned that Maudie's husband was the butcher at Shumpert's IGA. (Both, Jean Haggard.)

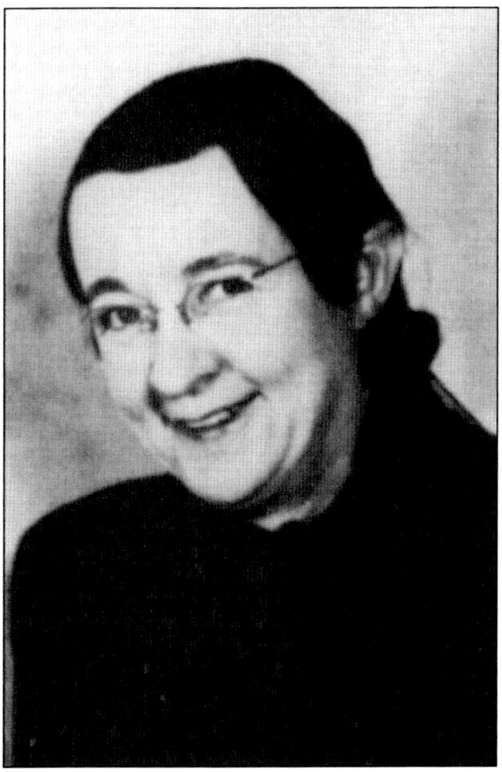

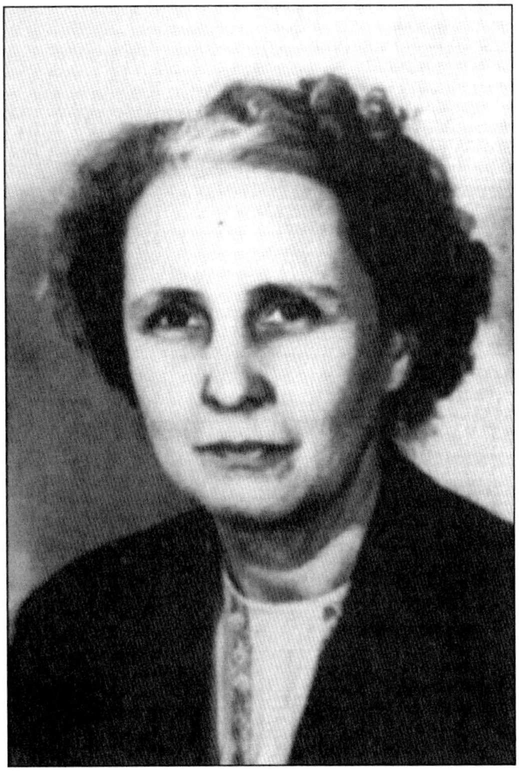

Lucille Derrick (left) taught second grade at Pelion Elementary. Iva Garvin taught first grade. The Honorable Kit Spires remembers both of these ladies teaching him not so very long ago. More information about the Pelion community can be found in two publications titled *Sandhill Recollections* and *Pelion, South Carolina—The Community and Its People* for sale at town hall. These two books were written by the local Pelion History Committee to preserve the rich stories and historical facts before they are no longer remembered. (Both, Jean Haggard.)

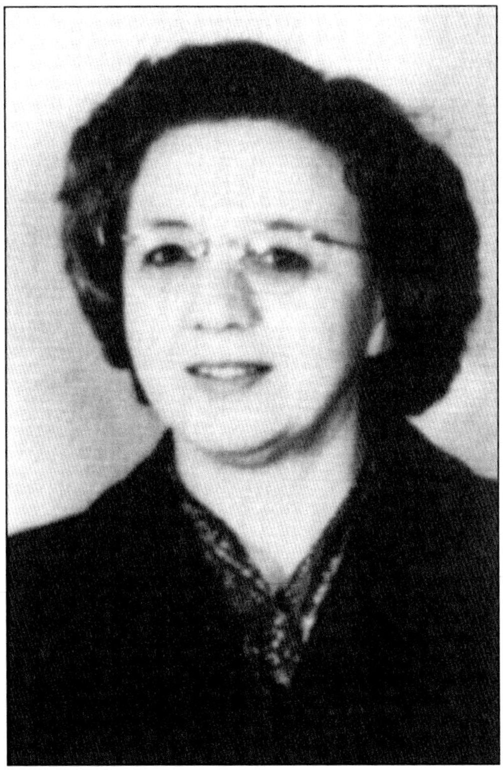

Batesburg-Leesville was known as the twin cities. Originally communities named for landowners, the two country towns began as stops on stagecoach lines. Later the railroad brought new life into the two cities, and an influx of mills, farming homesteads, and most importantly chickens was the making of their futures. Pictured here is an old postcard of a turpentine mill in Batesburg from the early 1900s. The towns finally merged in 1992 after sharing one school district since 1952. Batesburg-Leesville is known for its annual poultry festival, which brings people from miles around to enjoy barbecued chicken, crafts, entertainment, and rides every May. (Mathias family.)

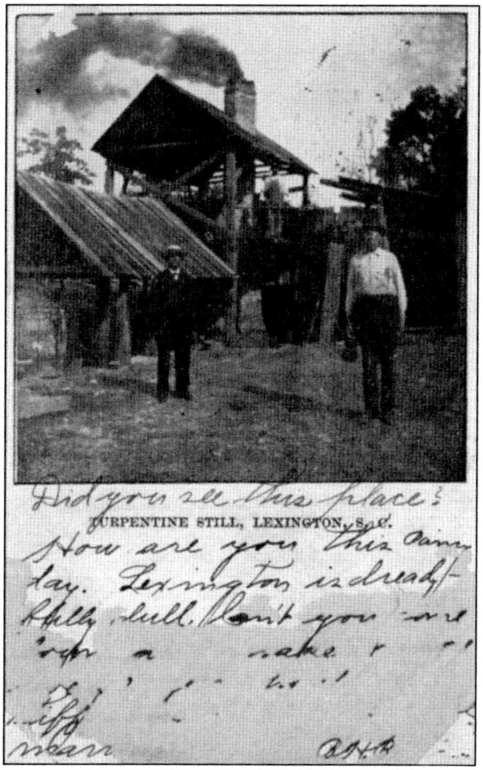

Joel Etheredge (1845–1893) was a schoolteacher and married Eudora Whittle (1853–1919), a traveling nurse who would act as a doctor because there were no doctors available that far out in the country. They had nine children. (Herb and Catherine Sharpe.)

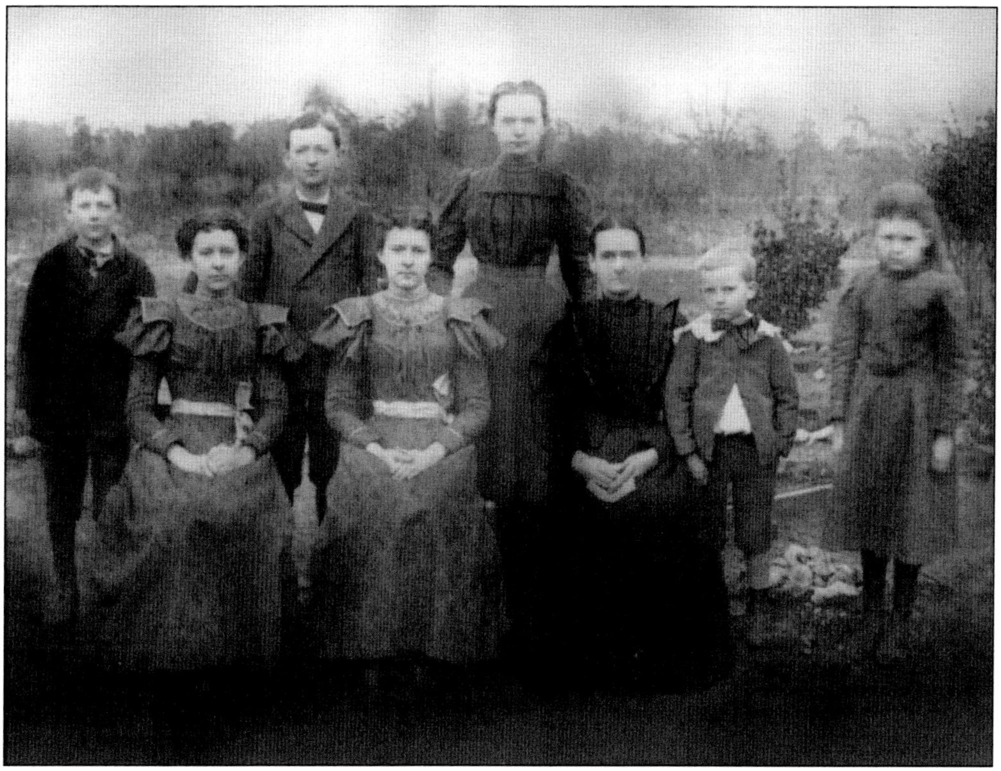

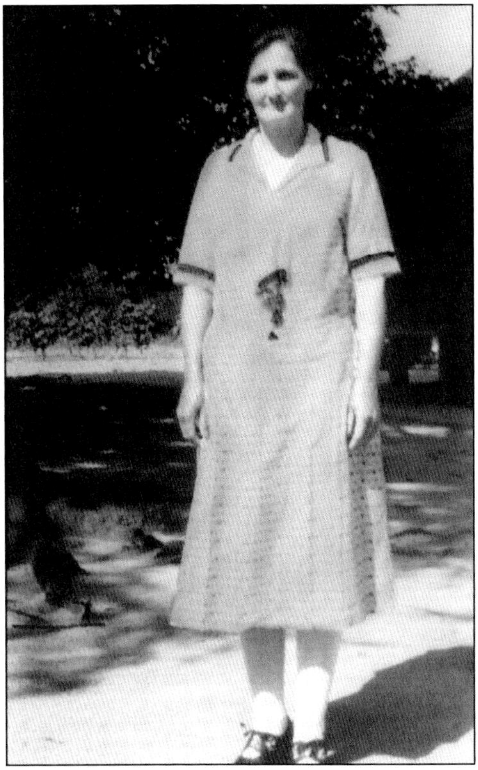

Herman Elwell Etheredge (1887–1959) married Eva Lucy Addy Etheredge (1890–1930). He was a farmer in Batesburg. They had five children. Herb Sharpe would visit his grandfather's farm, Kneece's Mill Pond, and there was a gristmill at one of the ponds on his property. Etheredge also had a threshing machine, which separated the seed from the grain. (Herb and Catherine Sharpe.)

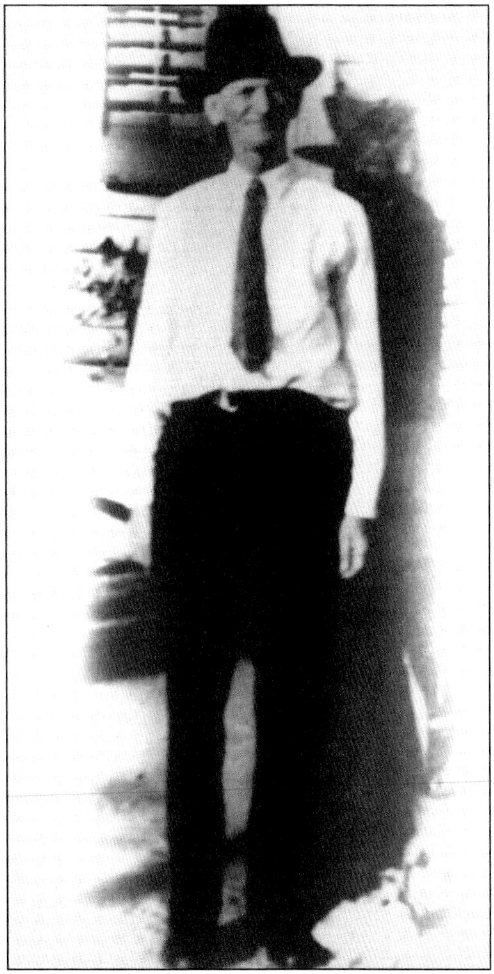

In the late 1950s, Herb Sharpe remembers spending time with his granddaddy, Herman Etheredge, pictured on the right. Herb and his Granddaddy Herman were walking around and saw a lizard. Granddaddy grabbed it and said, "Let's use this lizard for bait at the pond." The following day, sure enough, they caught a big catfish! Herb learned to skin and clean the catfish. His granddaddy asked him if he wanted to take it back to Columbia. There were no coolers and ice packs at that time. Granddaddy took the fish, wrapped it in newspaper many times, and packed it in ice. When Herb opened it in Columbia, it was actually so cold part of it was frozen solid. At that time, it took over two hours to return to his home in Columbia. (Herb and Catherine Sharpe.)

Evelyn Ruth Etheredge was a dietician in the Columbia city schools when she met William Herbert (W. H.) Sharpe, who worked for the Coca-Cola Company as a salesman. They had two children, Herbert and Herman, and lived in Columbia. Herb remembers that most of his aunts and uncles all went to college. During difficult times, that seemed very unlikely, but education was definitely emphasized in his family. (Herb and Catherine Sharpe.)

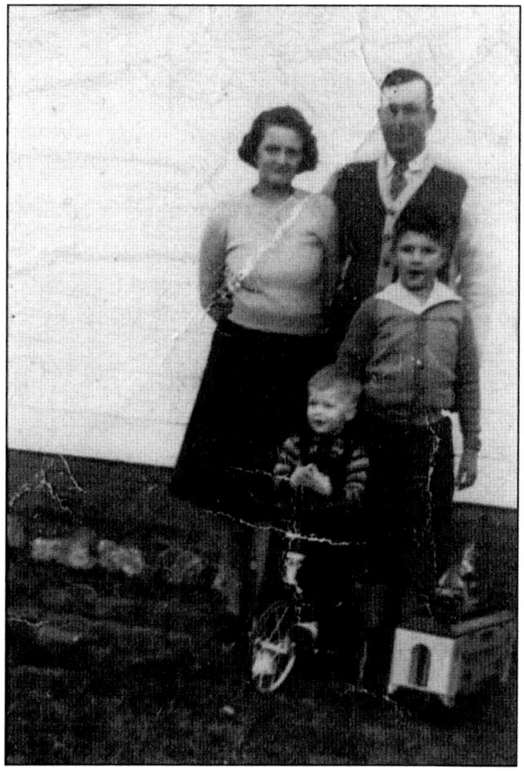

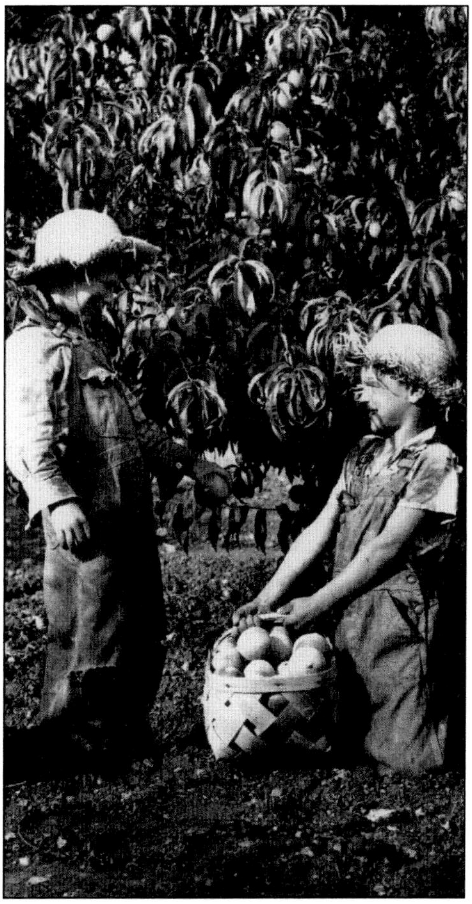

Home of the Lexington County Peach Festival since 1959, Gilbert has been the center of attention each July. For more than 50 years, this small town has inspired other county residents to share in the opportunities presented by this event. Since pageants, art contests, and recipe contests all require time for judging, they are held ahead of time so winners can be announced at the festival. (Lexington Main Library.)

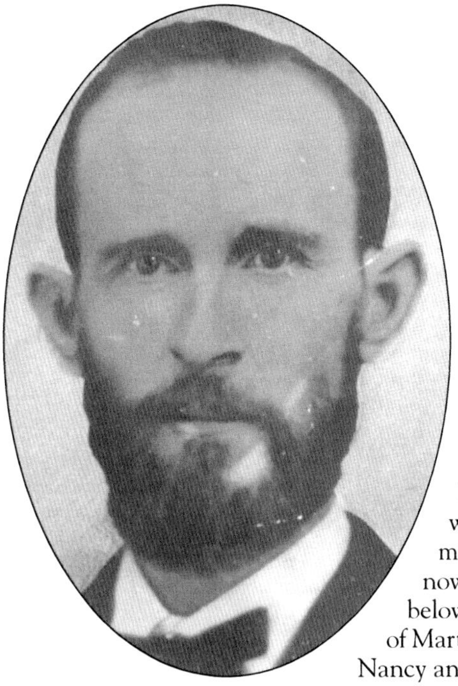

James Henry Lewie came from an old Gilbert family. Known as "Captain" Lewie for his service in the Civil War, James was admired and praised throughout the area. The town was renamed for him until 1899, when there was a terrifying train accident due to confusion between Lexington, Leesville, and Lewiedale. Captain Lewie owned a country store with Leaphart. Their store provided everything from mules to caskets. Lewie built a beautiful home, which now belongs to Gwyndell and Nancy Taylor. Pictured below is the Lexington Guards flag that was created out of Martha Ann Leaphart Lewie's silk wedding dress. (Both, Nancy and Gwendyll Taylor.)

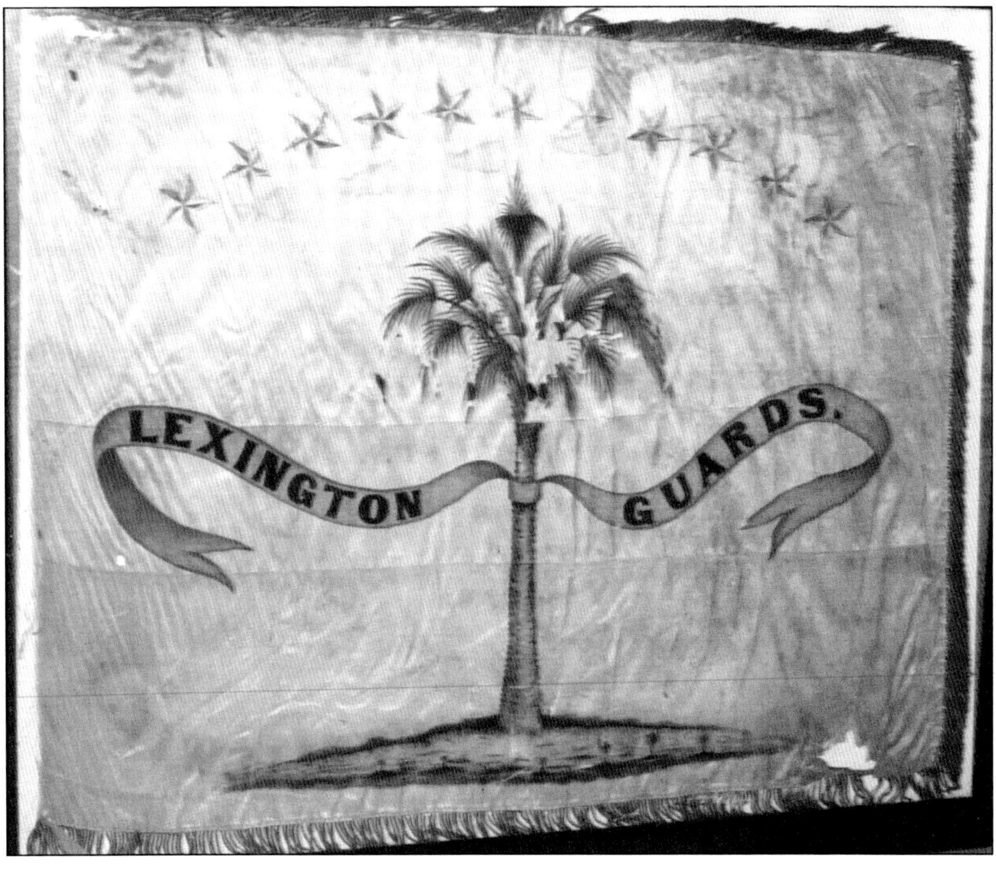

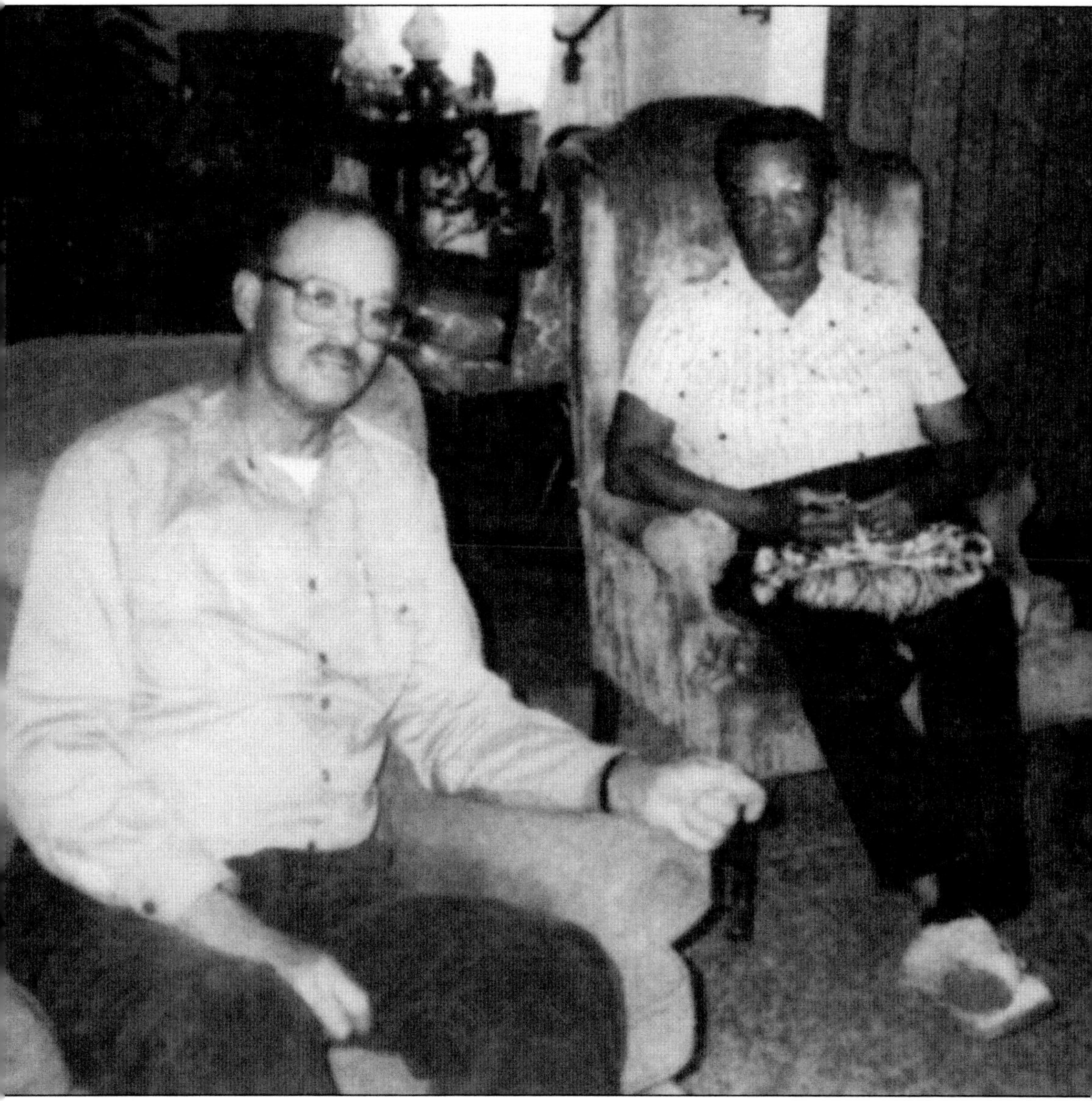

Dorothy and R. E. Summers were sharecroppers who lived in Gilbert. Dorothy recalls that she was only allowed to attend school for four months a year at a one-room schoolhouse heated by a fireplace. R. E. remembers a unique tradition called "box parties," parties held to raise money for teachers' salaries. Sharecropping was a way of life in the South. At the time, no one had freezers, so meat had to be cured to preserve it through the winter. An iceman would bring ice for the cooler. People would put the milk bottle down the well on a string to keep it cool. Buying groceries at a store was rare, since people grew everything they needed themselves. The landowner would share meat, milk, butter, and cream with the sharecropper. Most everybody had chickens, too. Although sharecropping was a hard life, it was a simple life. (Kathryn Liverman.)

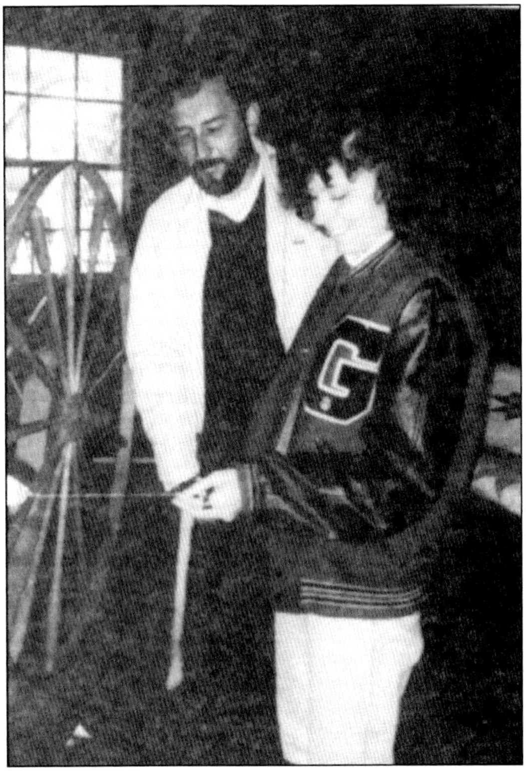

Horace Harmon is pictured teaching Katrina Craps how to spin thread on a spinning wheel at Gilbert High School. Harmon retired as the director of the Lexington County Museum and is considered an authority on Lexington County history. Many people from Lexington remember the museum from visits, hands-on activities, and events that taught them about local history. Keeping with that tradition, the Lexington County Museum continues to provide educational programs that demonstrate Colonial methods of self-sufficiency. (Kathryn Liverman.)

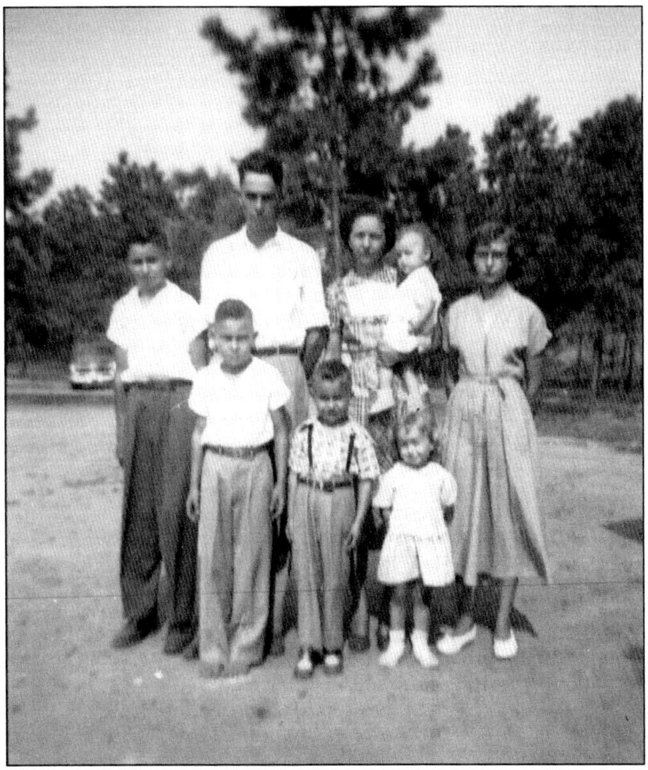

Faye Wilma Laphon Long met Colie Festus "Buck" Taylor through a friend of her sister when she lived on Priceville Road. The couple was married in 1932. Their son Gwendyll recalls that people who were participating in the WPA woke up at 3:00 a.m. to take their mules to the section of the lake nearby to move the logs that were being cut down, piled up, and taken to a sawmill. Every Sunday morning, they all rode to St. Paul's Lutheran Church in a 1932 Ford Model A. In later years, both Faye and Buck worked at Olympia Mill on the second shift, from 2:00 p.m. until 11:00 p.m. They would farm in the mornings. They had 6 children, 12 grandchildren, and 13 great-grandchildren. (Nancy and Gwendyll Taylor.)

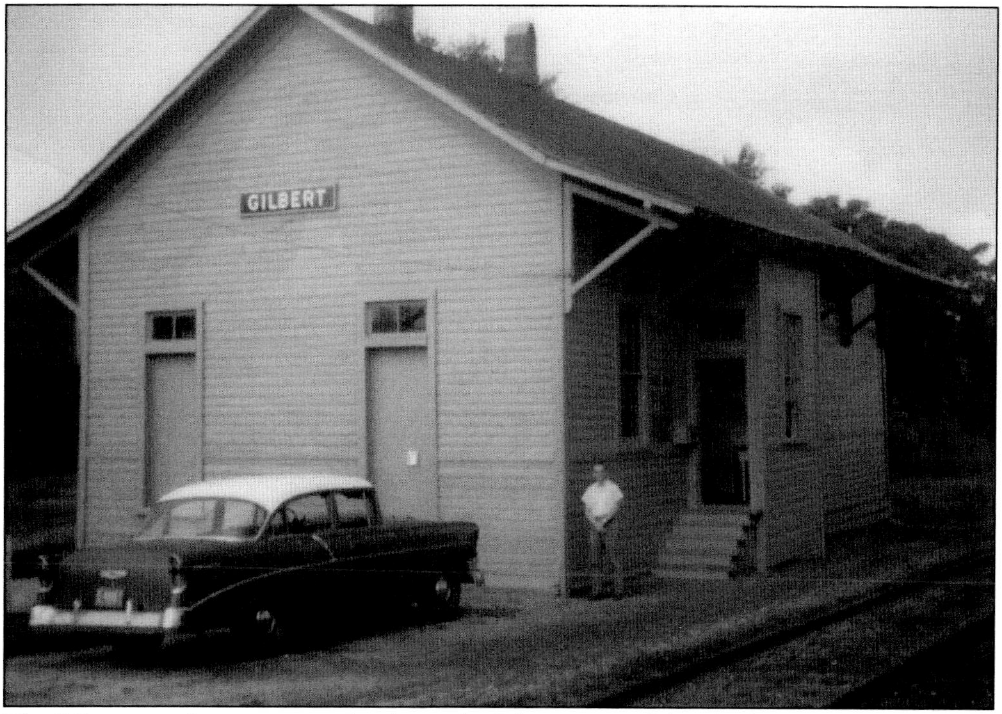

The Gilbert train depot was once the place to be. Like so many of the whistle-stops on the Southern Railroad, the town of Gilbert built up around the hustle and bustle of the railway. Pictured below is a map of the layout of the town of Gilbert in the early 1920s created by Pascal G. Corley and J. H. "Bunk" Keisler. More information can be found in the town book titled *Gilbert: Reflections and History*. (Both, Nancy and Gwendyll Taylor.)

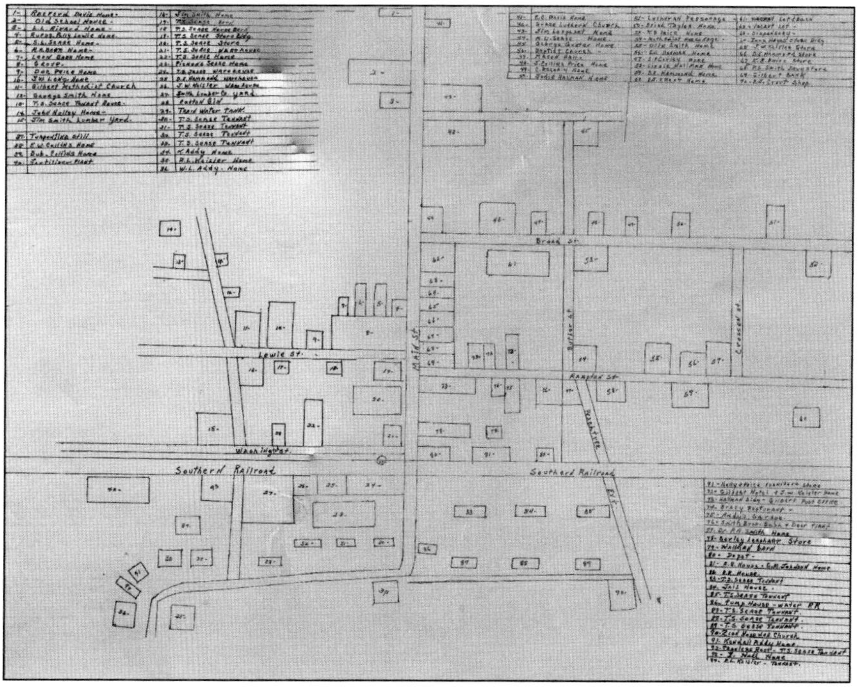

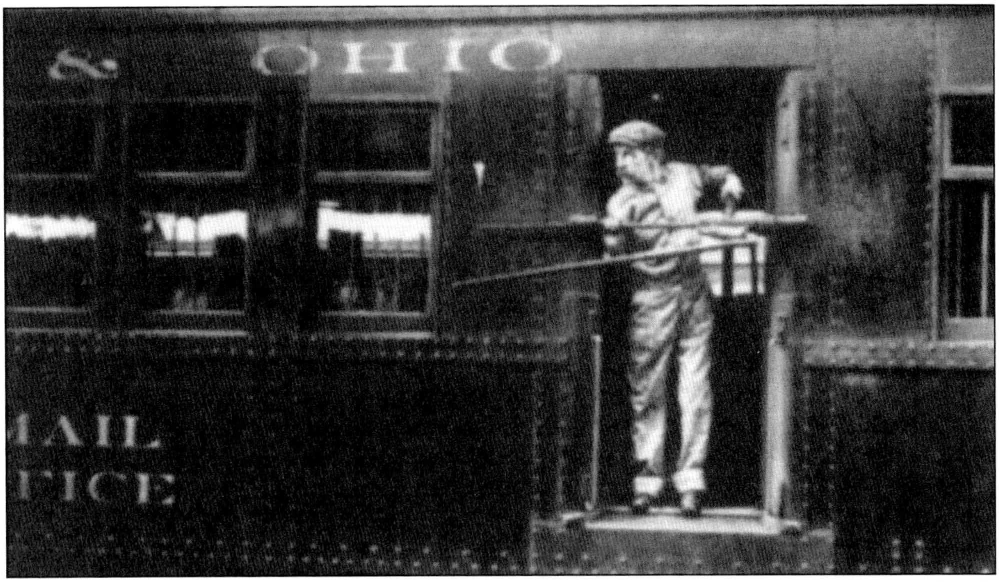

The early Swiss and German settlers expanded their search for homesteads toward the fertile riverbed areas and wound their way toward the Dutch Fork area, called Irmo today. These settlers were loyal to the king who had granted them their land and had a difficult time during the Revolutionary War. When the railroad came in the 19th century, this stop on the railroad line grew into a town. In the 1930s, Lake Murray enveloped many of its surrounding areas. The businesses that resulted from the new electric power plant were a boon to this area. There was a Rosenwald school for African American children located in Dutch Fork very similar to the one in downtown Lexington. Gene Able wrote a thorough and interesting text called *Irmo and the Dutch Fork Legacy: A Centennial Celebration*. (Kathryn Liverman.)

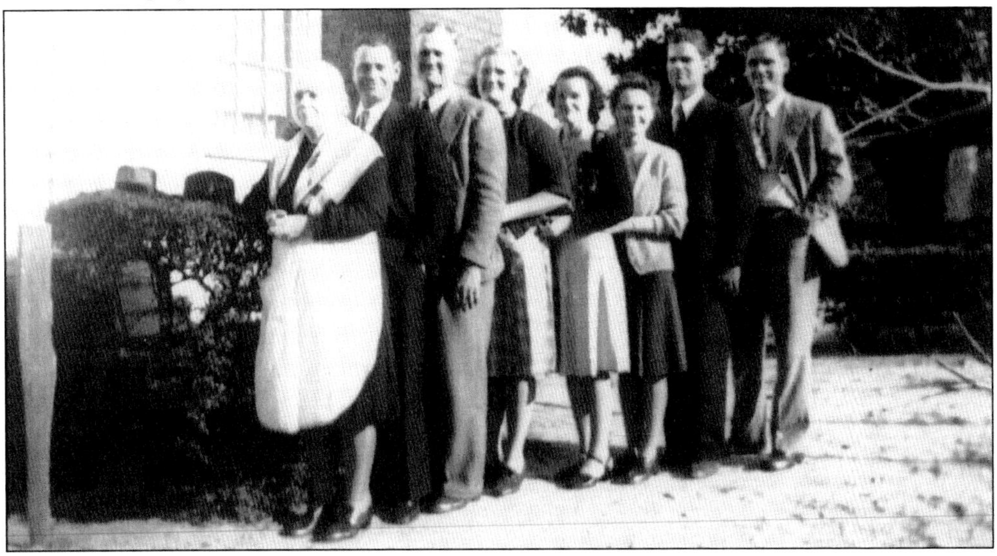

Annie Laurie Kennerly grew up near the small town of Swansea. Her parents, J. C. and Henrietta Kennerly, had eight children. J. C. was a cotton farmer. Annie Laurie remembers her childhood as a time of work, school, and church. During the Great Depression, families did not have money for many extra things, but they had an abundance of love and respect for each other because they worked, played, and prayed together. (Annie Laurie George.)

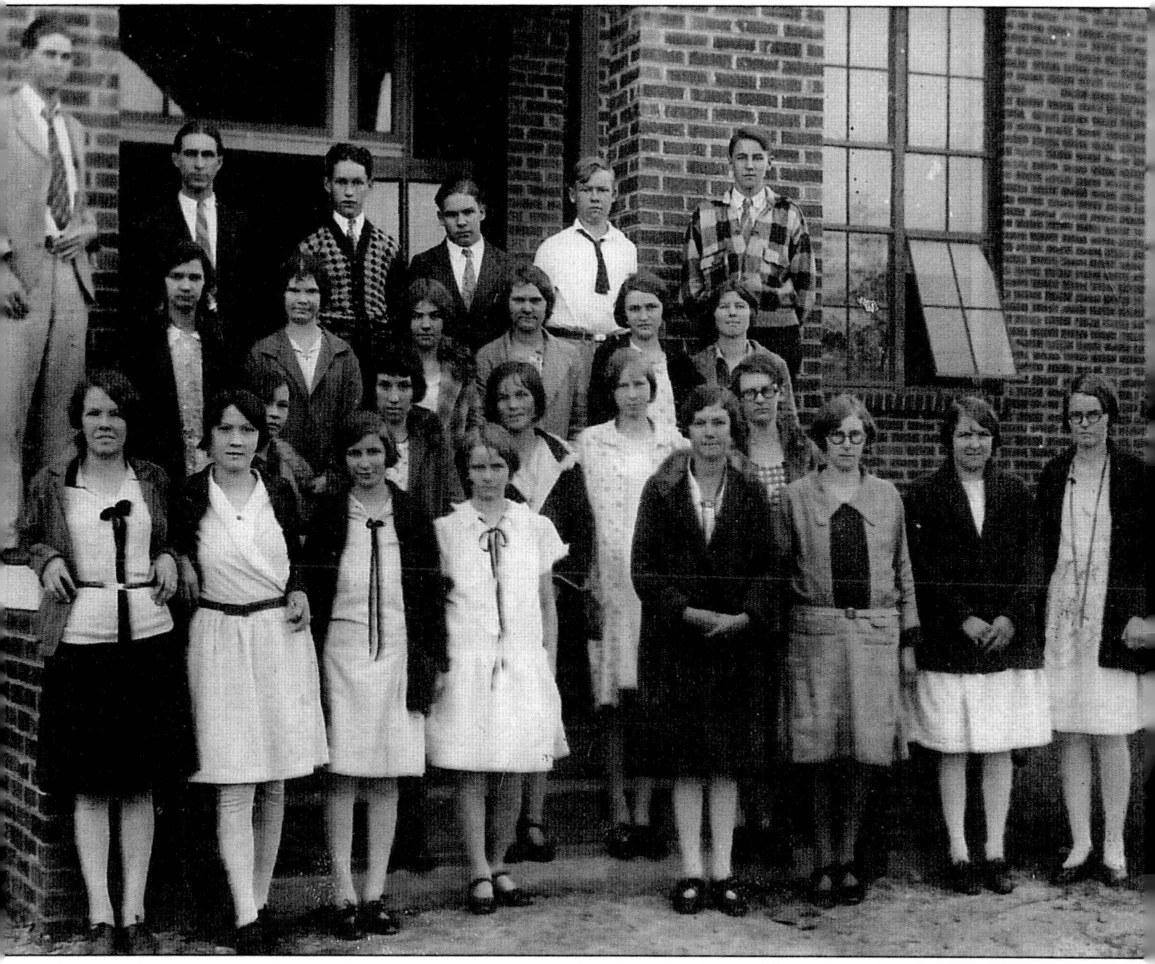

Pictured here are students who attended Swansea High School in 1929. The following students are included: Lynn Redmond, Evelyn Sturkie, Jettie Kirkland, Louis Jeffcoat, Madison Gunter, Thomas Hoffman, Leon Shectler, Mittie Argoe, Verna Brooker, and Woodrow Moore. (Annie Laurie George.)

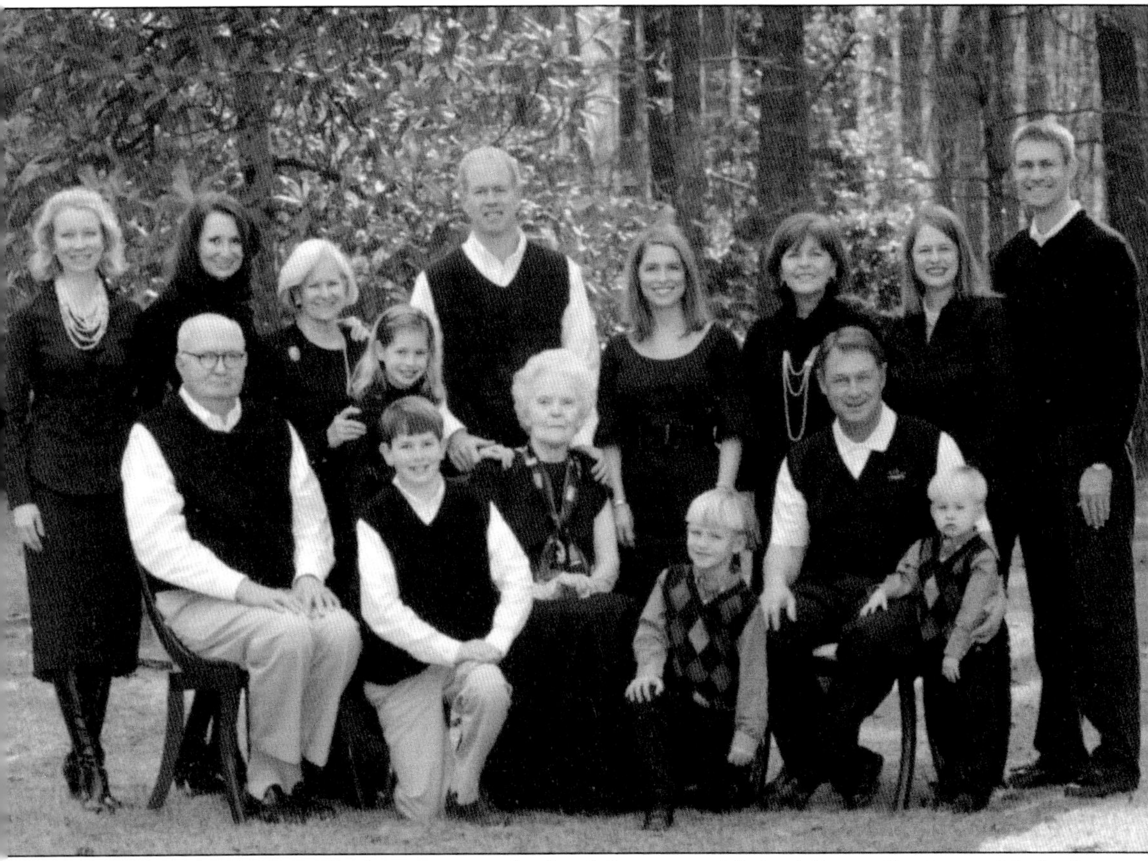

Annie Laurie George has been very involved with Lexington Medical Center, Lexington Methodist Church, preservation of local history, American Legion activities, and much more. She has cherished memories of being a young girl growing up in Swansea: bacon frying in the afternoon, cotton fields, driving at an early age (as soon as her feet could reach the pedals), and family outings. She and her husband, Sam A. George, had three children, four grandchildren and four great-grandchildren. (Annie Laurie George.)

Five

Churches and Traditions

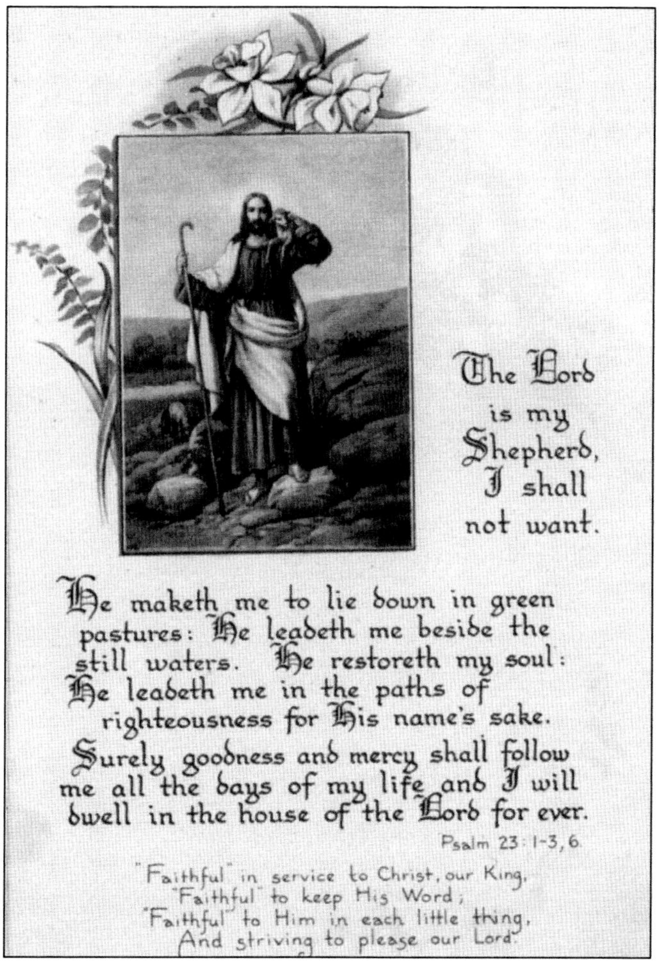

This excerpt from H. Odelle Harman's confirmation booklet signifies the common thread that binds this county. While each person may subscribe to a different denomination or even a different religion, together they believe in God and country. The people who have had the strongest influence in this county worked together, played together, and prayed together to build a strong future for their children. (Harman family.)

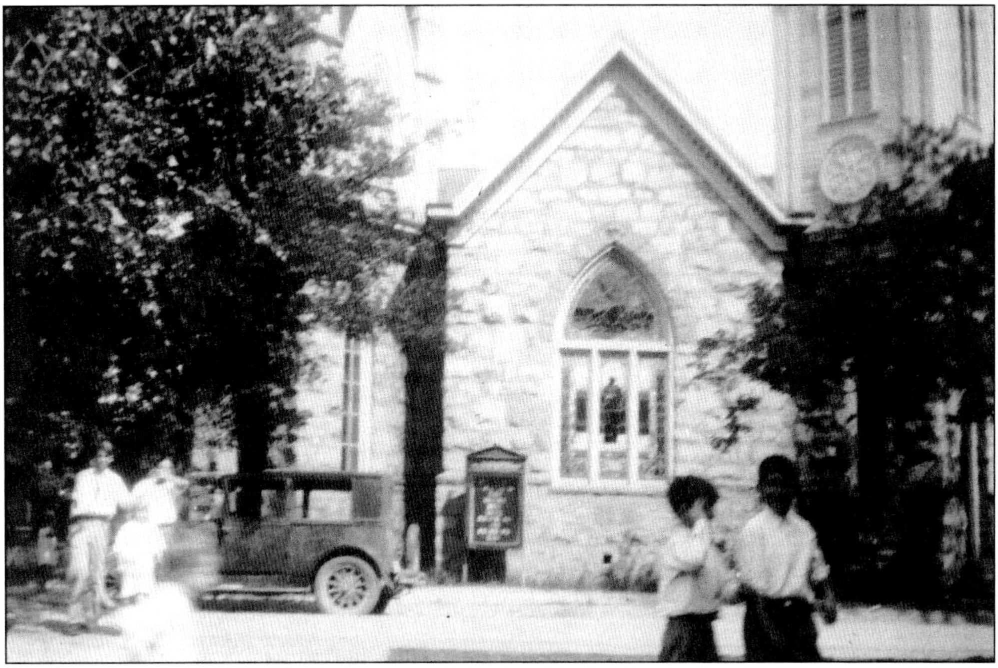

St. Stephen's Lutheran Church dates back to 1830. The congregation has weathered the Civil War and the loss of the church building, World War I, and the loss of the new church building to fire. During that time, other churches, "offspring" of St. Stephen's, were built closer to the local communities. St. Stephen's was destined to return stronger each time. The United Methodist church offered sanctuary until the time that the new "Rock Church" would open in 1900. (Mathias family.)

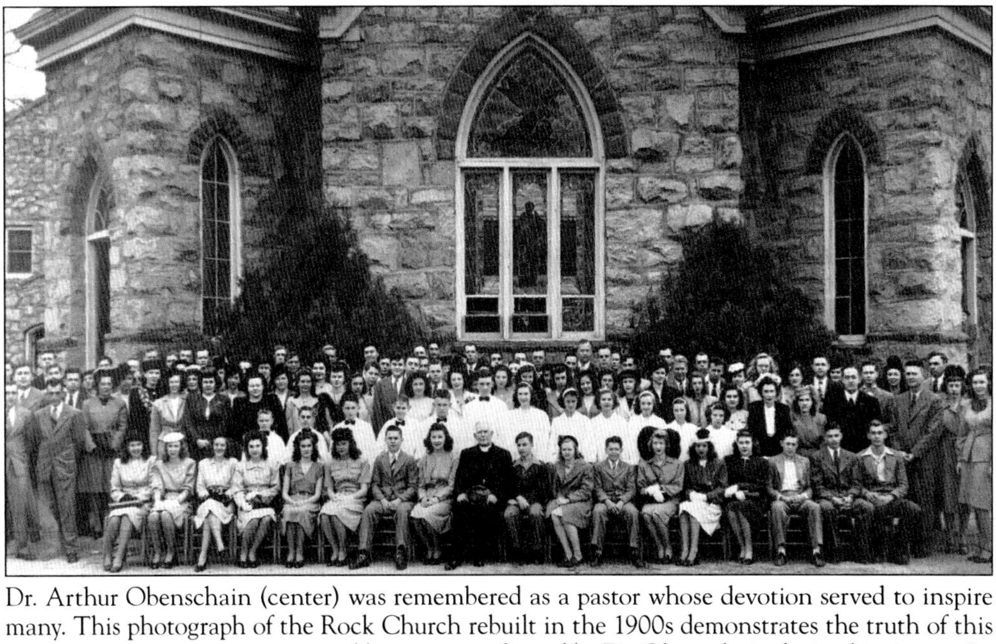

Dr. Arthur Obenschain (center) was remembered as a pastor whose devotion served to inspire many. This photograph of the Rock Church rebuilt in the 1900s demonstrates the truth of this statement, since everyone pictured here was confirmed by Dr. Obenschain during his time at St. Stephen's. (Courtesy of St. Stephen's Lutheran Church.)

Martha Barre was the first librarian at St. Stephen's library, which was funded by a member's significant donation. Here is her baptismal certificate from 1915. The wording combines with illustration to make a work of art; this was a special document for all church members. St. Stephen's is unique in many ways. (Mathias family.)

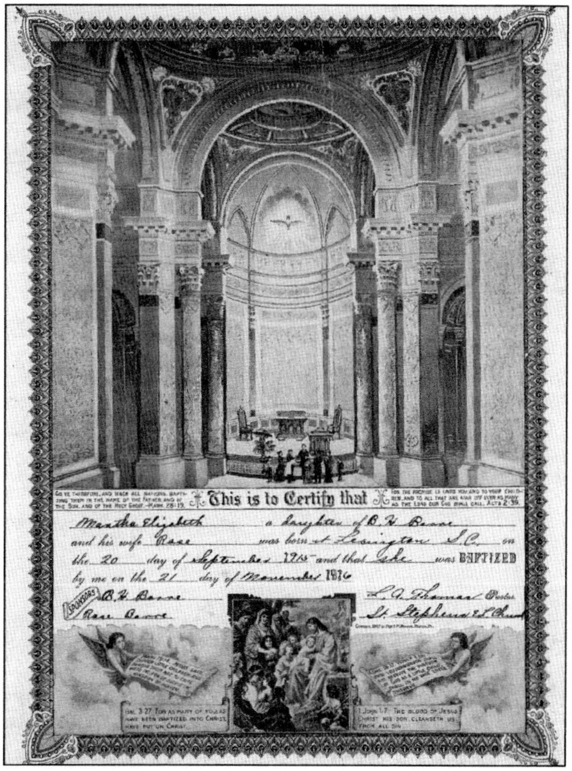

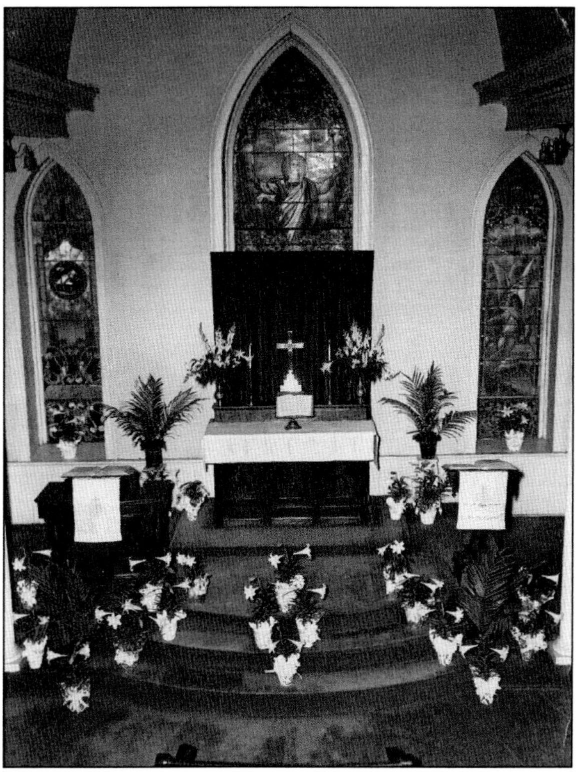

After 180 years of worship in Lexington County, St. Stephen's Lutheran congregation remains a community-minded group. The people of St. Stephen's are leaders in Lexington who serve through ministry, generosity, and discipleship devoted to the belief that "with God all things are possible" (Matt. 19:26). (St. Stephen's Lutheran Church.)

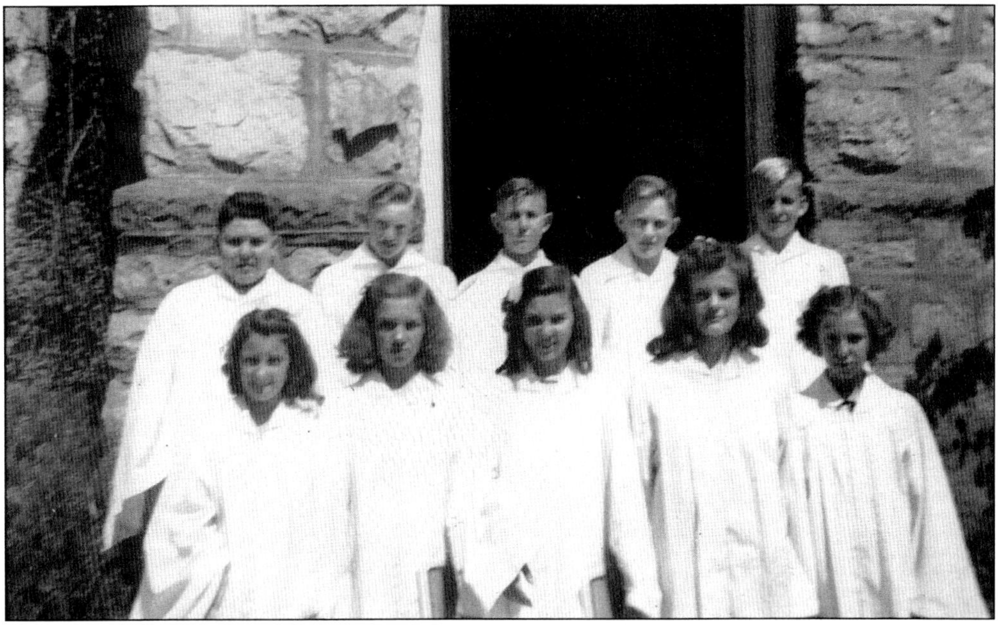

The Theological Seminary of Lexington began under the direction of Rev. Ernest Hazelius. While this was only one of his major accomplishments, it may be the most noted. The seminary was a source of pride for the Lutheran community for many years. Reverend Hazelius retired from teaching in 1851 and is buried in the St. Stephen's graveyard. The seminary building and grounds were donated to the Lexington County Museum in 1974 by the Leaphart family. (Harman family.)

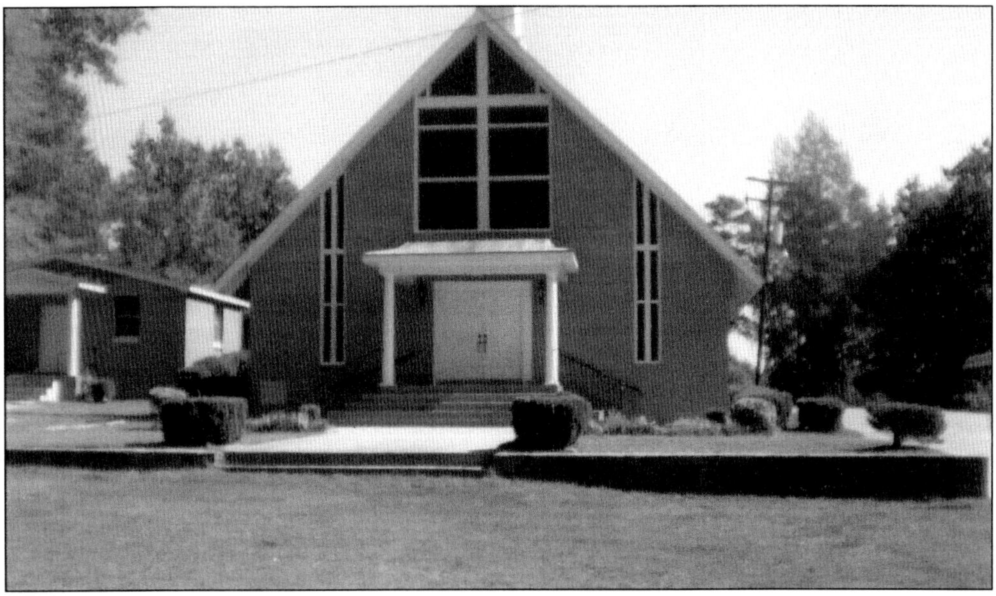

The AME church organized in 1865. The first African Methodist Episcopal church building was destroyed by fire around 1890. At that time, another church was built and was renamed New Bethel AME Church. It prospered until 1971, when a gas explosion again took their sanctuary. Mid-Carolina Co-op and Lexington Memorial opened their doors to the congregation until the new building could be built. The new building was opened in 1973. This church continues to demonstrate strong leadership in Lexington County. (Doug Jones.)

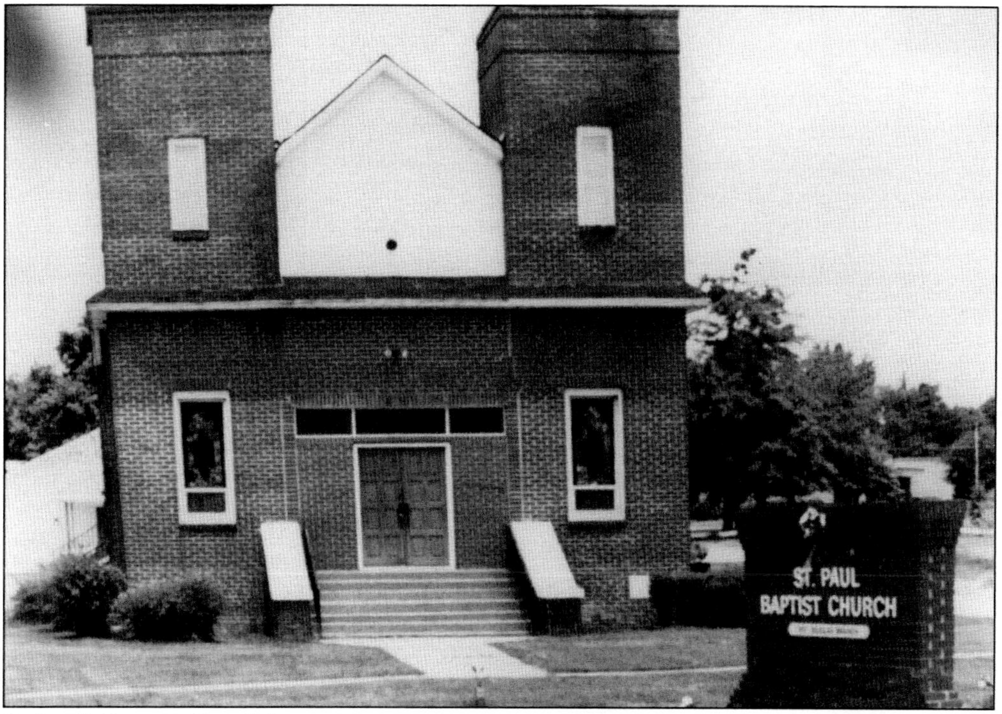

St. Paul's Baptist Church began before 1902. The African American community first built a wooden church and then worked to move the church in 1929 and make renovations. Brick and stained-glass windows were added along with indoor plumbing. Rev. Arthur Bailey served in the mid-1900s for 32 years. Rev. Douglas Branch served the next 10 years. These two pastors were the most noted for their service. Since 1929, the church family has grown and continues to make renovations and updates. (Douglas Strother.)

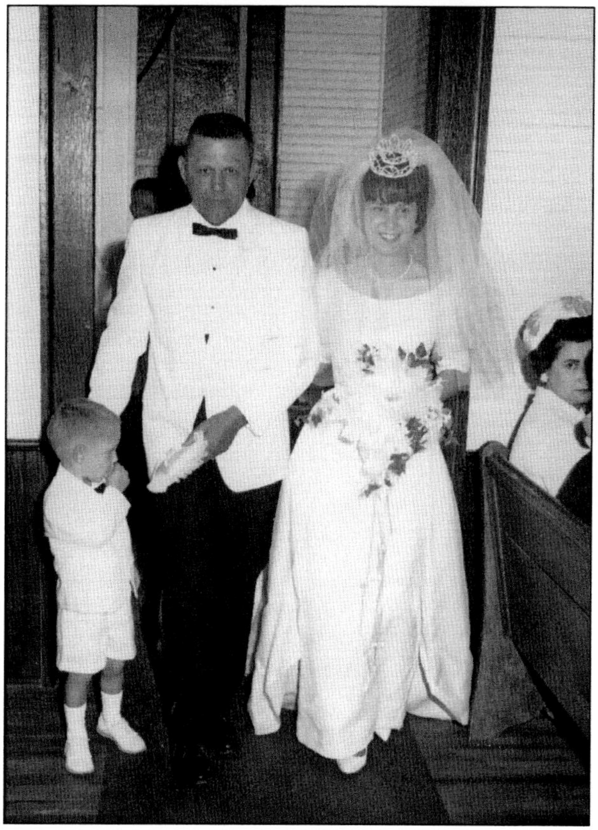

Jean Haggard and Roy Nichols walk down the aisle at Holy Trinity Lutheran, a small country church in Pelion. Many generations of Lutherans have enjoyed the camaraderie and community that Holy Trinity provides. Members have preserved the heritage of their ancestors by keeping the original worship areas the same. (Jean Nichols Haggard.)

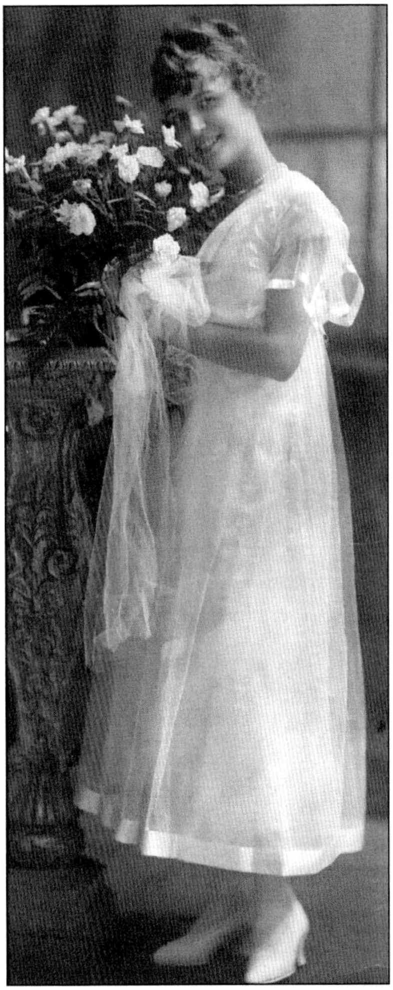

The Lexington Methodist Church dates from 1850, when it had a circuit minister. The preacher would ride to a different location to preach each day for 28 days. A little log church was built and served the area for 25 years. When the Civil War came, the Methodists were prevented from assembling and told to get out of town by Sherman's men. In 1867, there were only four members. A congregation of five built a new church in 1875. Since then, several new churches and additions have been needed because of the growth of their congregation. Today there are 1,100 members in a very busy and blessed church family. (Annie Laurie George.)

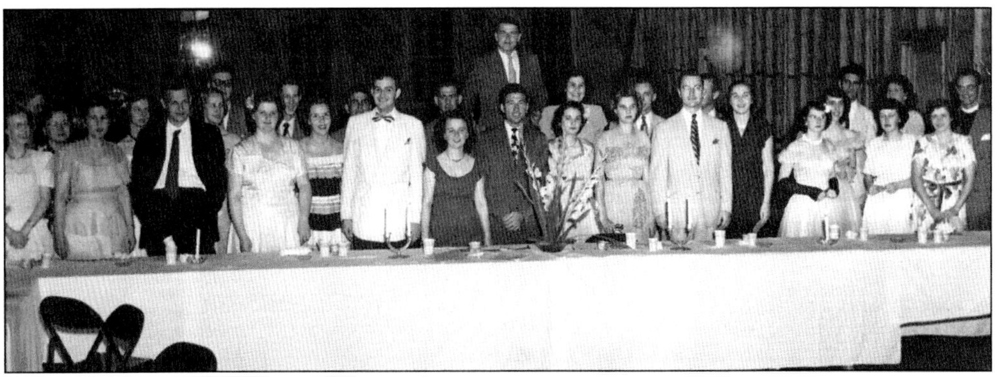

One tradition spanning the county was the Junior-Senior Banquet. Every year, high school juniors would spend hours decorating and planning a formal banquet honoring the senior class. Young people would prepare for months in advance for this day as they made or shopped for clothes, hairstyles, and accessories. Most of these events would have elaborate themes revolving around popular trends of the day and/or music. This tradition was a form of the modern prom night. (Mathias family.)

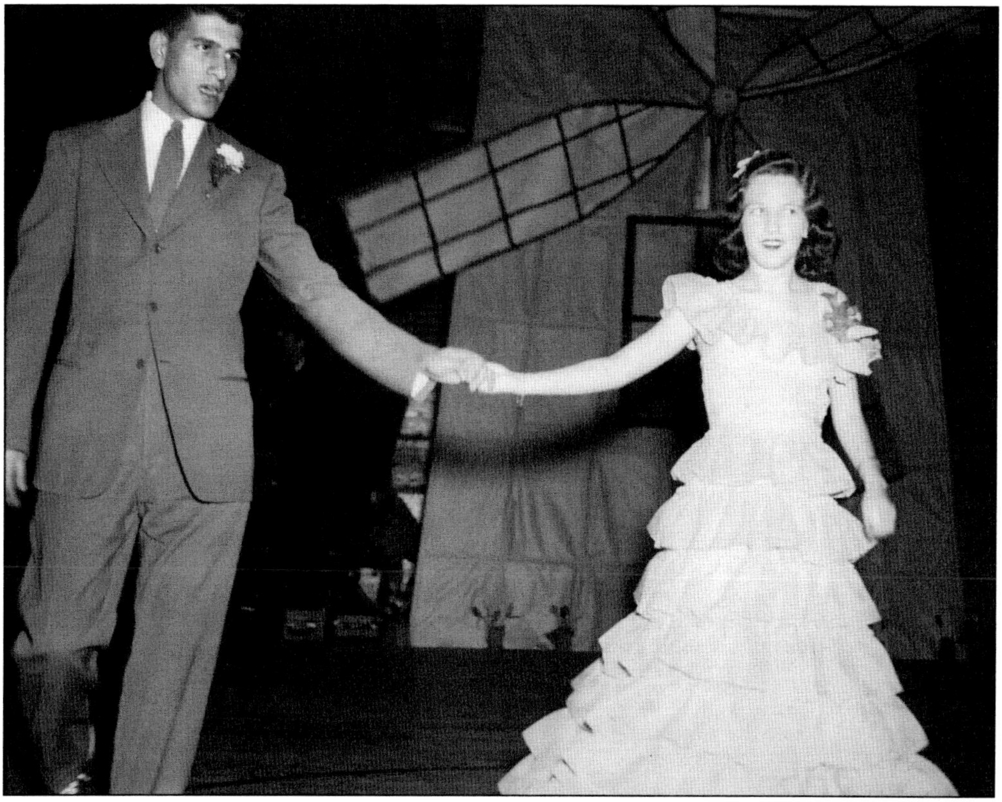

Arthur Mack and Nancy Web are dancing the night away at the Lexington High School Junior-Senior Banquet. Many times, students would come to the dance as couples and take photographs as mementos of this occasion. Young ladies and gentlemen cherished the opportunity to socialize and share this evening with friends. (Mathias family.)

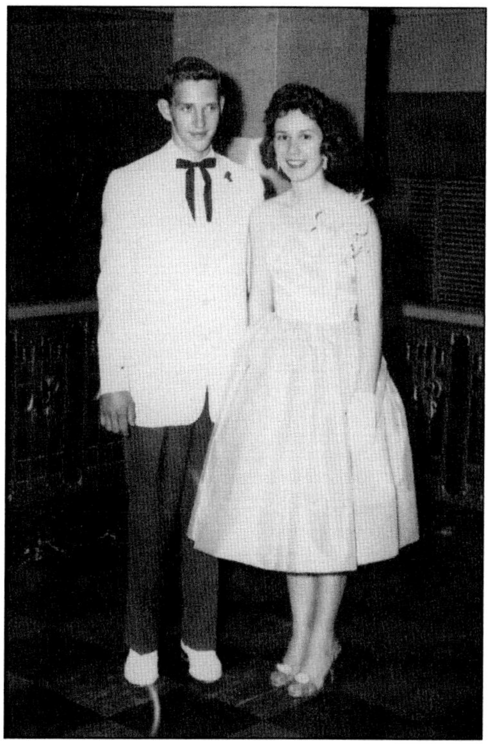

Jean Nichols remembers the excitement leading up to the Junior-Senior Banquet. The juniors would spend time thinking of ways to create a wonderful night to be remembered by the seniors in hopes that the next class would do just the same for them. Jean and her date had their banquet at Jefferson's Hotel instead of at the school gym. Everyone thought that was very elegant. (Jean Nichols Haggard.)

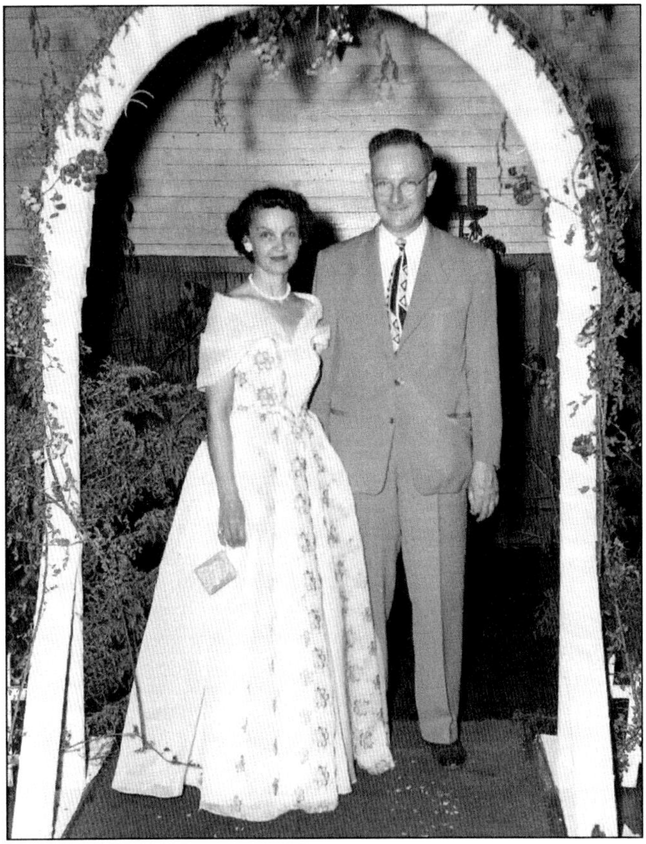

Lois and D. F. Shumpert attended the Junior-Senor Banquet. The gym at Pelion High School was decorated for a country garden theme. Each year, Lois looked forward to dressing formally for this date. Her daughter, Laura Shumpert McMahan, remembers shopping at Haltiwanger's ladies clothing store in downtown Columbia for their gowns. Street photographers would snap people's photographs and mail them to their homes. Pictured here from left to right are Laura, Betty Stover, and Lois. (Both, Laura Shumpert McMahan.)

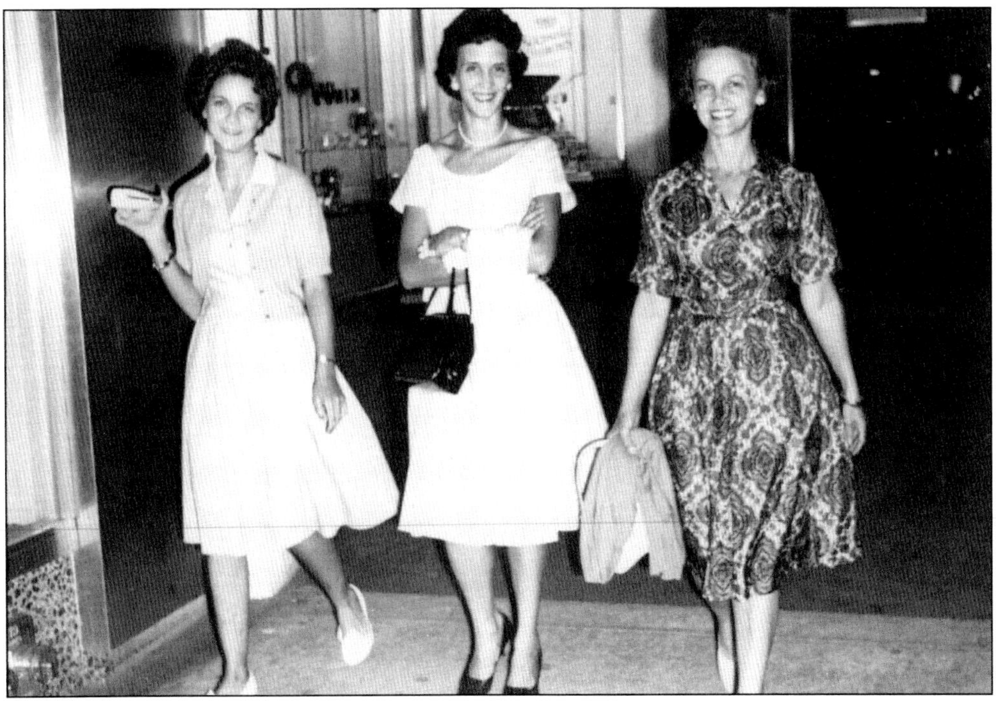

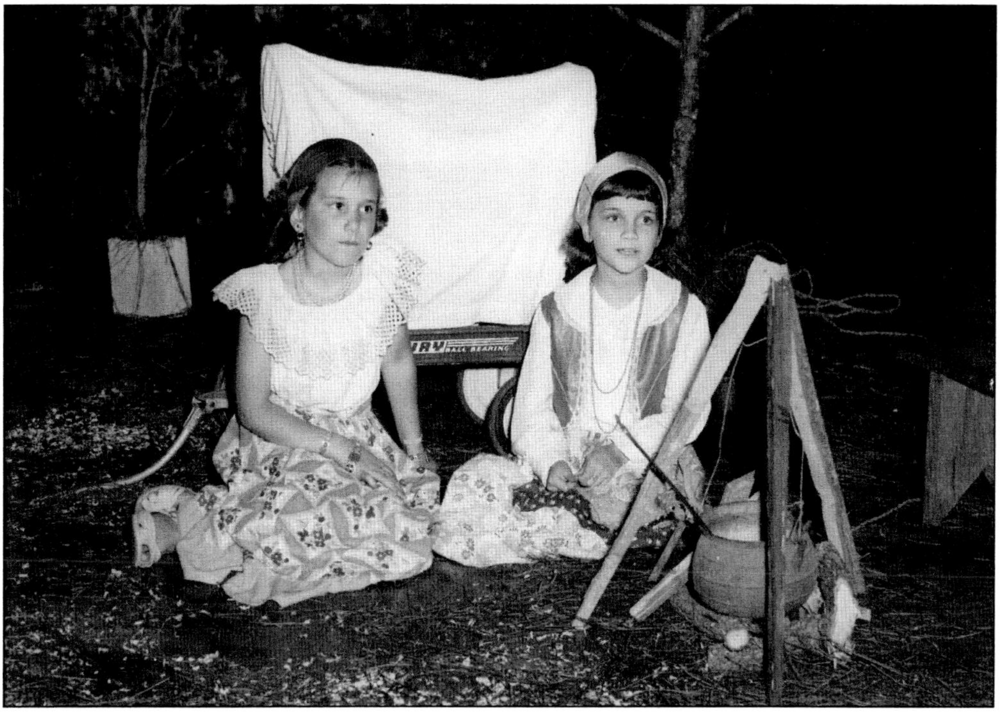

Sometimes younger students were able to help with serving and decorating for this big event. Jean Nichols Haggard (left) and Laura Shumpert McMahan are dressed as gypsies to play a part in the theme of this Junior-Senior Banquet. (Laura Shumpert McMahan.)

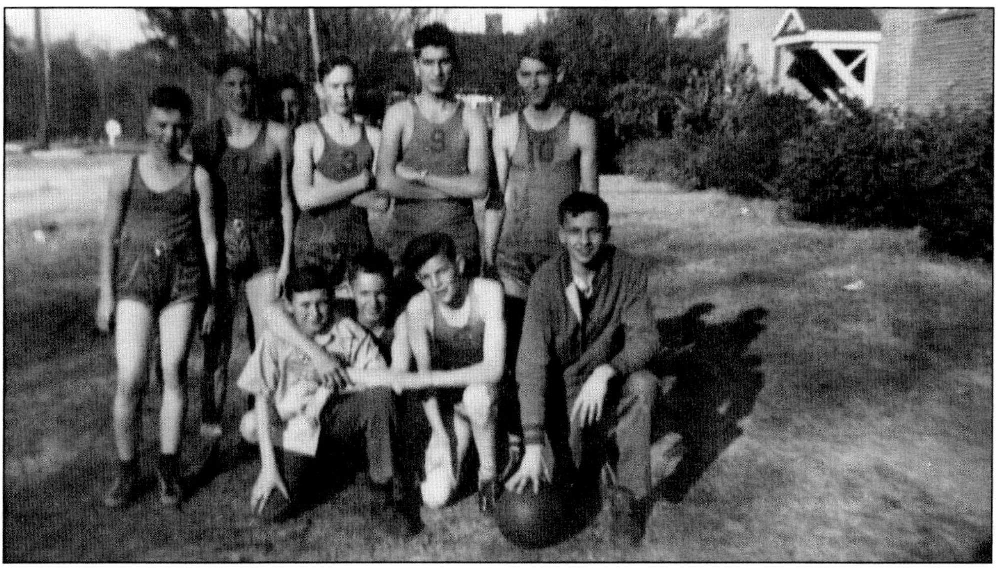

The Lexington High School football field was located directly behind Hite's Restaurant. Many people remember going out to football games and practices and stopping by the Dairy Bar for some refreshments. Football is the most supported sport in Lexington County. Everyone seems to be a part of the age-old rivalry of Clemson versus Carolina. The fan base for these two teams expands beyond alumni boundaries. People from all walks of life get together on game days to cheer on their favorite teams. (Mathias family.)

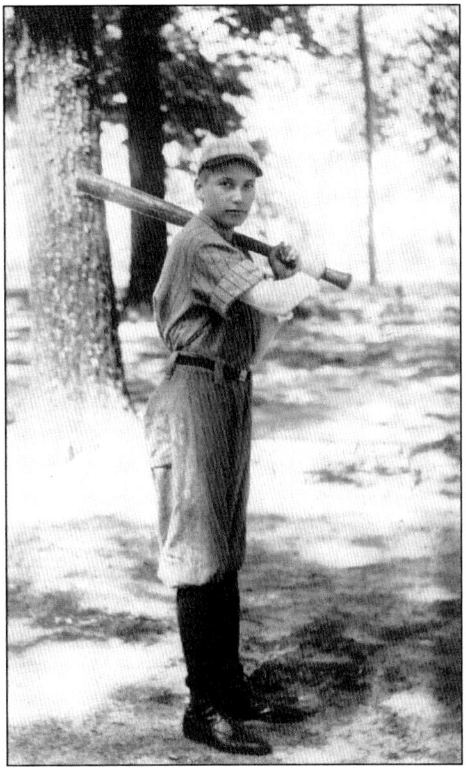

Baseball was one way in which people in the communities had a chance to visit and share news. The idea of sports recreation did not become a part of the working-class family until the 1930s, when inventions made work around the house and farm much faster. Then families had more free time to spare. Also, artificial lighting made ballgames possible after working hours, which helped all people in the community participate. Community centers were built by the local governments and through donations from individuals. Sports were run from these community centers, as the schools were too spread out and too small to have large enough teams. In a unique way, this built a united community without school boundaries. (Both, Annie Laurie George.)

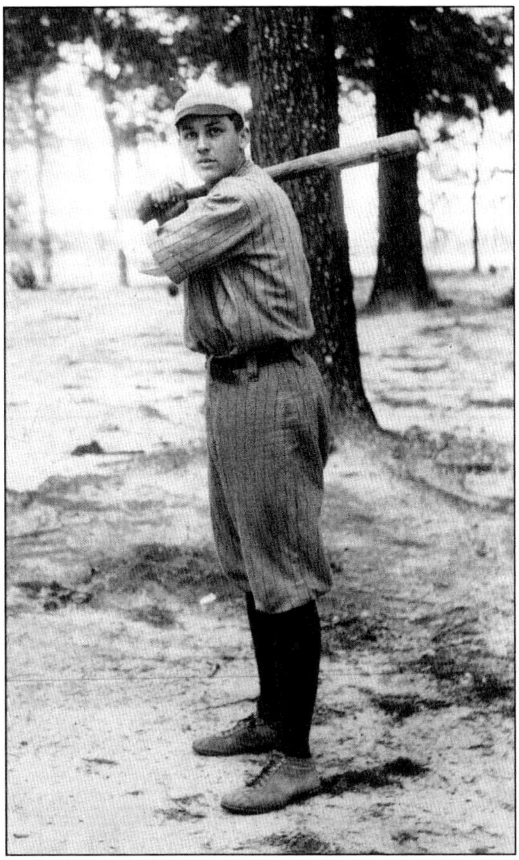

Rep. Floyd Spence (left), pictured here with his brother Allen, was an alumnus of Lexington High School whose impressive career included the military, law school at the University of South Carolina, and, in 1952, the South Carolina House of Representatives. Representative Spence then served in the U.S. House of Representatives from January 1970 until August 2001. Friends who knew him say that the late congressman was known for many things, among them being an athlete. He was recruited by Clemson and USC. After Spence was elected to Congress, the late Frank Howard, a former Clemson coach, told him if he had come to Clemson instead of USC, he would have become president instead of a congressman. (Mathias family.)

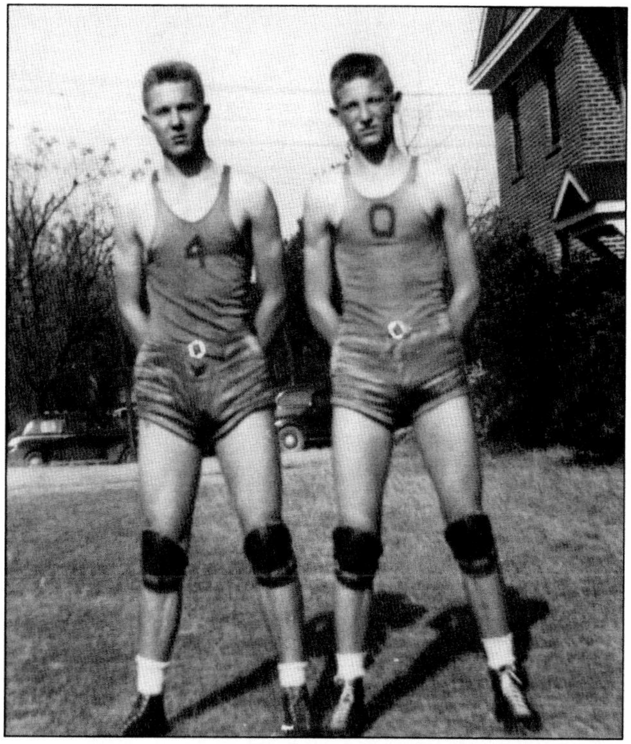

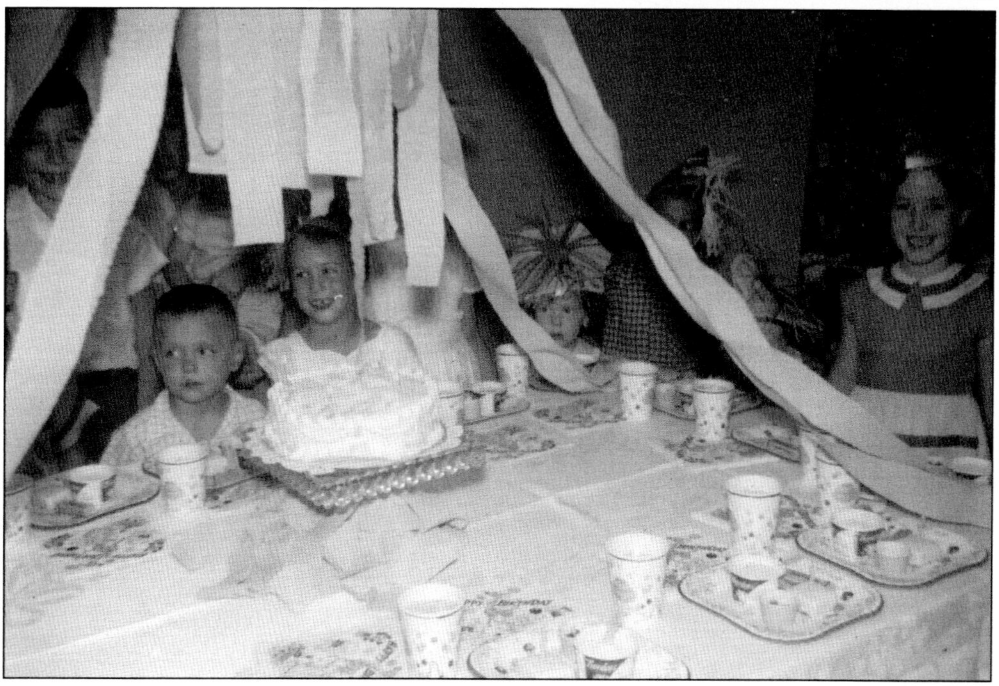

Other traditions in Lexington County were local events such as picnics, banquets, fishing tournaments, and golf tournaments. A birthday party such as the one here at Ron Redd's home was a great time for everyone. Getting dressed up and having a fun time with friends was all that was needed for entertainment. (Ron Redd.)

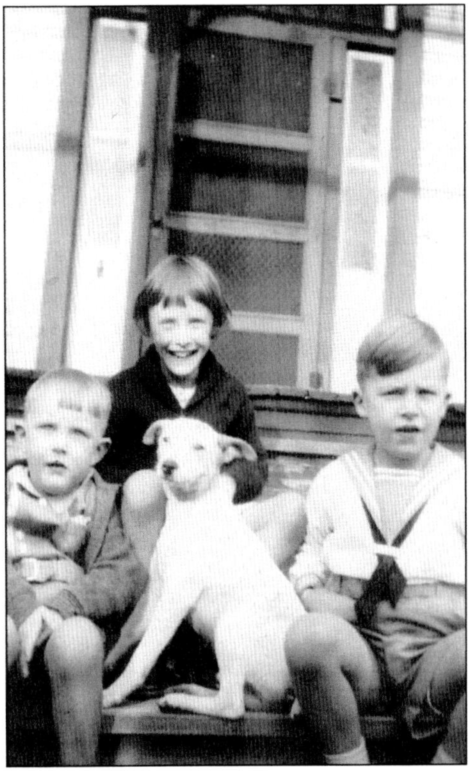

Local organizations would hold fund-raising events, but the biggest calendars were those for sports and church events. Communities would coordinate all activities so families would be able to attend all events. Due to many fires and growing communities, fund-raisers were often held to retire building debts. The joy of retiring a building debt is often recorded in histories of organizations in Lexington County. (Mathias family.)

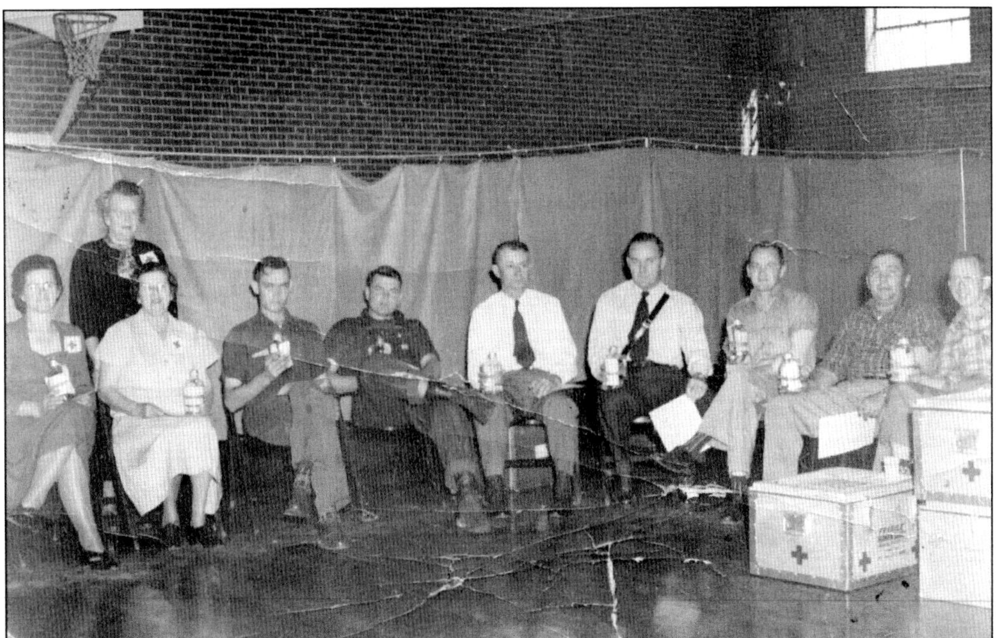

Another common event was a Red Cross blood drive. Here is a blood drive at the Lexington Community Center. Pictured are, from left to right, Ethel Wingard, Katherine Taylor, Pearl Mitchell, Clark Harmon, Boyd Wingard, Odelle Harman, patrolman C. C. Parrish, Ralph Steele, R. H. Caughman, and Roundtree Sessions. (Harman family.)

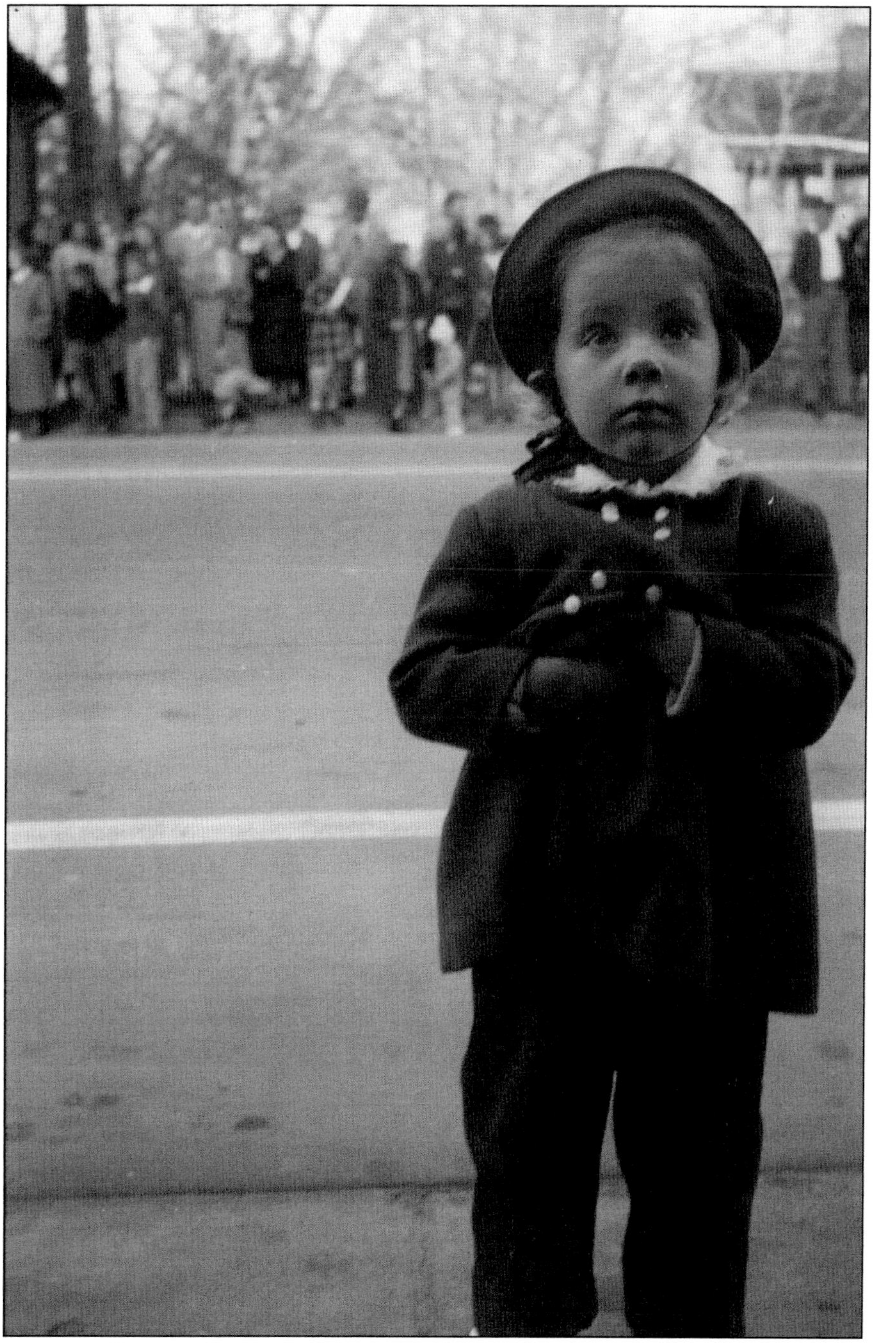

The Lexington County Christmas Parade has been a family tradition for many years. Drew Glover Welch is pictured here participating in the parade. People would come to watch their friends on business floats and fire trucks; politicians would ride along and visit with people; last was always Santa. Drew remembers families visiting and celebrating during the parade. The tradition continues today with organizations such as the Boy Scouts, Girl Scouts, school bands, local businesses, and politicians participating. Children still wait to see Santa at the end of the parade. (Drew Glover Welch.)

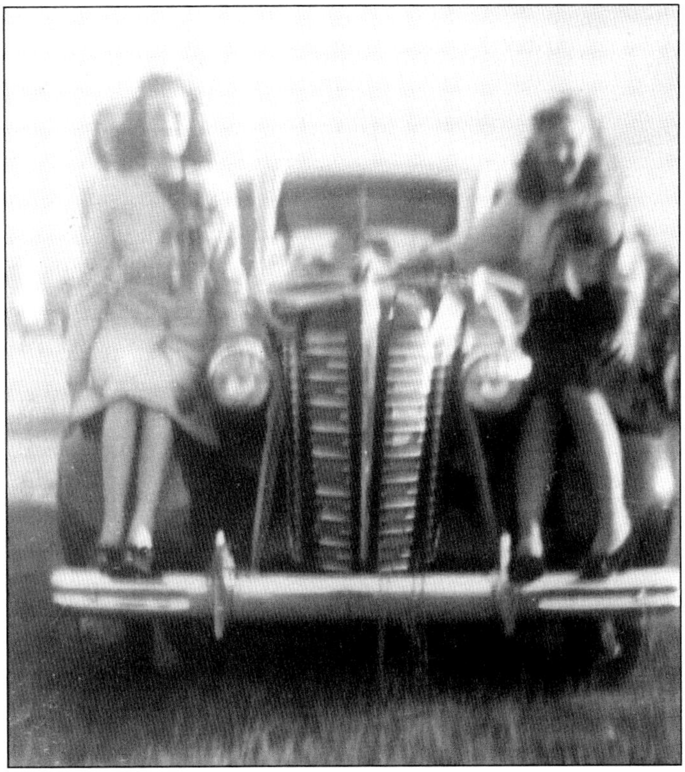

The South Carolina State Fair has been held since 1839 in Columbia. The agricultural nature of Lexington County and its proximity to Columbia made a match for many generations of participants in the fruit, vegetable, nut, and flower categories, as well as all of the baking categories. Lexington County participants have won many blue ribbons for their efforts. In 1861, the fair buildings were occupied by Confederate authorities and used in the manufacture of war munitions. In 1865, Sherman's army burned the buildings. The buildings were rebuilt, and the fair resumed in 1869. (Left, Mathias family; below, Kathryn Liverman.)

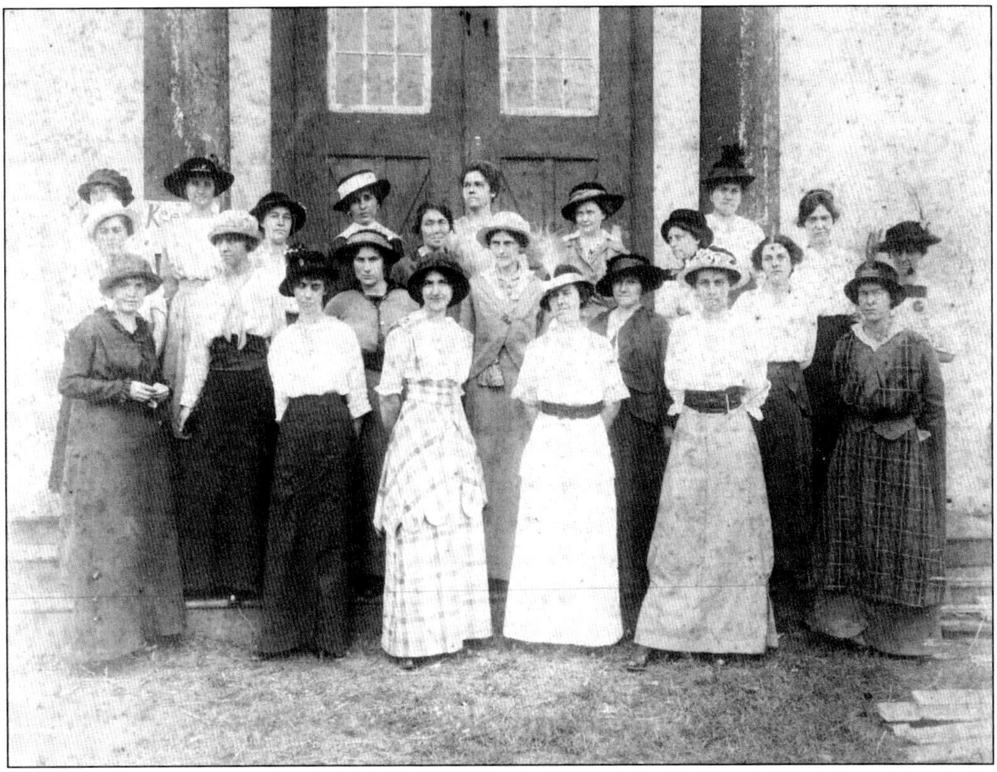

Six

Military Involvement

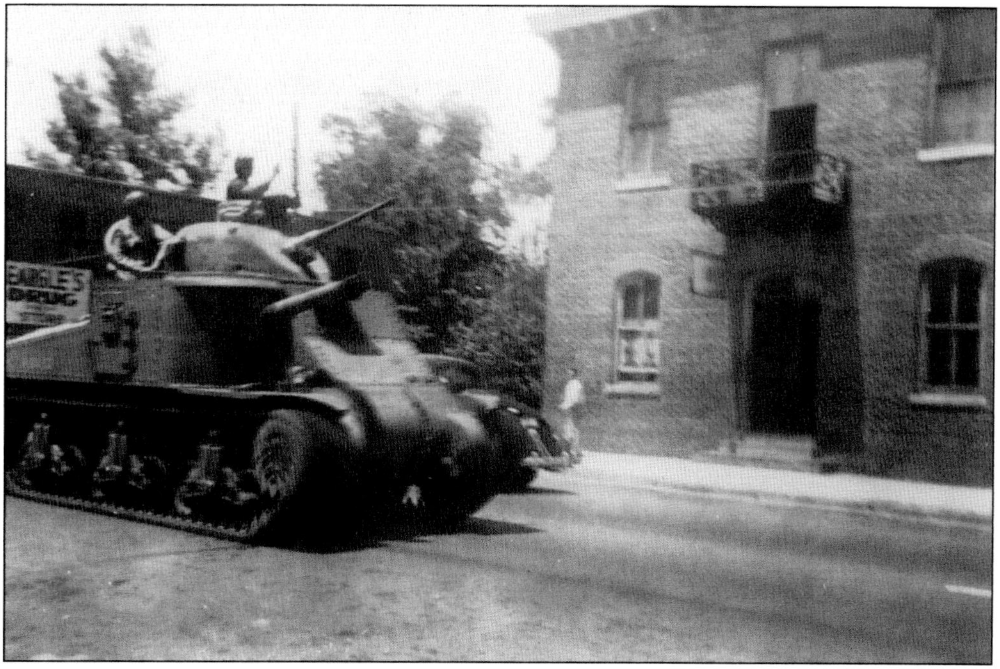

It is hard to believe that this tank was coming down Main Street in Lexington during the 1940s. Lexington County residents have a history of being heavily involved in military forces since they were first called upon in the late 1700s. The rugged land, American Indians, Regulator battles, and having to take care of one's own made these immigrants difficult to defeat. (Mathias family.)

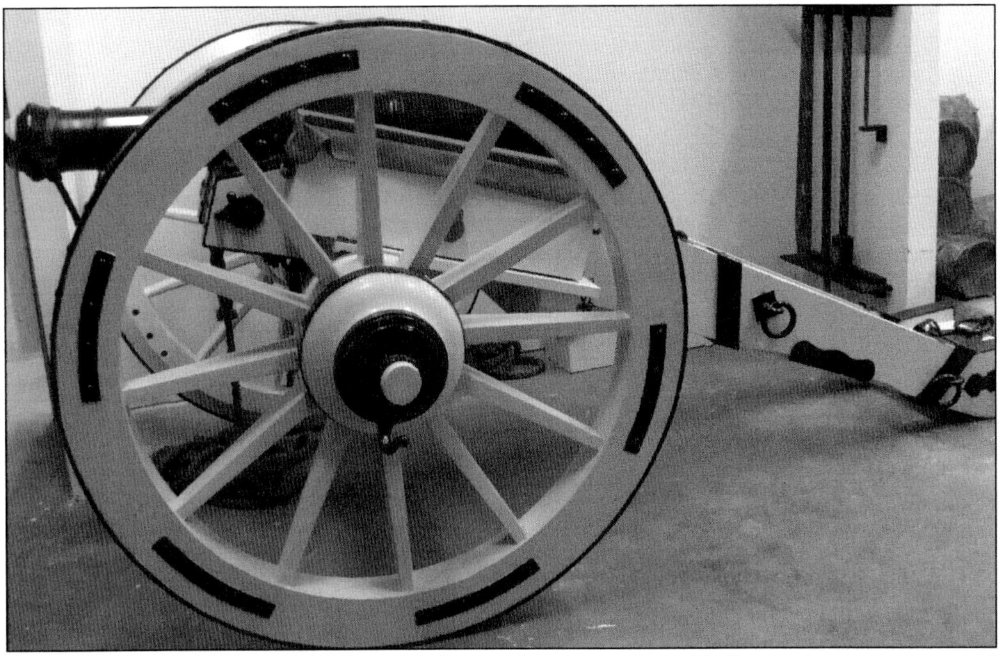

South Carolina was where the Patriots truly met the Tories. Over 130 battle sites have historical markers to preserve the details. Twice there were skirmishes at Fort Granby in what is now Cayce. The Battle of Tarrar Springs was fought just east of Lexington on November 16, 1781. Possibly the most famous battle in Lexington was Eggleton's Capture. John Armstrong was the mastermind behind this daring ambush. A small group of Legion Dragoons was dispatched to scout ahead and look for enemies. Armstrong spied on General Rawdon and set a trap for his company. They captured 2 officers and 45 privates. In 1785, Lexington County was established, changing the name from Saxe Gotha to Lexington in honor of the Massachusetts Revolutionary War battle. (South Carolina Military Museum.)

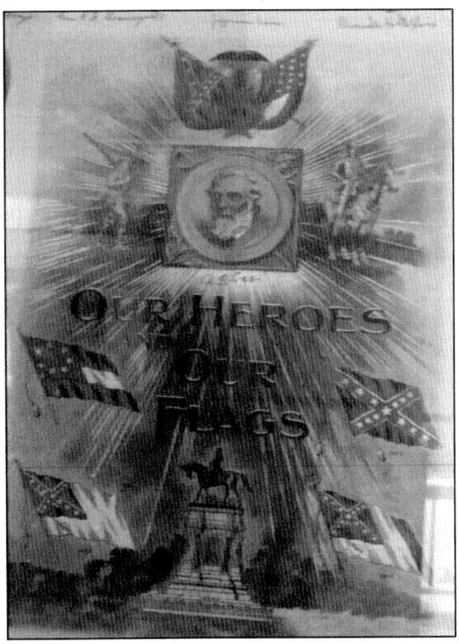

After the families of Lexington County had put behind the arguments of Whigs and Tories, a new argument arose. The farming area was ripe to house many slaves. According to *Uncle Josh* by Godfrey M. Harman, in 1850 there were 7,352 whites, 21 free African Americans, and 5,557 slaves in Lexington County. In other publications, a majority of the people in Lexington County were said to be anti-slavery, as they came from serfdom in Germany and valued freedom. The reality of being able to farm large tracts of land made some slave labor hard to ignore. (Paeth family.)

The 5th South Carolina Cavalry, also known as the South Carolina Mounted Cavalry, made several attempts to halt Sherman's march on Columbia. Many accounts in journals have shared the inhumanity and the wastefulness of this campaign. A Pelion resident recounted hiding as a child in the woods among chickens, cows, and horses while Union officers came through the family property. These officers would purposefully ruin whatever they could not eat by throwing it in the dirt or crushing it. Sherman's march ravaged the Lexington area, especially downtown. Pictured here is Joseph Slice, father of Andrew Slice, serving in the Confederate army. (Bennett Roof.)

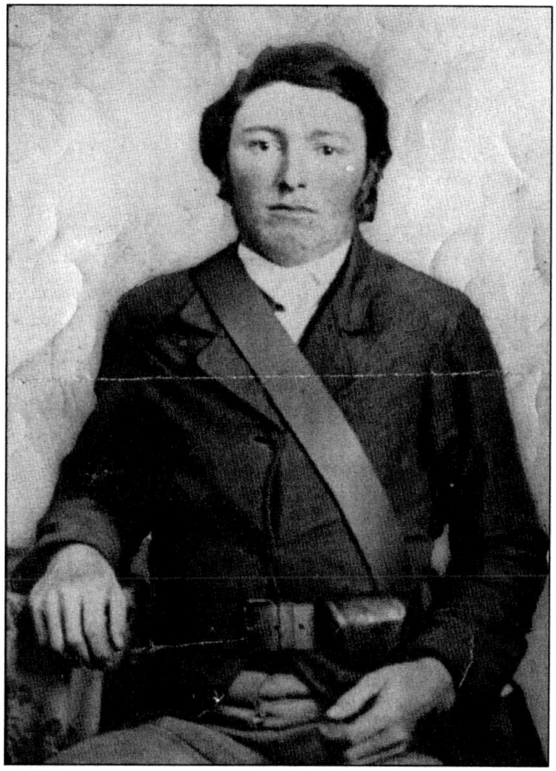

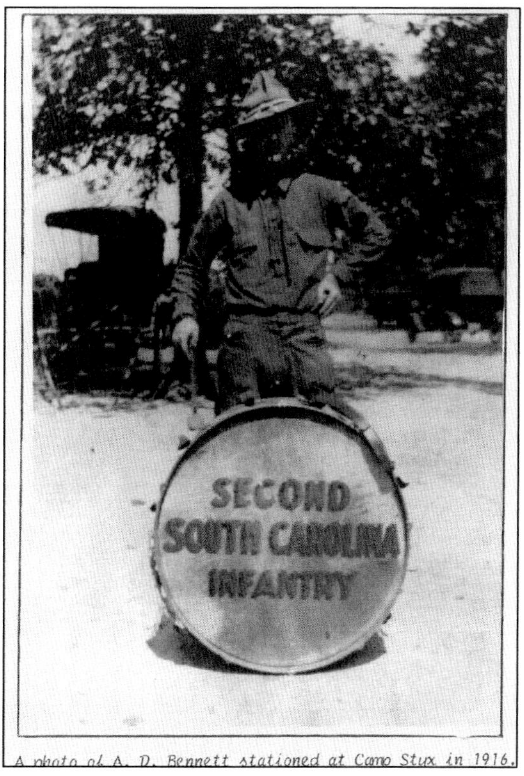

A. D. Bennett is pictured in 1916 at a military training camp located in what is now the town of Pine Ridge. This site was first used during the Civil War as a training camp. The 2nd Infantry Regiment, South Carolina National Guard, was stationed at Camp Styx for eight weeks in the midsummer of 1916. Troops trained in the heat, bugs, and swamps to prepare for battle overseas. At the same time, other camps in the area were being created, such as Camp Jackson, now Fort Jackson. (Town of South Congaree.)

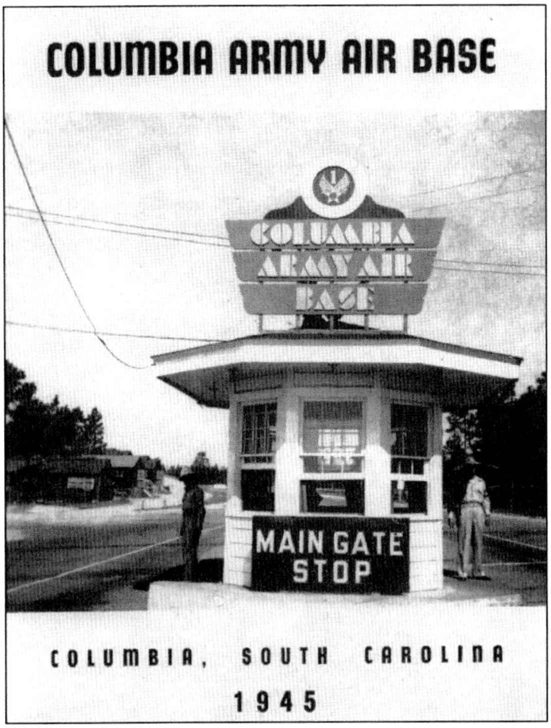

In the early 1940s, early aviation pioneers established a landing area in Lexington County known as the Lexington County Airport. The site was selected because of elevation, the nature of the terrain, and the good soil in the area upon which to construct facilities such as taxiways, aprons, and runways. Around 1941, the U.S. War Department acquired the airport from Lexington County and expanded it dramatically to serve the effort for World War II. (Cayce Historical Museum.)

Pictured here is the building of the water tank at what was then called Columbia Army Air Base. There are many accounts from the people of Lexington about how the air base impacted their lives. To some, it was the introduction of a spouse, to others, the beginning of their service in the army. (South Carolina State Museum.)

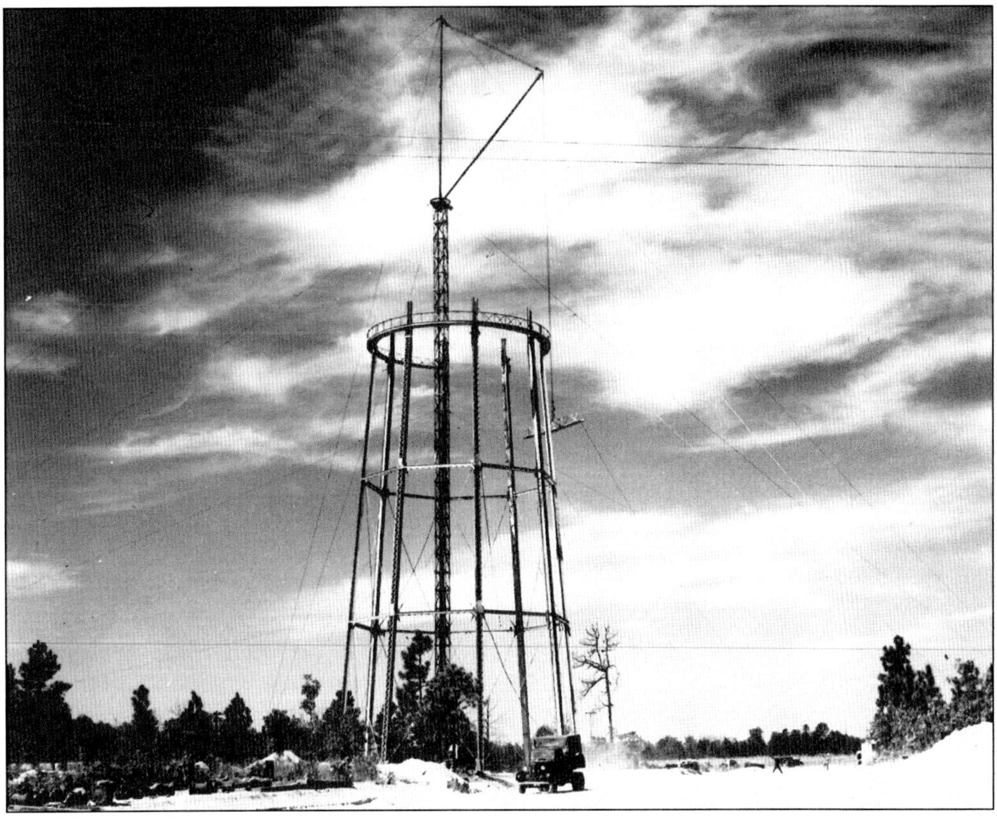

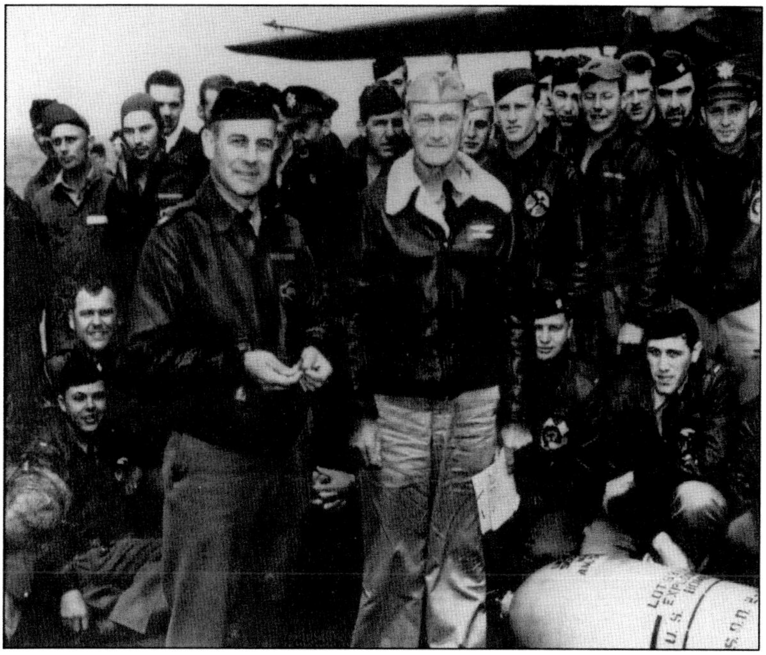

In 1942, Jimmy Doolittle, a military legend, traveled to Columbia and called volunteers for a secret mission. Approximately 25 of these B-25 flight crews practiced bombing islands in Lake Murray. They later flew the famous Doolittle Raid over Tokyo. The Doolittle Raid was the first good news from the Pacific theater of operations. (Cayce Historical Museum.)

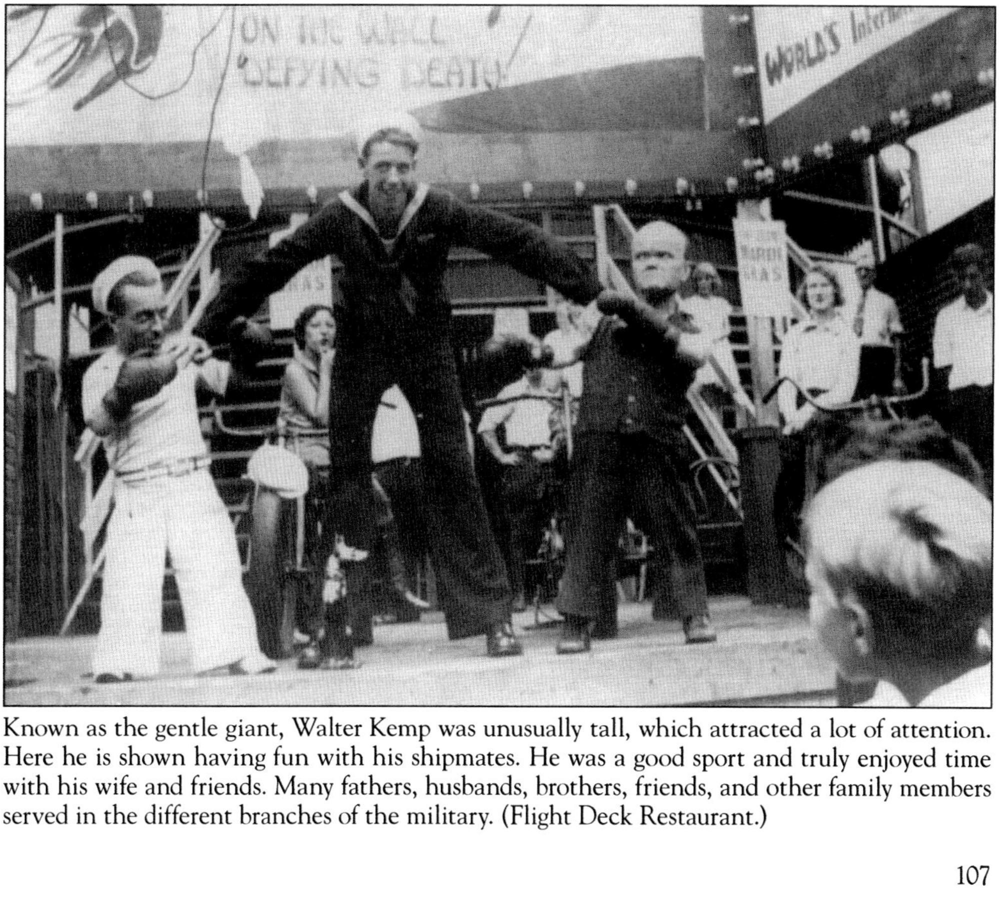

Known as the gentle giant, Walter Kemp was unusually tall, which attracted a lot of attention. Here he is shown having fun with his shipmates. He was a good sport and truly enjoyed time with his wife and friends. Many fathers, husbands, brothers, friends, and other family members served in the different branches of the military. (Flight Deck Restaurant.)

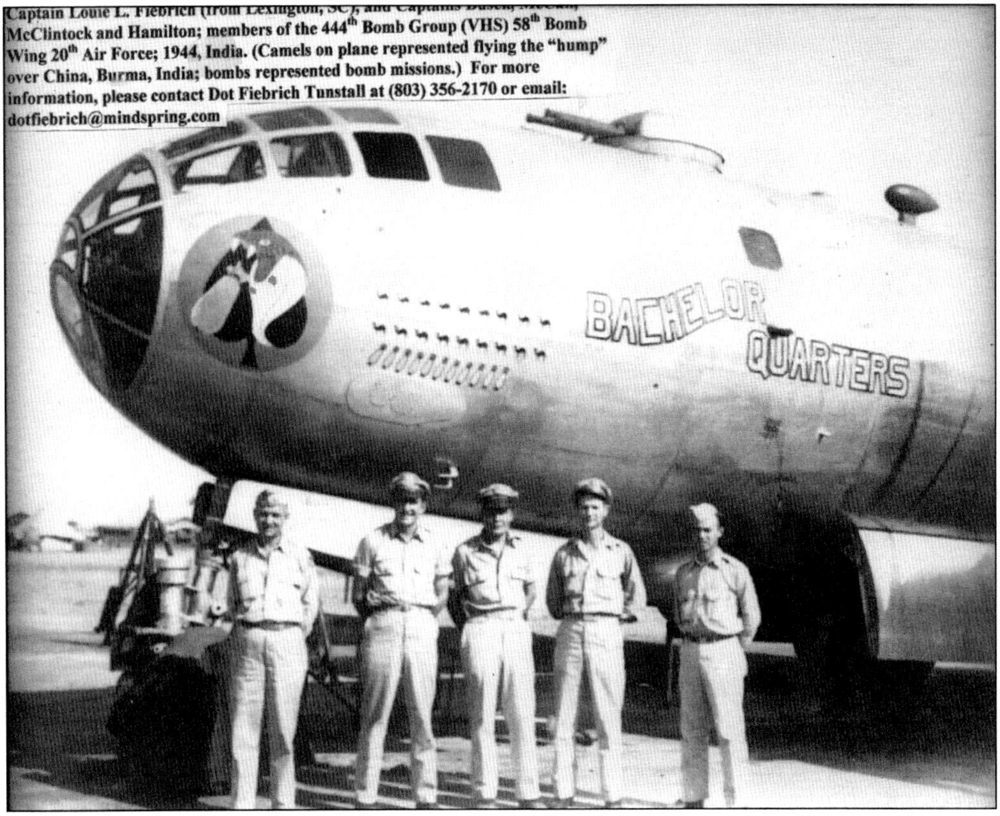

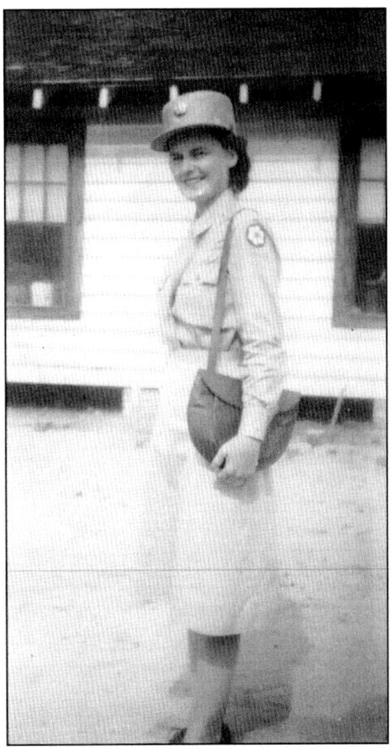

Members of the 444th Bomb Group (VHS), 58th Bomb Wing, 20th Air Force in 1944 stand in front of a B-29. They are, from left to right, Capt. Louie L. Fiebrich (from Lexington) and Capts. Busek, McCall, McClintock, and Hamilton. This mission served as a test run for the planes. The nine camels on the plane represent flying the "hump" over China, Burma, and India; bombs represent bombing missions. Fiebrich served in both world wars; he was awarded nine medals for exemplary service. (Dorothy Tunstall.)

Gussie Kennerly from Swansea served as a first lieutenant in the Women's Army Corps (WAC). The Kennerly family was very proud of their daughter, who helped protect democracy and freedom. (Annie Laurie George.)

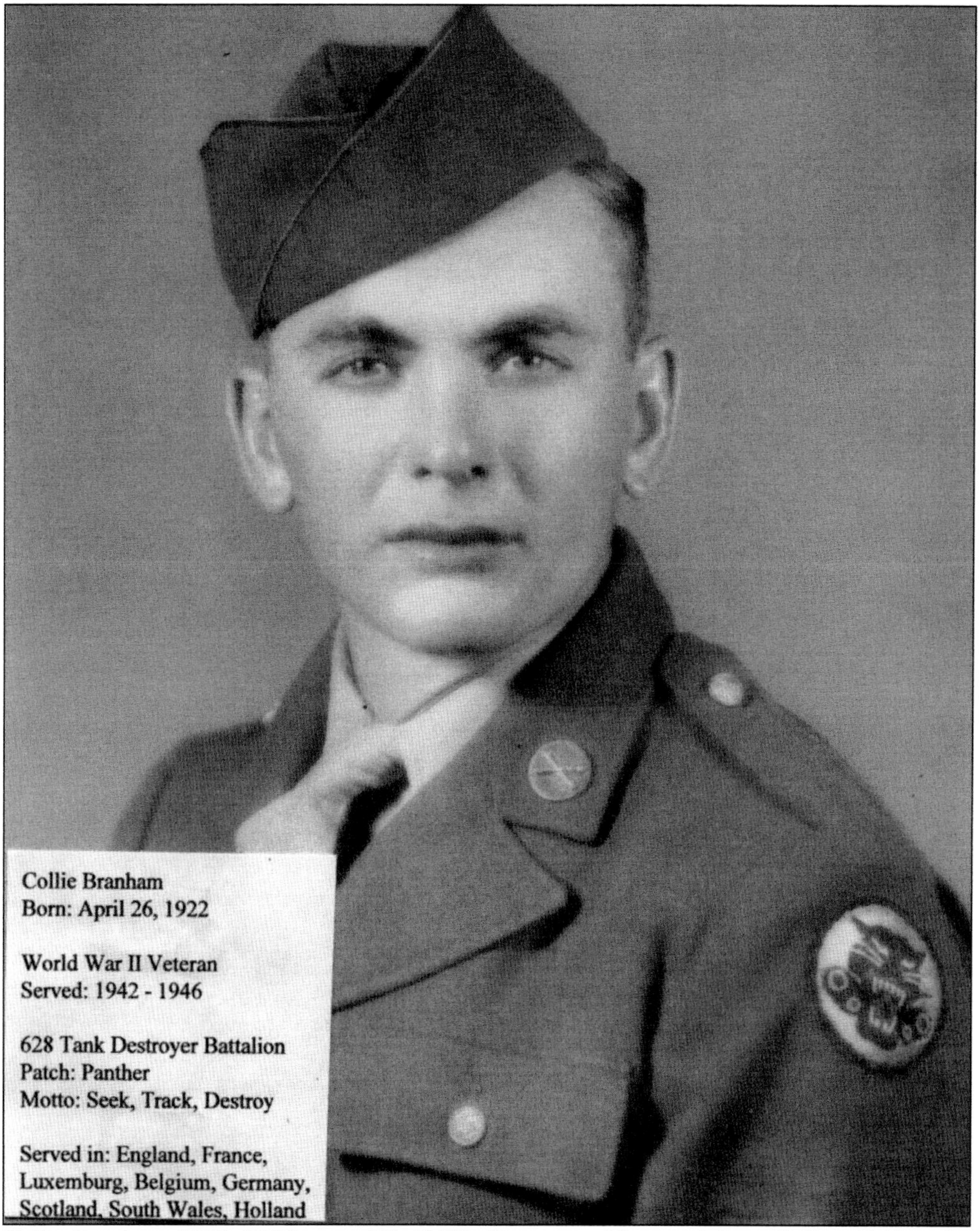

Collie Branham (1922–2007) was a World War II veteran. He served from 1942 to 1946 in the 628th Tank Destroyer Battalion in England, France, Luxembourg, Belgium, Germany, Scotland, South Wales, and Holland. Their patch was a panther, and their motto was "Seek, Track, and Destroy." Branham came from a family of 12 and left home to enlist in the military. He received five medals: Army Good Conduct; Medal Set American Campaign; Medal Set, European, African, Middle East Campaign; Medal Set Honor Service Lapel Button; and Victory World War II, Medal Set. He sent money to his mother out of his army pay to help feed his younger siblings. After returning from the war, Branham worked and provided for a wife and eight children. He had 13 grandchildren and 11 great-grandchildren. His personal motto was, "If you want something, work for it!" (Branham family.)

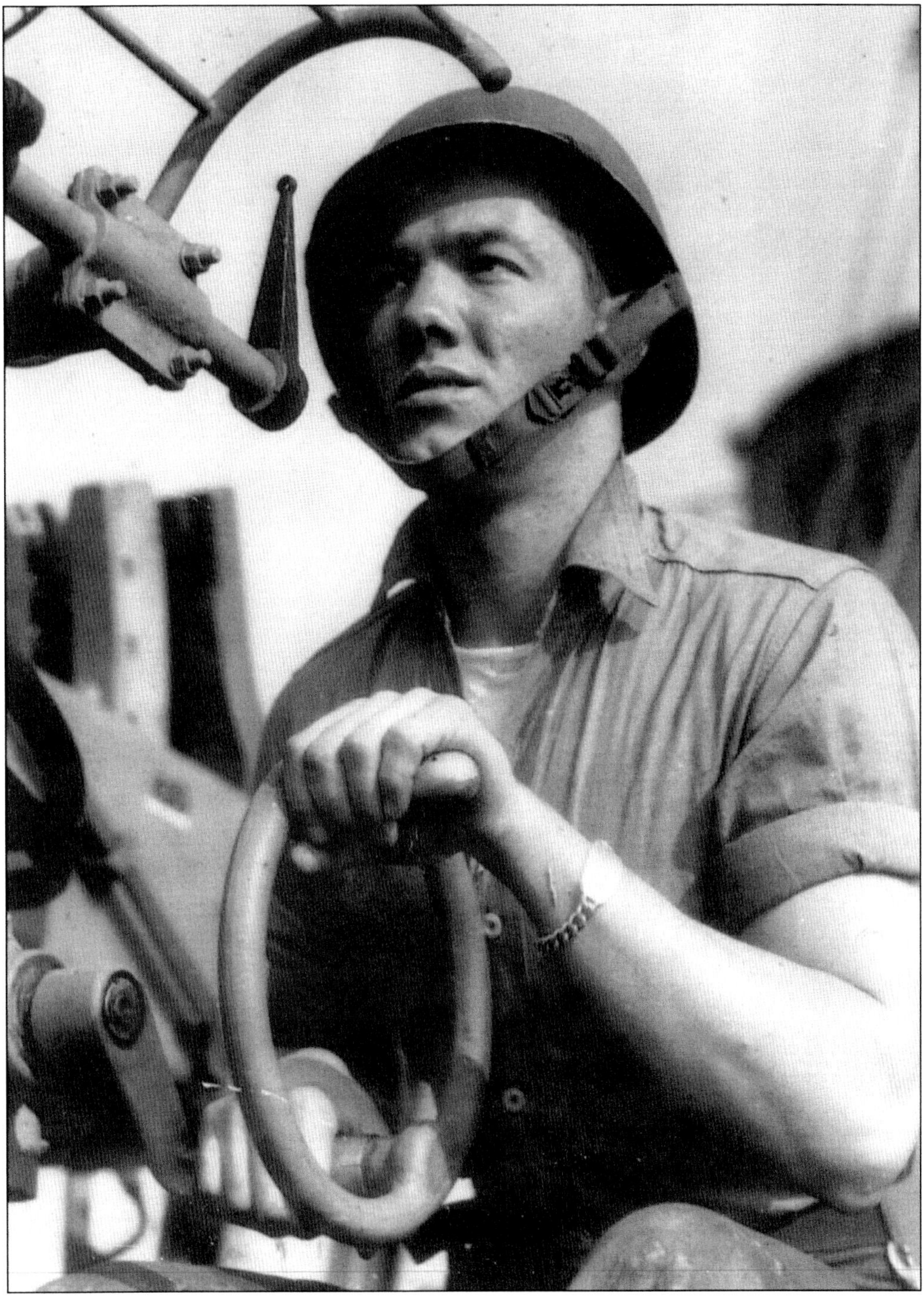

H. B. Liverman served four years as a seaman first class in the U.S. Navy in the European theater of operations during World War II and 20 years in the U.S. Army serving in Korea and Vietnam. He was a recipient of the Silver Star Medal. (Flight Deck Restaurant.)

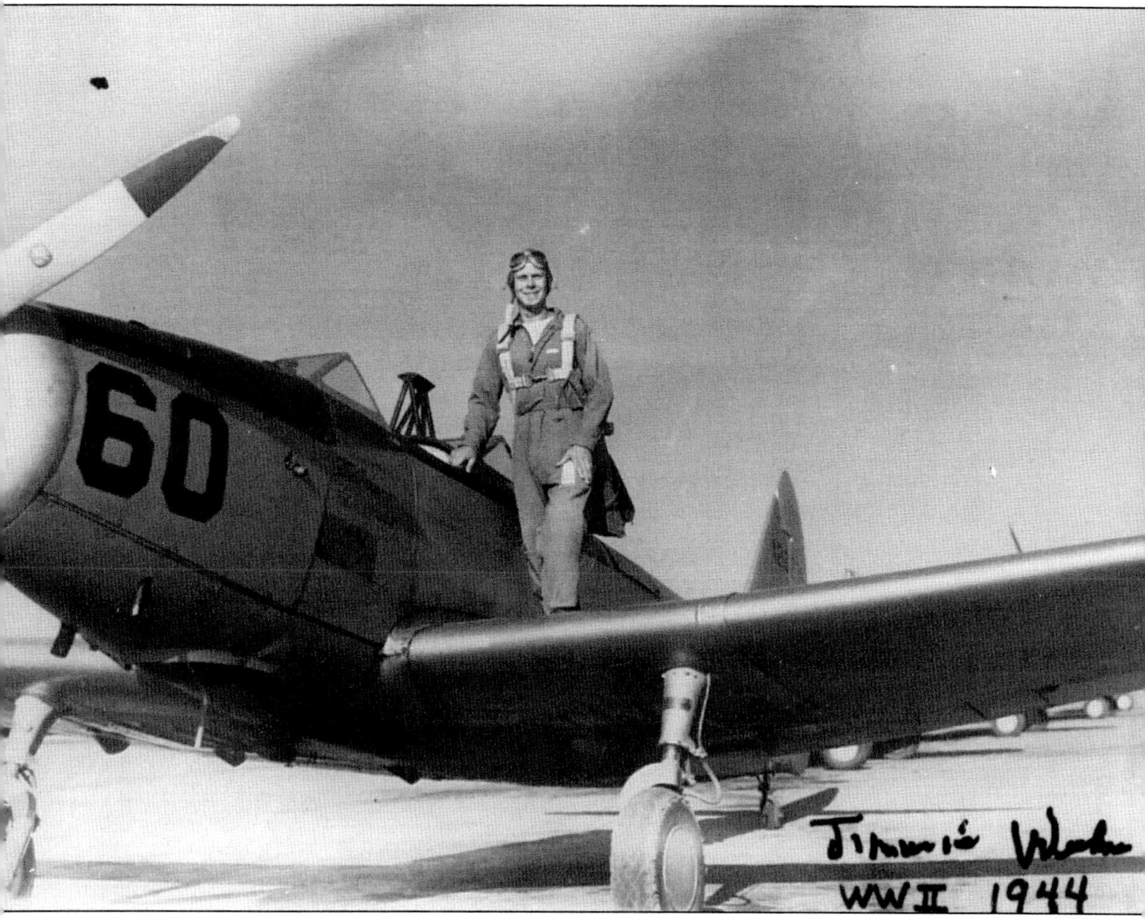

Another native Lexington son is Jimmy Weeks, a pioneer in aviation. Jimmy could fly anything, especially if it were experimental, and was instrumental in creating the Lexington County Airport. People remember him as having no fear. He was loved and respected in the Lexington community. (Flight Deck Restaurant.)

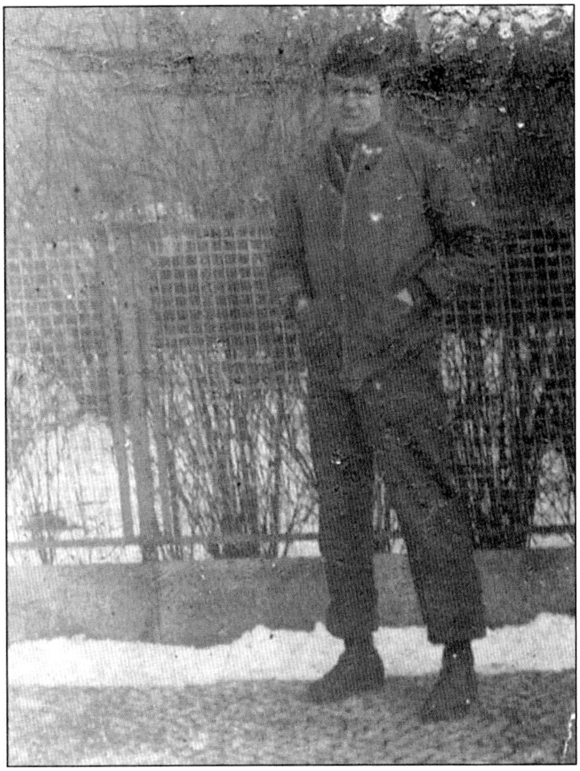

Redd Reynolds served in the 78th Division of the U.S. Army and also with the Armed Forces Radio Network during World War II in the European theater. Later he was in broadcasting and did news coverage with the South Carolina National Guard in Fort Stewart, Georgia. There was not much at Fort Stewart for the men in their free time, so he arranged for some shows. They were approved, and that was the beginning of entertainment shows for servicemen at the fort. The shows were always free for National Guard members. The performers were people that gave their time and God-given talents to the men and women who served. Many friendships were forged and will not be forgotten. (Both, Redd and Doris Reynolds.)

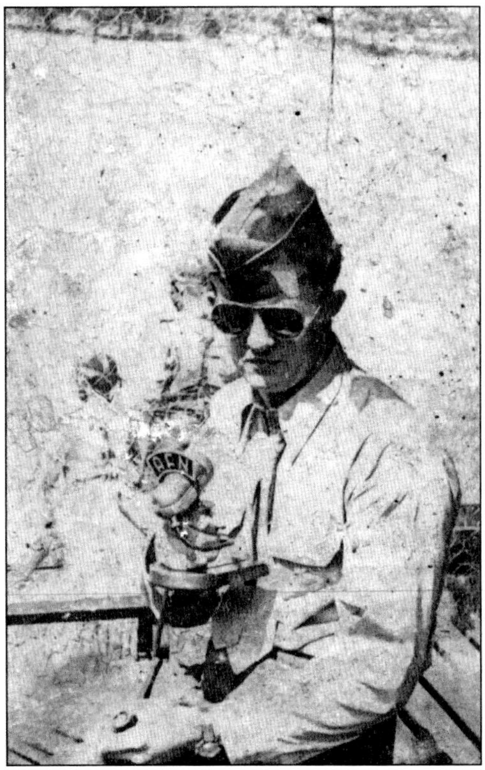

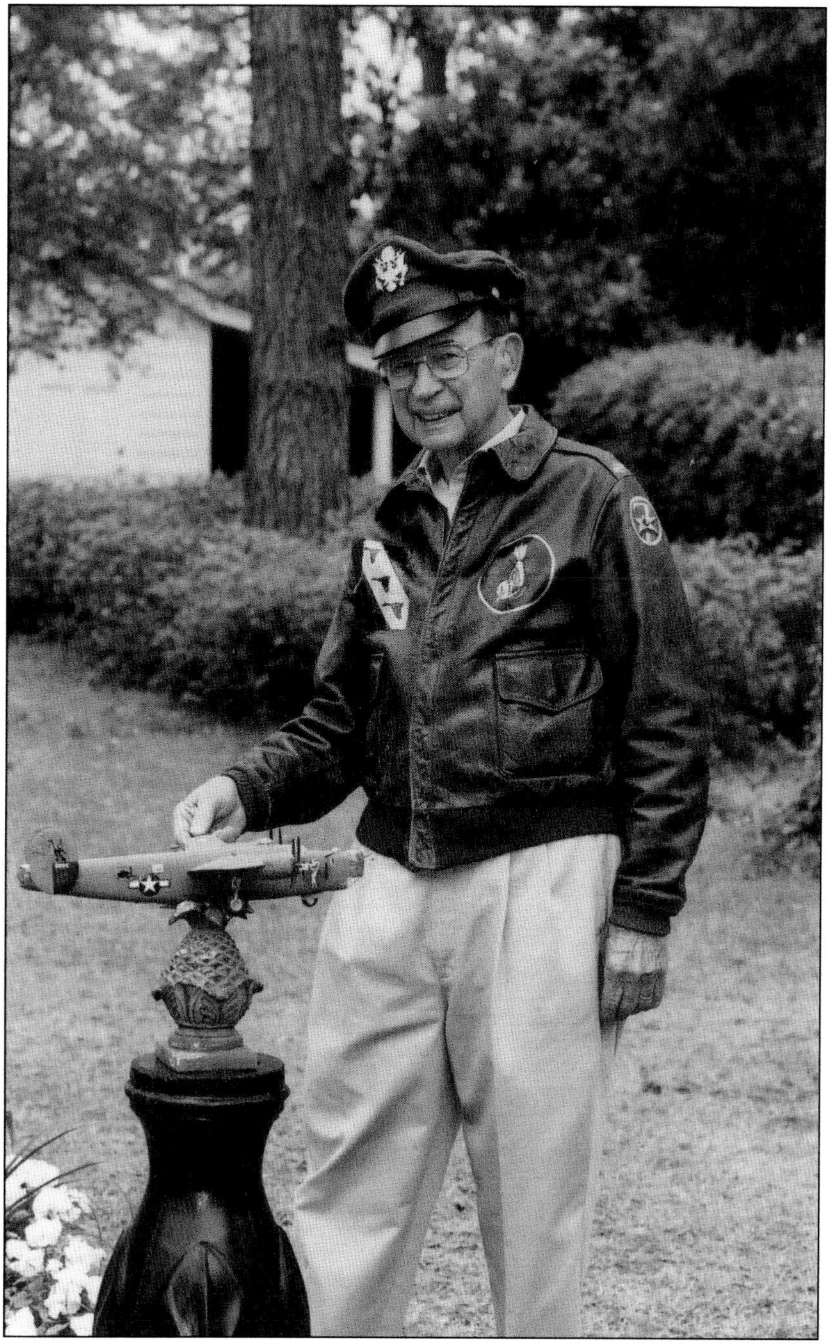

David "Murray" Price is a typical small-town boy from Lexington. He worked in a cotton mill as a high school student and enlisted in the air force when World War II struck. He piloted a B-24 four-engine airplane with a crew of 10. Murray went on over 40 successful bombing missions in the Pacific theater and was involved in Iwo Jima from the air. Murray and his crew bonded in their life-or-death missions, at least a few of which they were uncertain if they would return from or not. Murray fondly remembers his crewmates and, in later years, reunited with them to reminisce. (Murray Price.)

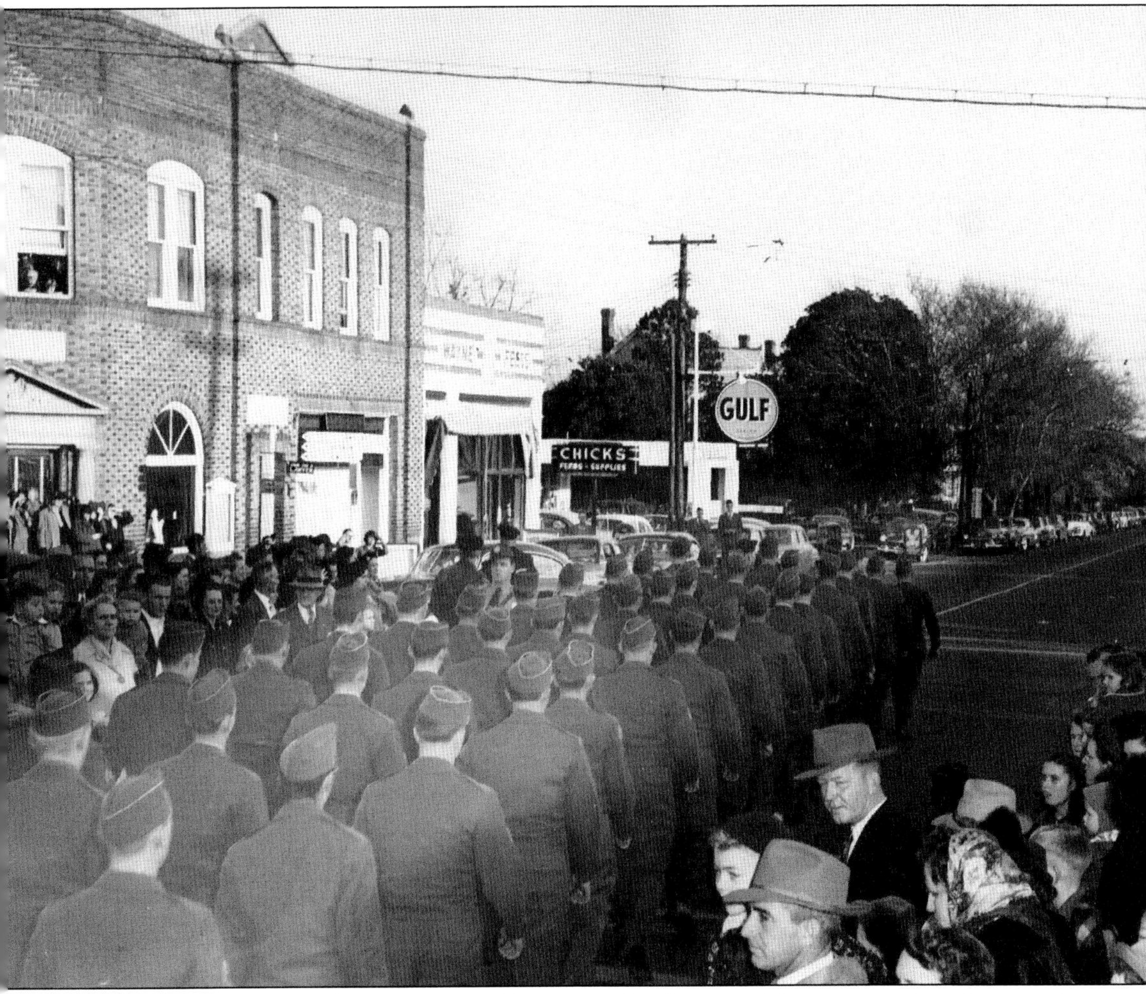

Just like these men and women pictured here returning from war, Murray remembers the receptions he received when he returned. People gathered in the streets to show support for all of the people who protected them and kept their freedom safe. Murray now enjoys his wife, four children, seven grandchildren, and two great-grandchildren and volunteering in the Lexington community. He has been very involved with the local YMCA, St. Stephen's Lutheran Church, and activities related to veterans. Murray is someone who is not afraid of hard work to get a job done. Being thrown into a melting pot at age 22 and leading men from all walks of life with only the common thread of country taught Murray the big picture. He will be the first to say that his happiness comes from knowing that he helped preserve freedom. (Ron Redd.)

Thomas Thain moved to Lexington in the late 1970s. He had an interest in aviation from a first flight experience in a "Tin Goose." During the war, he left Clemson University to join the U.S. Army Air Corps and became a skilled P-51 pilot. Conditions were so bad that most flight was done by instruments. He sadly witnessed friends die from weather and flight obstacles as much as enemy fire. Tommy worked hard to inspire people in Lexington to vote and have a political voice. He enjoyed his farm and cheering on the Clemson Tigers. He and his wife, Randy, had three children, five grandchildren and two great-grandchildren. (Thain family.)

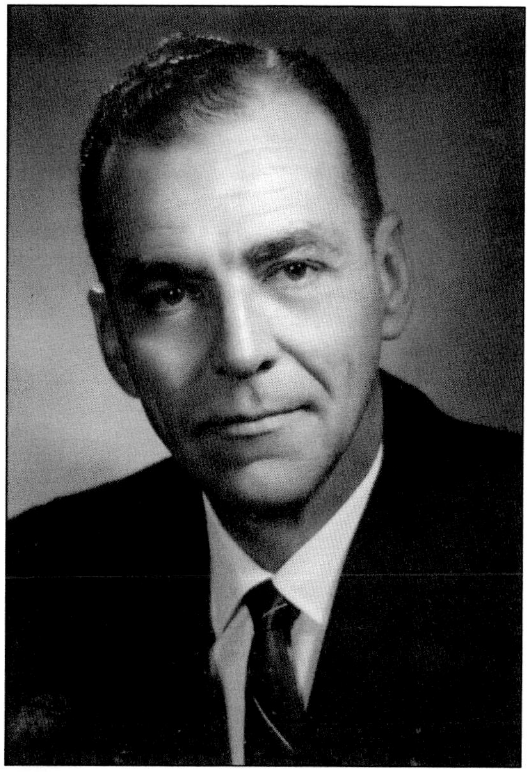

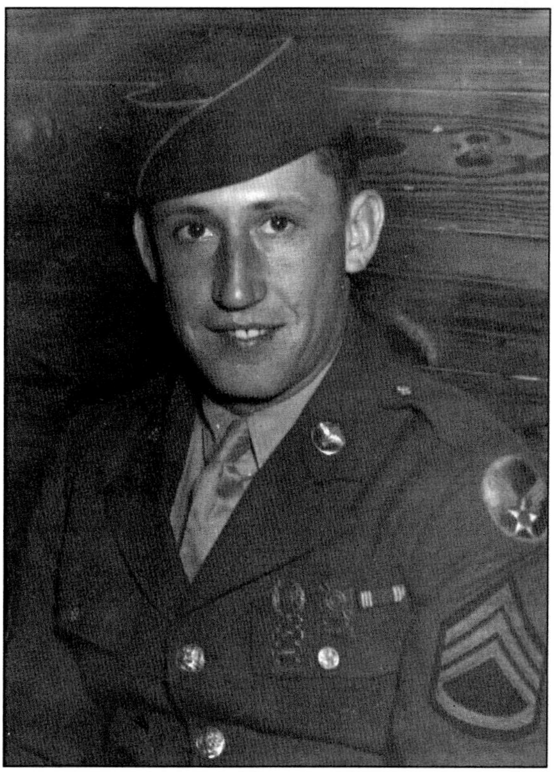

Harry Hite said he lied about his age and joined the U.S. Army when he was 17. He became part of the 8th Infantry Regiment in 1934 at Fort Screven, Georgia. He served four years and returned to Lexington in 1938. After Pearl Harbor was attacked, he enlisted in the Air Corps, serving in the 395th Fighter Squadron of the 9th Air Force. (Susan Wade.)

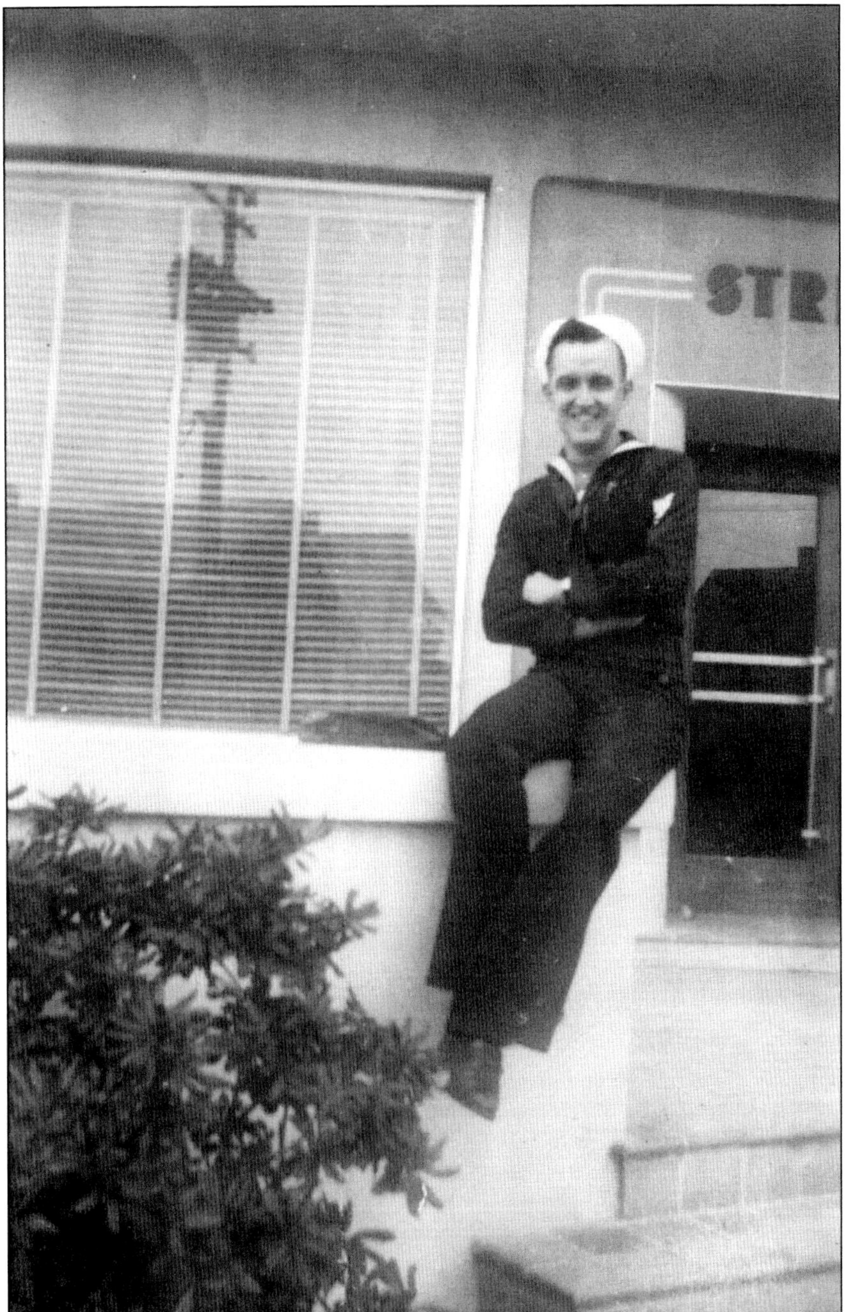

Wallace Redd enlisted in the U.S. Navy during World War II. He served on an aviation repair barge in the Pacific theater and was charged with issuing repair parts to the surrounding ships. During the war, somehow, Wallace's commanding officer (CO) found out that Wallace's brother's ship was in a port they were scheduled to visit. The CO made arrangements for Wallace to go ashore, meet his brother, and bring him aboard the ship for the night. They had not seen each other for almost two years. They spent about a day or so together and did not see each other again until after the war. (Ron Redd.)

Ron Redd joined the naval reserves on a delayed entry in 1970 prior to graduating from Newberry College. In 1971, he was assigned to the USS *Sampson*, a guided-missile destroyer. Ron left the military but reenlisted a few years later to make it his career. His parents, Doris and Wallace, were very supportive and even visited him on the USS *Eisenhower*. Redd retired from the military in 1995 as a first-class petty officer. Redd's son, daughter-in-law, and two grandchildren live in Prosperity. (Ron Redd.)

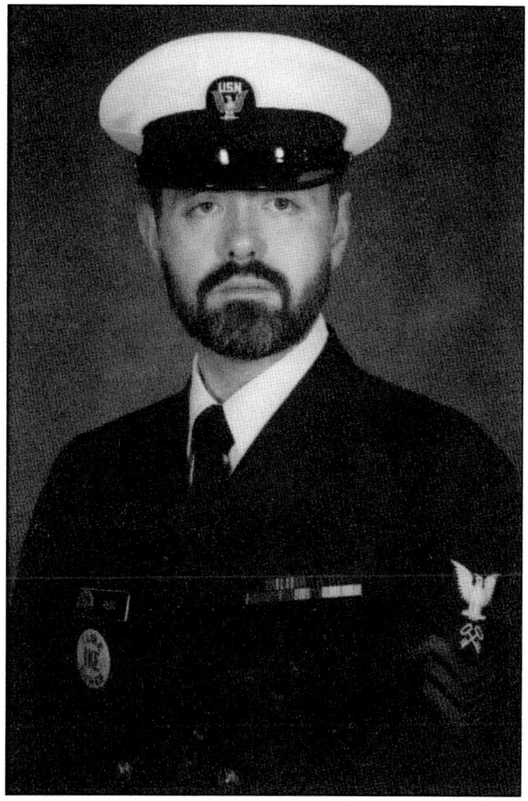

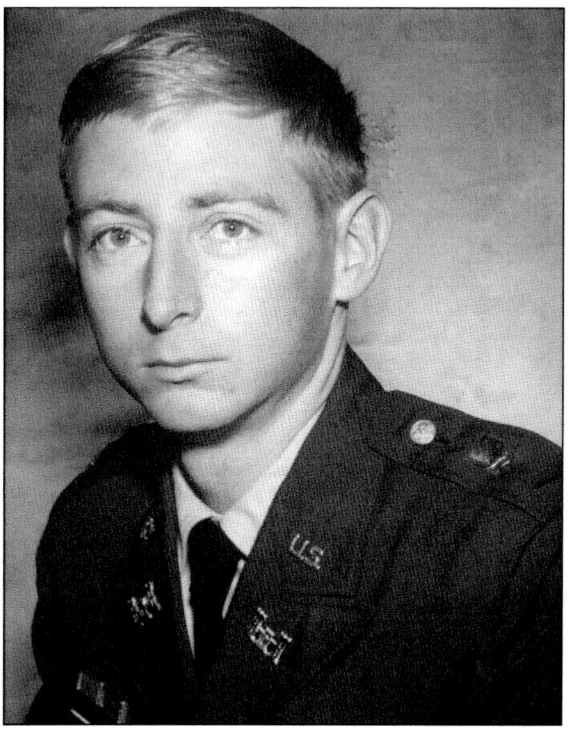

Sam Jackson is a farm boy from Pelion. After graduating from Clemson University, he was commissioned in the army. He served as an officer in Vietnam for two years. After the war, he came home to farm with his father. (Jackson family.)

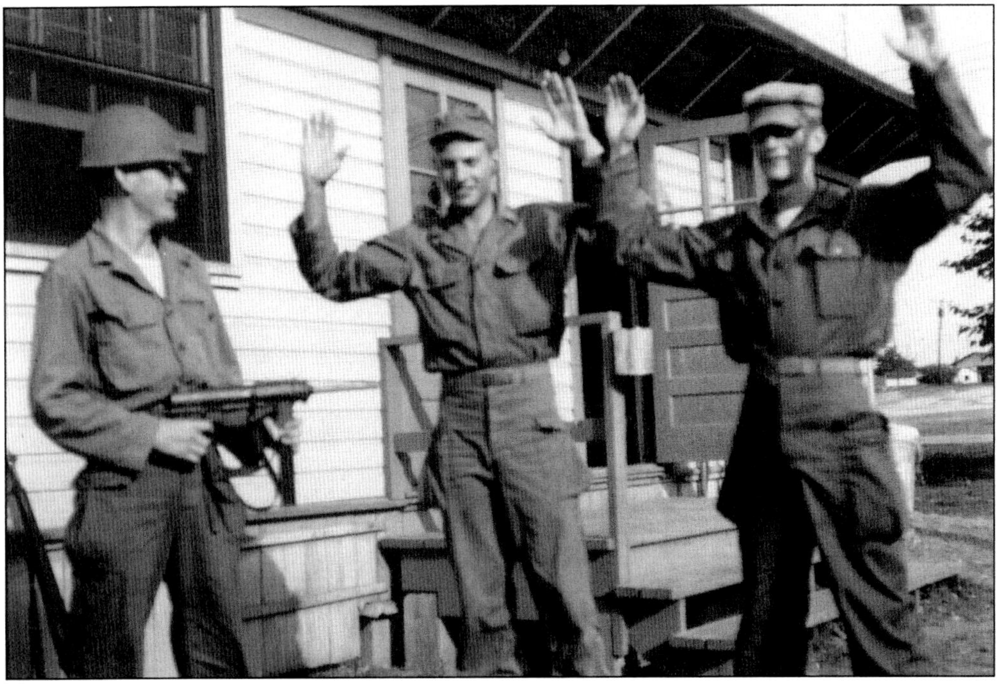

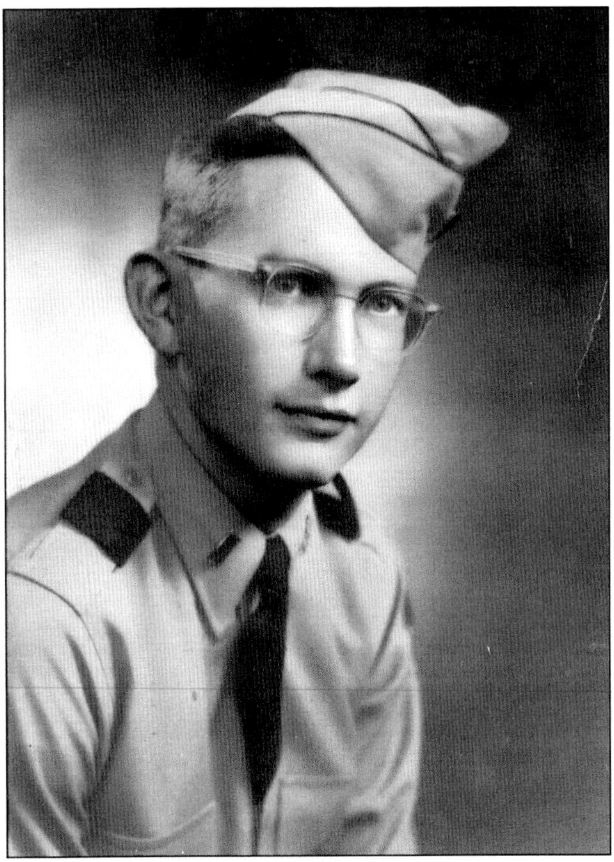

Lexington native Bill Mathias has some fun at ROTC summer camp. This program is still active in high schools today preparing young men and women for a military career. During the Korean Conflict, Bill served in Germany in an army tank battalion. He was engaged to Carolyn Newman from Batesburg at the time. He served until the end of the war and came home to return to college at Clemson University. Many young men were called away from jobs and college to fight. Those pictured here represent the strong belief in country that can be found in Lexington County. Always remembered are the ones who gave the ultimate sacrifice of their life and future. (Both, Mathias family.)

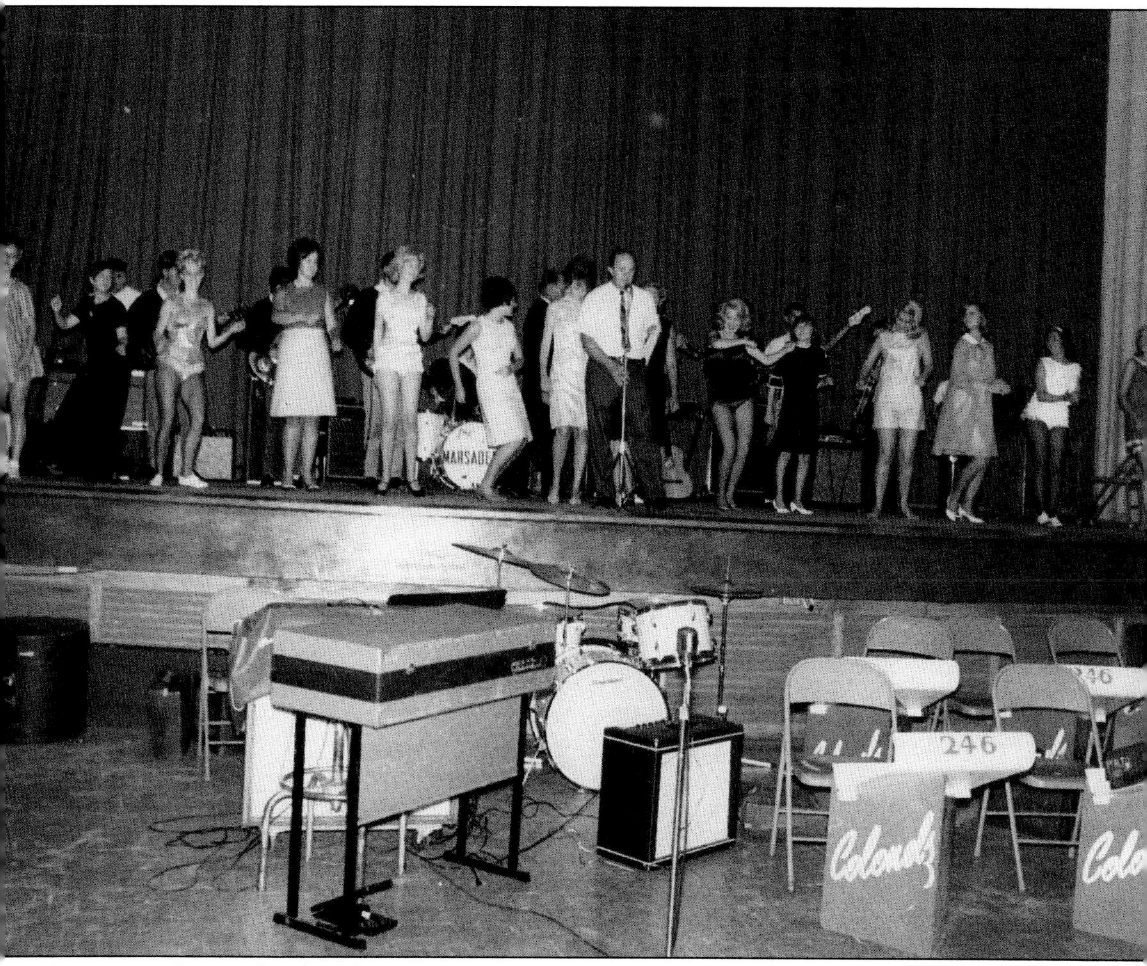

Lexington County has long been a supporter of its men and women in uniform. For 30 years, Redd and Doris Reynolds produced and directed free Caravan of Stars shows for the South Carolina National Guard during its annual training. Redd was once referred to as the Bob Hope of the National Guard. Many of the young people that were part of these shows are now some of Lexington County's leading citizens. (Redd and Doris Reynolds.)

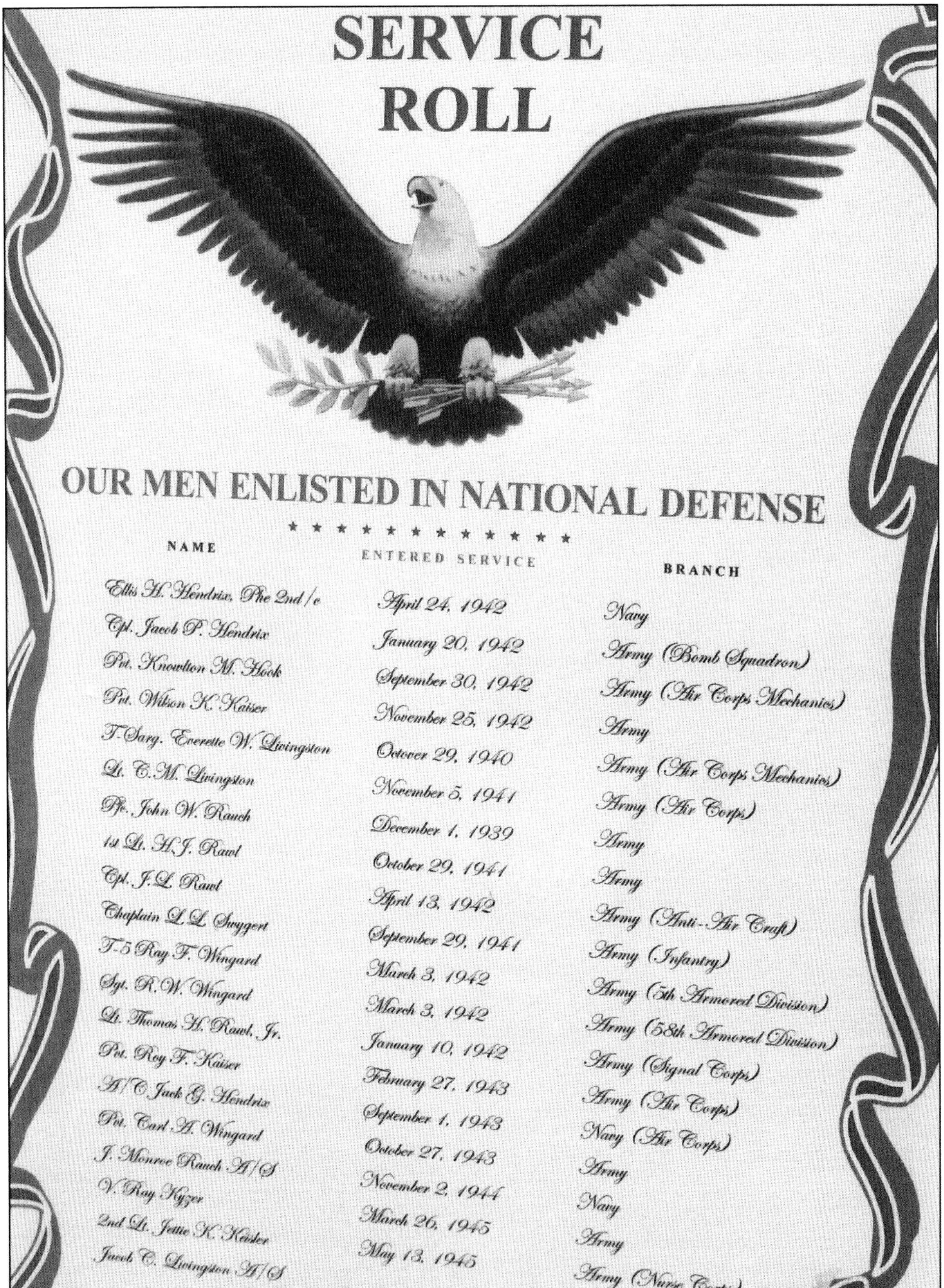

This banner is symbolic of all of the efforts Americans made to honor their loved ones. At St. John's Lutheran Church in Lexington, there is a banner and scroll with names of 20 church members who served during World War II. Thankfully, none lost his life; however, one soldier was captured and held as a prisoner of war. The names on the scroll and the blue stars on the banner were added as each of the 19 men and 1 woman entered the U.S. Army or Navy. The scroll and banner were a project of the Women's Missionary Society. St. John's is proud of the support and contribution of its members to their great nation. (Redd and Doris Reynolds.)

Seven

Historic Sites and Parks and Recreation

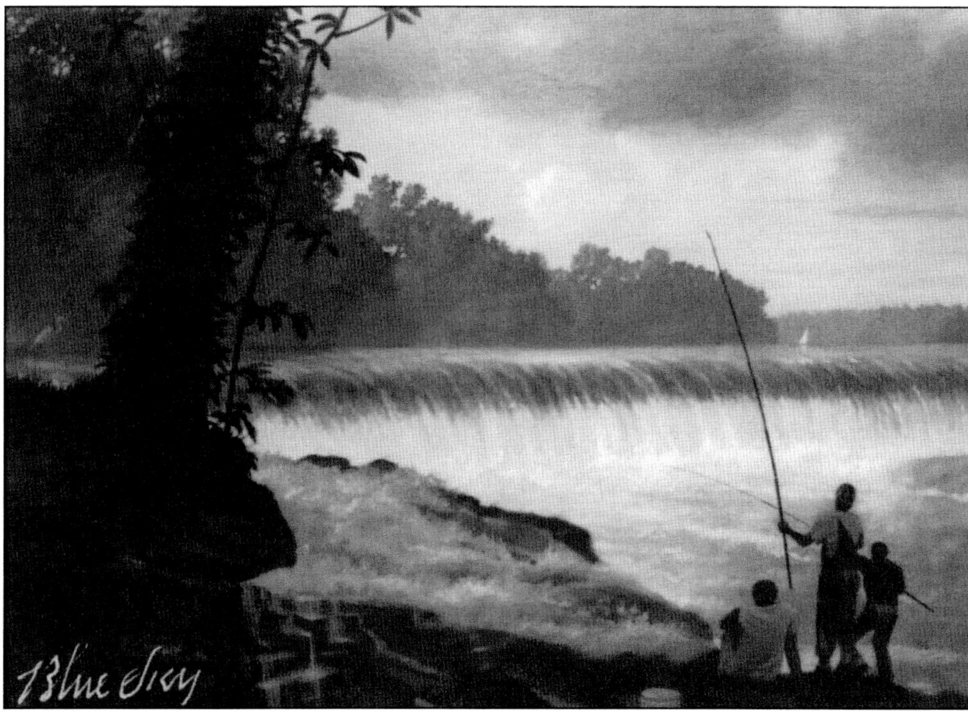

Lexington County is home to a variety of parks and historic sites. The local museums have complete handouts for historic site enthusiasts. Many have enjoyed visiting the sites of Revolutionary and Civil War events. There are a multitude of outdoor activities available for children and adults to share. Special events, seasonal festivals, parades, and family events are frequently planned annually. Local artist Blue Sky shares an idyllic afternoon of fishing on riverbanks in Lexington. (Artist Blue Sky.)

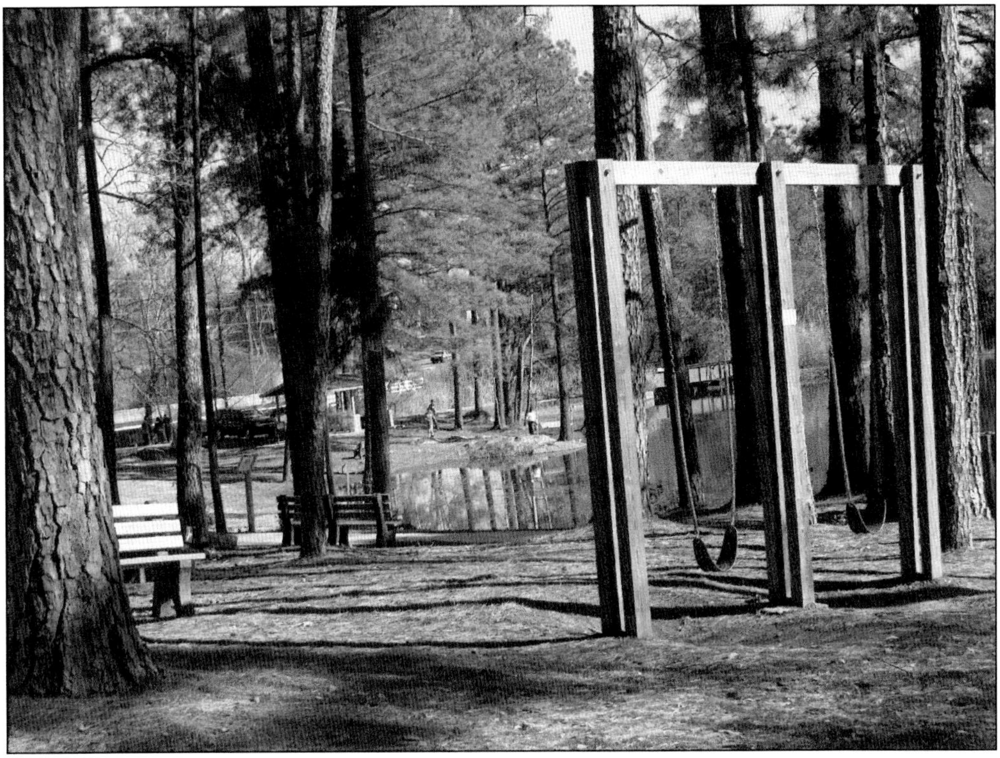

Back in its heyday, this quiet woodland spot called George's, then Gibson Pond, had quite the reputation. One Lexington lady remembers it as the place for everyone to meet and relax—swimming in the pond, dancing with a special friend, and for some, a first kiss. This site began as a mill, which was destroyed by fire and later became one of the first local recreation buildings. It was then sold to the Gibson family and renamed. Today it has been purchased by the Town of Lexington and has once again become a place for family picnics, fishing, and outdoor recreation. (Paeth family.)

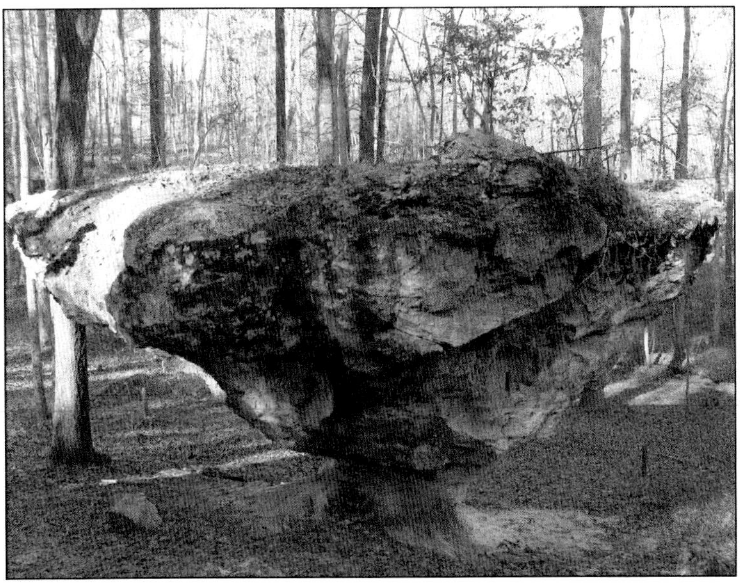

The history of the unusual formation known as Peachtree Rock has baffled many people. The surrounding area has been preserved for the future generations to visit. Now home to walking trails, picnic areas, and quiet reflection areas, Peachtree Rock is a place where memories are made. If this rock could talk, it would have amazing things to tell. (Paeth family.)

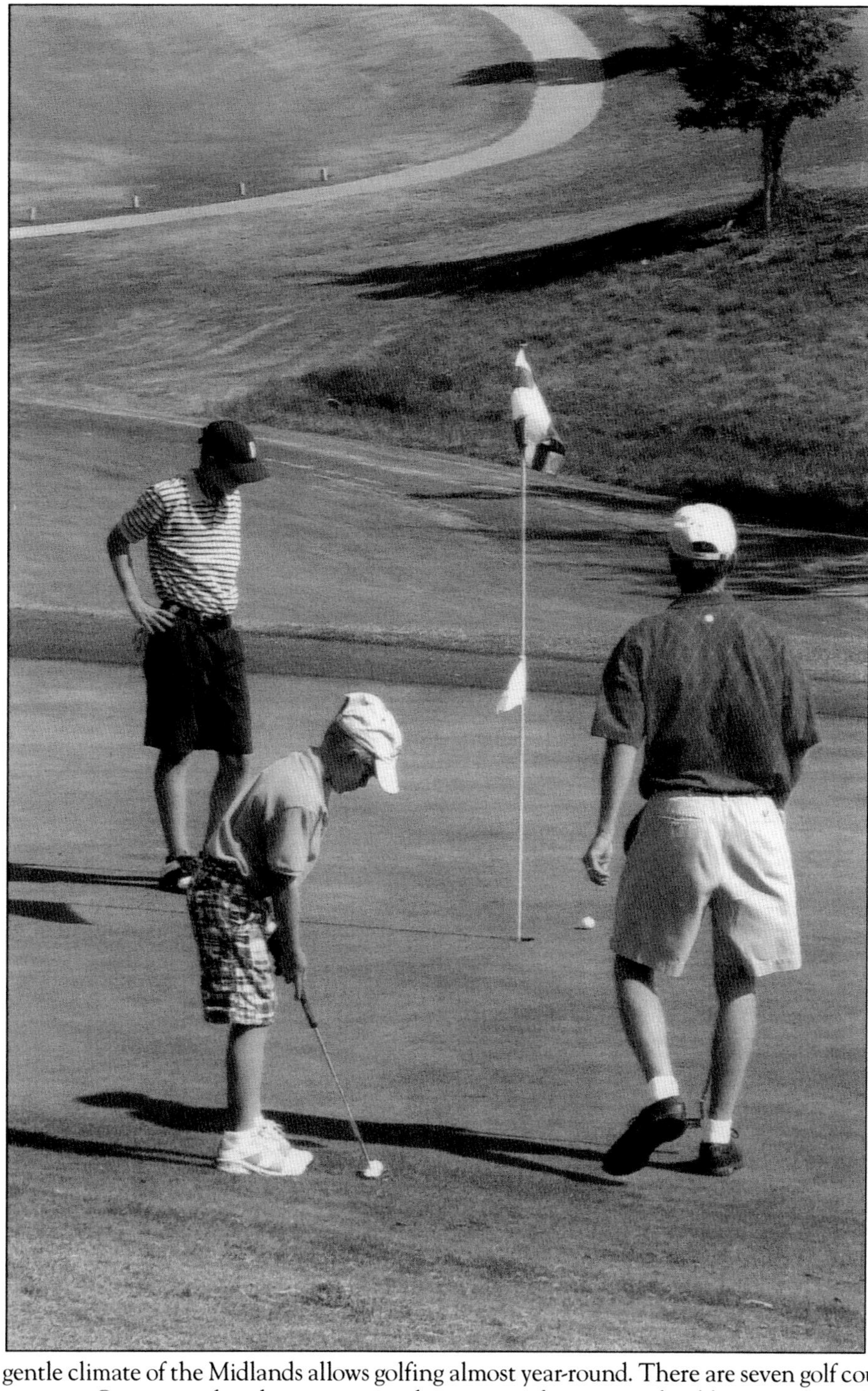

The gentle climate of the Midlands allows golfing almost year-round. There are seven golf courses in Lexington County, and enthusiasts enjoy the variety of private and public courses available. Local organizations frequently hold golf tournaments to raise funds, and local high schools boast excellent golf teams that often go on to higher competitions. Sam Jackson Jr. and his sons, Sam III and Tim, are enjoying an afternoon of golf. (Heather Jackson.)

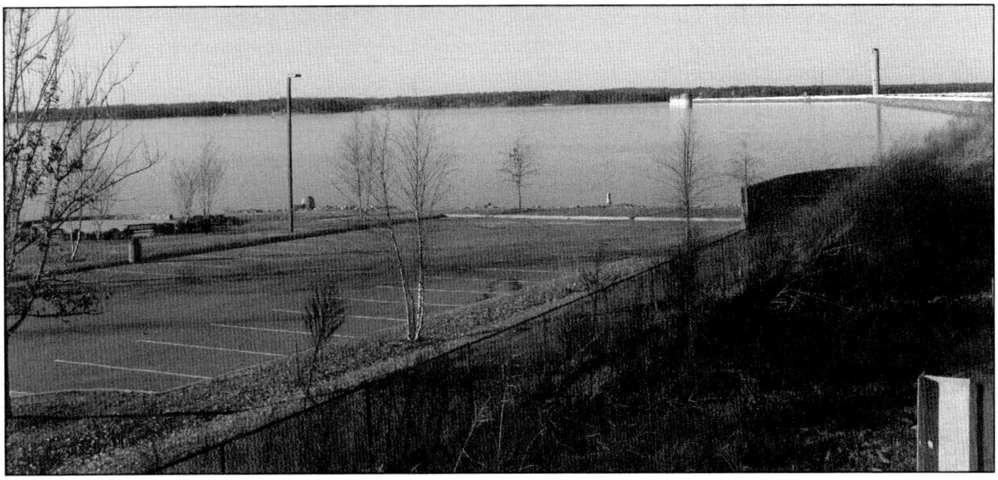

Lexington County residents enjoy the benefits of the Congaree River. Runners, kayakers, canoeists, tubers, rollerbladers, fishermen, picnickers, painters, photographers, and bird-watchers all enjoy the 9 miles of trails along the Three Rivers area in Cayce. Grandby Gardens Park and Guignard Park offer benches, shade trees, and small trails for outdoor activities. Saluda Shoals is close by the Saluda Dam and offers 359 acres of outdoor recreation. Virginia Hylton Park, in downtown Lexington by the courthouse complex, offers a playground, small pond, and short walking trails. For the more adventurous nature lovers, Harbison State Forest has 12 miles of challenging wooded trails. Riverbanks Botanical Garden is located on the Lexington side of the Saluda River, and the zoo section is at the end of a lovely woodland trail or tram ride over the river in Richland County. (Paeth family.)

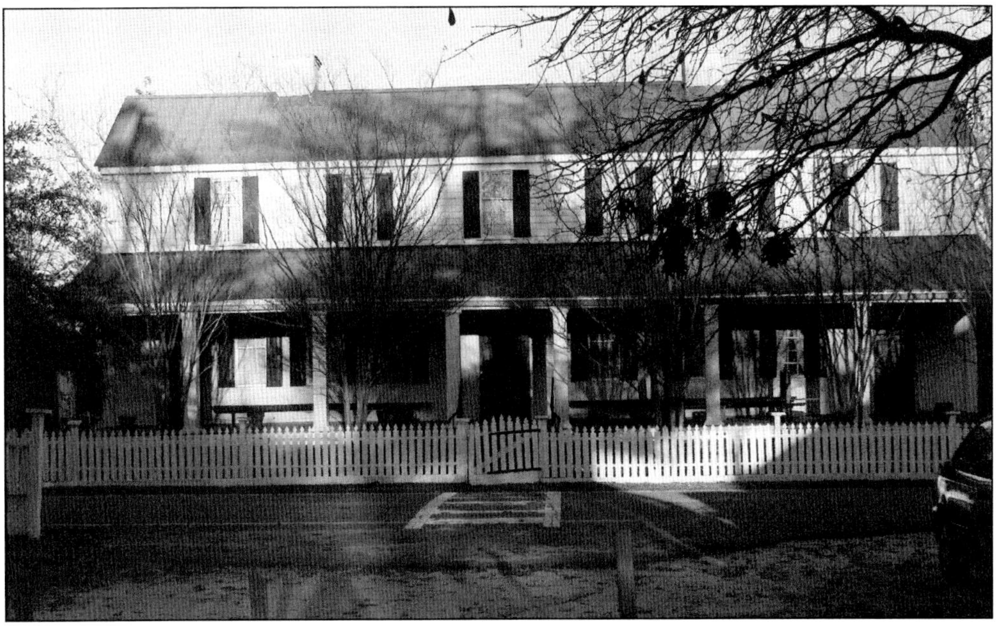

The Lexington County Museum is composed of 30 historic structures, including the oldest building in the town of Lexington (the c. 1832 John Fox House) and a building used by the Lutheran seminary when it was in Lexington. The museum has an impressive display of times gone by. Visitors will be greeted by guides dressed in period costumes even in the hottest of seasons. (Paeth family.)

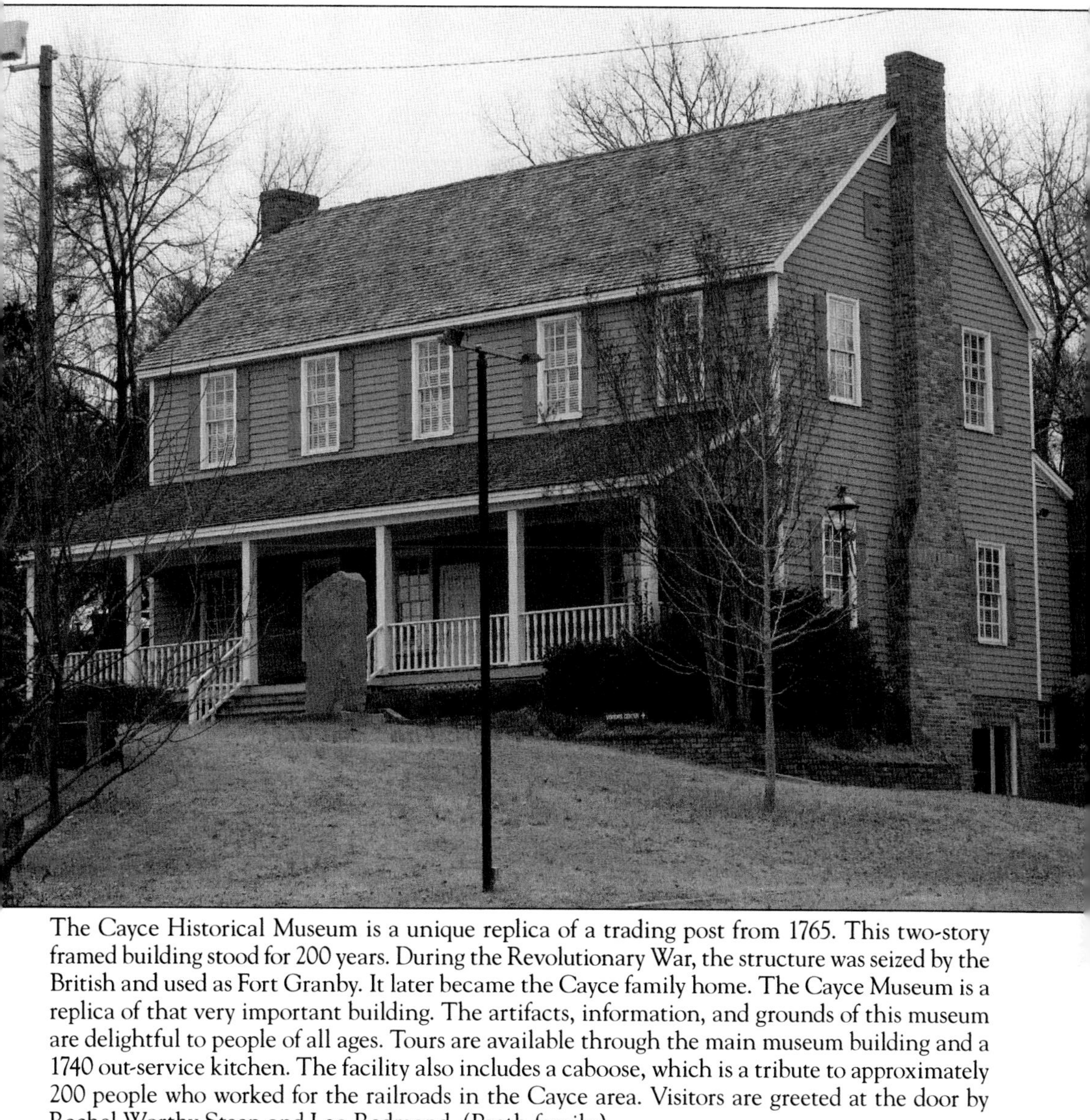

The Cayce Historical Museum is a unique replica of a trading post from 1765. This two-story framed building stood for 200 years. During the Revolutionary War, the structure was seized by the British and used as Fort Granby. It later became the Cayce family home. The Cayce Museum is a replica of that very important building. The artifacts, information, and grounds of this museum are delightful to people of all ages. Tours are available through the main museum building and a 1740 out-service kitchen. The facility also includes a caboose, which is a tribute to approximately 200 people who worked for the railroads in the Cayce area. Visitors are greeted at the door by Rachel Worthy Steen and Leo Redmond. (Paeth family.)

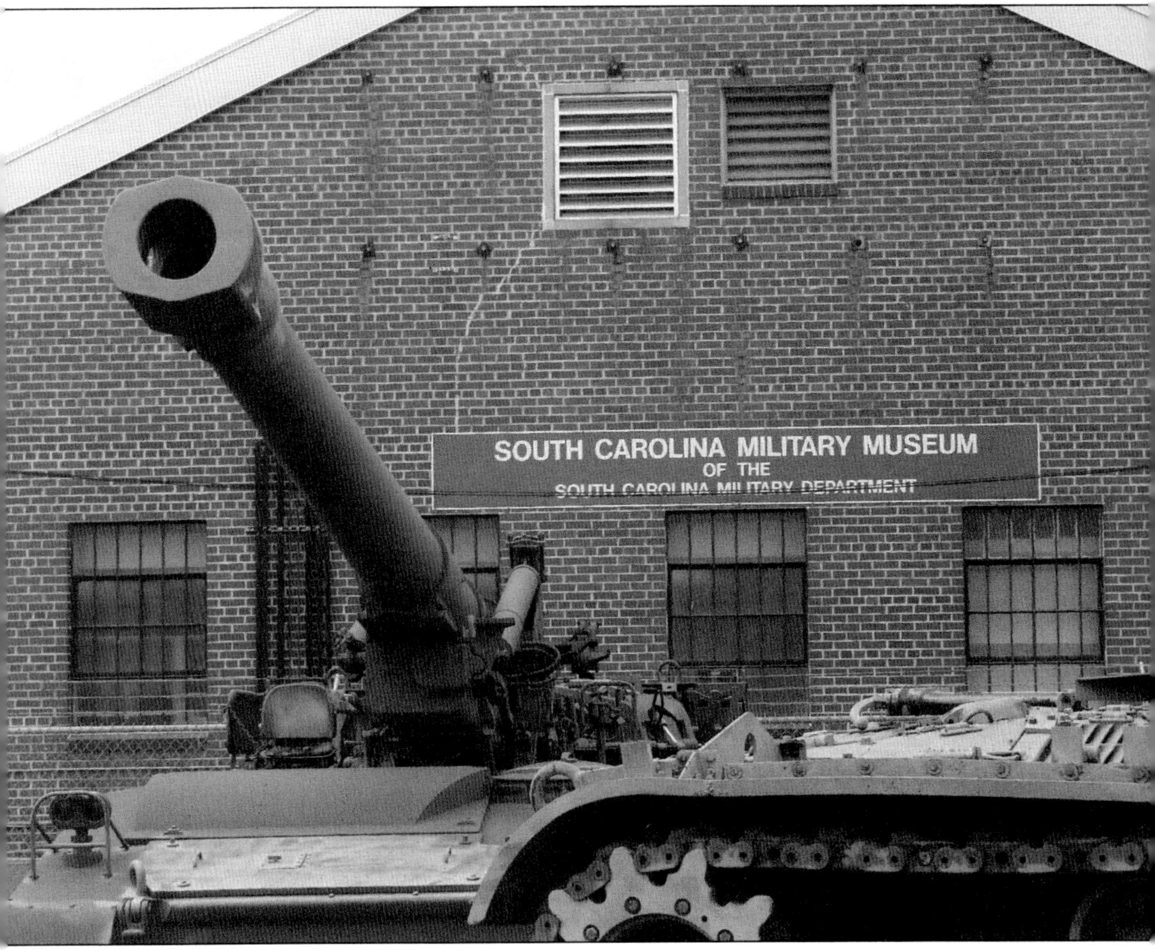

The South Carolina Military Museum showcases the state's military history from the first militia in 1670 at Charles Towne to today's citizen soldier deployed in the global war on terror. The militia is known as the father of the South Carolina Army National Guard. The museum is a must-see for anyone interested in our state's military history. (Paeth family.)

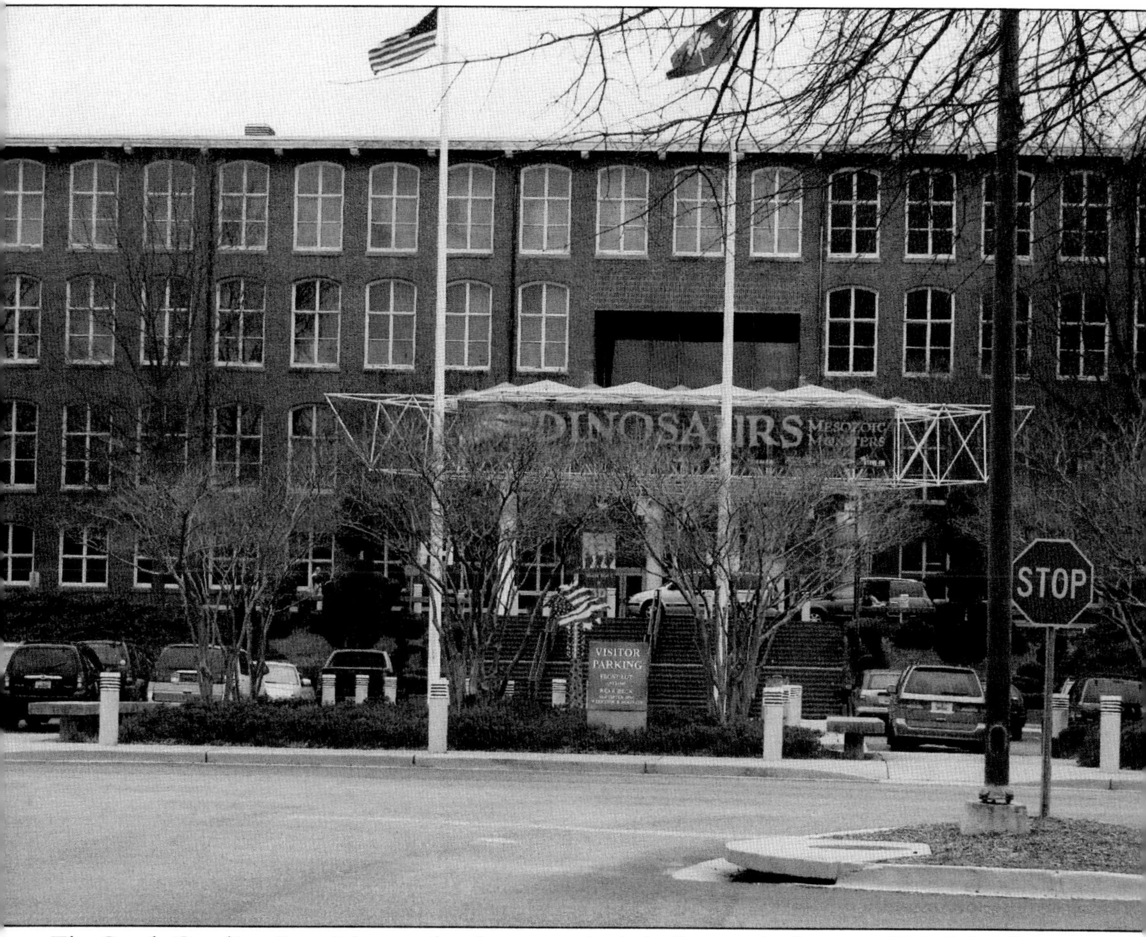

The South Carolina State Museum has been creatively built into the historic 1893 Columbia Mill textile building. Its four floors provide an abundant selection of material showcasing the many wonders of the state of South Carolina. Visitors enjoy hands-on displays that teach about the time periods significant in South Carolina history, fine and decorative arts, natural history, and technology. (Paeth family.)

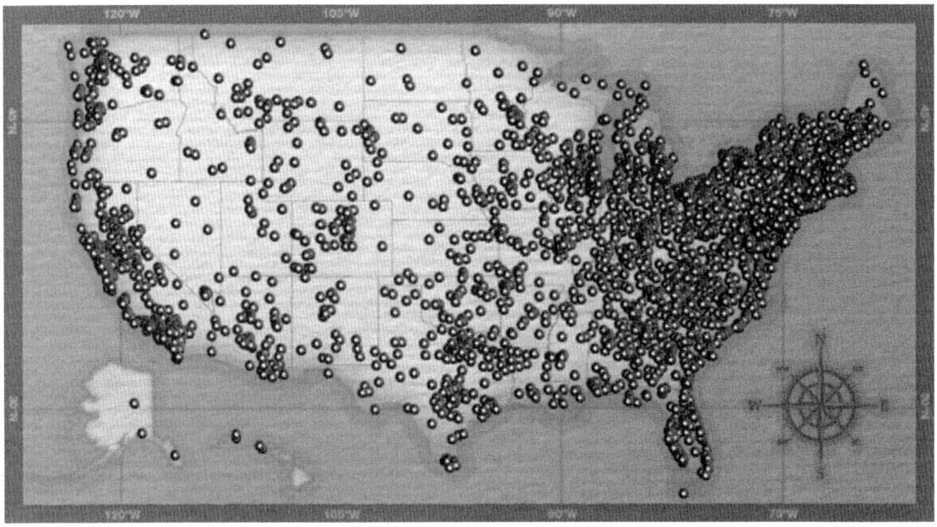